LEAVE YESTERDAY ALONE and MUSINGS

LEAVE YESTERDAY ALONE

and

MUSINGS

BY RICHARD MATHESON

GAUNTLET PRESS
■ 2014 ■

FIRST EDITION
10-digit ISBN: 1-934267-40-6
13-digit ISBN: 978-1-934267-40-0

Interior Page Design by Dara Hoffman-Fox

Manufactured in the United States of America

Gauntlet Publications
5307 Arroyo Street
Colorado Springs, CO 80922
(719) 591-5566
www.gauntletpress.com
info@gauntletpress.com

LIMITED EDITION

INTRODUCTION

~~~~~

Musings and *Leave Yesterday Alone* are among the rarest of my father's writings.

The first is a personal diary chronicling his remarkable life; a confessional of secrecies and revelations. The second is an unpublished, non-genre novel. Written in 1950, when he was twenty-four, it captures the idyllic thrall of campus life but also its cruelties of heart and doomed dreams.

In this troubling and thoughtful book, time is a slow murder. Though the characters trade in wit and nonchalance, like sinking ships their vulnerabilities slowly drown them. Nothing lasts forever, youthful idealism the first to perish.

The novel's descriptions of college life as self-consumed theater scathe and though student's lives are asylum from the real thing, for them, life takes more than it gives. Fate's acceleration forces outcomes few can flee, and while amusing distraction, their cynicisms cannot save them from deeper wounds. Only the truest heart among them escapes. But typical of my father's talent for irony, we're left to wonder how truly that heart ever beat.

Central in this conflicted oasis is Erick, a mercurial student who charms and bruises, his inner monologue a twisting fascination. With aspirations of becoming an author, his talent is real but insecurities about his life haunt; a self-obsessed fever that will not break. He fixates on women, their perfection or indifference infecting his thoughts and the novel with something unnerving. And while there is the implication he may be homosexual, as with the books other ambiguities, answers unprovided resonate most.
~~~~~

INTRODUCTION

Written over six decades ago, the choking morals of that time seep through the story, fusing lust with restriction. Fueling it all is sexual craving; seductions of mind and flesh that bring thrills and despair to nearly every character, poisoning what passes for love. And while disdaining the puritanical, the story exacts judgmental penalties on the uncaring.

Everywhere in the novel, amid its hurt psychologies, is the author's gift for character and telling detail; the daggered humor of the collegiate, the longing for things unearned. Like all promising tomorrows, *Leave Yesterday Alone* is wish-filled, often tragic. Golden futures are only that, and the young are falsely blessed by what they cannot foresee.

Privilege, in this harrowing novel, not only compels them to become something greater, it makes them forget what they truly are.

—Richard Christian Matheson
2013

MUSINGS

~~~~~

In which I write one page per day
(unless I don't)
for the rest
of my life.

(Begun 11/8/94)

by
Richard Matheson
~~~~~

I am calling this book MUSINGS because, although I plan (and hope) to write one page of it each day—probably before bedtime, it will not be a diary. What I do each day in the way of chores or accomplishments or—more rarely—recreation, is of no significance to this book.

Not that I will not record what happened on any particular day if the events of that day warrant comment. I will, in fact, write in this book anything I choose. These are to be *my* musings. So I will detail my thoughts, my beliefs, my likes and dislikes—in brief, any subject I choose to deal with.

To begin with, I am Richard Matheson. But already I am wrong. I don't believe that I am Richard Matheson. Not fundamentally. Richard Matheson is the name of the body and brain I have occupied in this life for almost 69 years. What I am really goes far beyond Richard Matheson—I believe. What I am has existed innumerable times in other lifetimes. This time around, this entity that is truly me, is called Richard Matheson.

So I have begun this book. I wonder when—and where—and *how* for that matter—it will end.

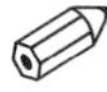

Well, here I am breaking my own rule first crack out of the bag. Why? Because it is the day after Election Day and I have to say something about what happened.

Sad, very sad.

One more vivid proof that no one who votes these days (and when did this sort of thing *start*?) ever votes *for* a candidate, *for* a belief, or *for* an honest conviction.

They vote *against*. Negative voting. Well, it fits, doesn't it? Because the campaigns are negative, too. Not "What I believe in, Folks," but "Let me tell you what a swine (or swiness?) my opponent is."

MUSINGS

They interviewed people on TV. Asked them, "Whose fault is it that things are the way they are? The voters or the politicians?"

To the last man (and woman) they answered, "The politicians."

And therein lies the problem, doesn't it? The Constitution gave the control of the government to the people.

The people have given it to the politicians. Sad?

Pathetic. Criminal. Until the voters realize that it's their responsibility alone, the problems will go on—and on—and *on...*

I wonder what will happen to California?

I was trying to inquire (of myself, I suppose) what will happen to California after the passage of Proposition 187?

A sidetrack here. When Ruth Ann and I attended a class lectured to by E.M. Esfandiary (Turkish, I think they said) on future aspects of all parts of society (or at least 10 years ago—which would be 1984). E.M. cited the newly created idea (newly created?) of the Proposition system. Instead of electing a politician and giving him carte blanche to vote yay or nay on all issues, the Proposition system would allow the voter to segregate issues and vote on them individually.

Great idea—but like all great ideas, replete with side effects. The side effect of the Proposition system is that groups with ulterior motives who can garner enough signatures, can sneak in all sorts of crap and try to get them passed by lying about their true purpose—aggrandizement, both financial and personal, i.e. Prop 188 backed by Philip Morris whose protestations of concern for your smokers provided a smoke screen for their real agenda—to cripple smoking laws already in operation, ergo make more addicts and, consequently, more money. Contemptible—yet there it was on the ballot.

Happily, the voters saw through that one—if not 187.

But back to California. Prop 187 is like one more nail in the rapidly taking shape coffin for the state. Other nails are faltering economy, street crime (in all its innumerable variation), gang warfare, polluted air and, need I add, *earthquakes*.

Where will my family and I be when the fan is finally hit?

Chris is gone already. Tina. Ali may leave soon. Us? Richard?

Time will tell.

I seem to be breaking my one-page-a-day rule, too,

So sue me.

Richard has been telling me about an astrological reading he had today. A Natal reading—what his character is, his basic personal components. Vedic, a form of astrology created (or, at least, evolved—and perfected?) in India.

He said that according to Vedic astrology, he is now in the second Virgo. How this works I have no idea since, as he said, his fundamental Libra aspects remain the same.

We saw two old friends tonight. John & June Hoffstadt. Took them to dinner at Brandy Wine. John is 77 now, older but still the same. June as well. John is, of course, retired as June is.

Interesting point—they have always been dedicated, ardent liberals. Yet they voted *for* Prop. 187. Odd how values change.

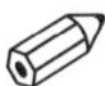

MUSINGS

I saw Shelly Weil today—has his own agency. I don't know if I'll go with him.

This day entry(ies) has (have) been inconsequential. Can't win 'em all.

I am getting bored with vampires. Well, not the critters themselves (if they really exist) but with the literature abounding on them. I wish someone would turn off the spigot.

I have contributed to it myself, of course, with *I AM LEGEND* and a few short stories, and did a script for *Dracula* and did *The Night Gallery* script. But, really, it's getting only harder.

Why?

Contrary to what is done to present these neck-biting guys and gals as sexy creatures—all the men are handsome and inclined to dress suits—all the females are inclined toward low-cut gowns and are almost invariably lusty.

But hey. Vampires are *dead*, aren't they? They are corpses who smell like shit and have no interests other than draining someone's jugular. Sexy? Romantic? Not so.

Maybe it's that immortality that appeals to viewers—readers. I don't know.

But they *don't* appeal to me anymore, if they ever did to begin with.

Sunday, Thanksgiving approaching. Christmas approaching. Ruth Ann and I went shopping for Christmas clothes for grandchildren William and Kate, Chris's two. We already bought clothes for Mariel (Ali's daughter) yesterday but Grandma Ruth could not resist several more outfits for her and we got them as well.

RICHARD MATHESON

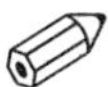

We are watching a program about wolves, narrated by and "starring" Timothy Dalton. I suspect they have programmed it because he is also playing Rhett Butler on CBS tonight—the sequel to *GONE WITH THE WIND*.

Anyway, it is a sad story. There are so many endangered species in the world (man being the primary one?), but wolves seem special—like dolphins and elephants. They are so *social*, for one thing—and so beautiful to look at. What will happen to Tina's hybrid wolf dog Kuana(?), a gorgeous animal. But if Tina returns to California, she can't take it with her. So what will happen to it? It is endangered in a different way.

I saw Lee Halloway today (my astrologer) to see why her predictions on my last major reading have gone so wrong. She has been *right* so regularly that I can't just negate her effectiveness. But she told me that I would earn more money this year than ever before—so much work, in fact, that I would have to be careful about my health since I was in a vulnerable state.

Au contraire. My health has had some problems this year, true, but my earnings this year have been relative bottom. I haven't had a major assignment out here in a year.

She was taken back by it—said that she had assumed that my status out here was such that it would overcome the Saturn-Pluto stuff going on.

Apparently not.

Well, I am going to find different agent representation, to begin with. What else I'm going to do, I don't know, I am frankly getting bored by my writing. It still works (as in my latest novel, *THE MEMOIRS OF WILD BILL HICKOK*) but my dejection of not being able to succeed writing material with a "message" is increasing daily.

Quo Vadis. Big Dick?

Triglycerides 470!

Ye gods! Granted I should have fasted before the blood test, but still…

I knew I've been eating badly of late. Mystic Mints indeed. Chocolate chip cookies. Mocha Cappuccino coffee. English muffins. Bagels. Chopped Liver.

Now it has to stop. I can't just kill myself with lousy dieting. Not with such a sedentary occupation.

So tonight I began. Turkey, broccoli, carrots, cauliflower. Shouldn't have added that soup even though it only had 65mg of sodium and 10g of cholesterol. Better, though.

Now it's back to my diet. For chrissakes, last May I had my triglycerides down to 184! And Dulin says it should be less than 100! Yikes.

If I die tonight, it's my own fault.

But as Scarlet said, "After all, tomorrow *is* another day."

It is.

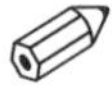

Collected stuff today to show the new agent. Scripts—four novels.

We'll see.

11/16/94. Am I really tired of writing? At the moment it seems so. Why? Because it has not brought in the return I hoped for? Money-wise, certainly not. But I must always confess that it is to my fault, no others. Harry altogether once said that I wanted to write like an amateur and be paid like a professional. I took offense at this when he said it. And certainly I can write professionally per se. But be may have been right in another respect. A professional concentrates on one thing. Steve King did. Dean Koontz. John Saul. The millionaire pros. Why not me? Is it a lack on my part? Must be. I lose interest in subjects so quickly. I've written fantasy. I've written mystery. Romance. Metaphysical. Westerns, for God's sake!—five of them and maybe I'll do a sixth. I even wrote a war novel. So what does it all say? An inability to concentrate? A lack of professional dedication? I don't know. I do know I was born with a talent. If I have failed in this lifetime—and I hope I haven't too much—it has been a failure to use that talent adequately; a failure to carry it as far as I think I might have gone. I will have to wait for the judgment on that.

Triglycerides 470, my ass! I went to Dr. Sapkin today to set up my next wonderful adventure with having my butt roto-rooted—and he said that a person should fast, fat-wise, for *two days* prior to the blood test, I didn't of course. I didn't fast at all. So the results are very suspect. Not that I will not go back on my diet—hell, I lost *four pounds* yesterday! (Water, mostly, I suspect.) But I will not continue in a state of shock.

Cohen's office phoned today (his nurse Michelle) to tell me I should watch my diet. I'm not sure if he knows about the erratic nature of triglyceride test results.

I have discovered that out of five of our (my) doctors—Sapkin, Spigelman, Fenmore, Shapiro and Cohen—only Harry is not a Preferred Provider for insurance. Why?

I met with Michael Siegel today regarding his possible agenting. (Jeez, as against my vow, this *is* turning into a damn diary.) Anyway, I liked him, he's young, intelligent, well-spoken, well-educated, reads. What did he tell me? He said that when he became an agent, he very quickly got a good reputation because he reads and returns phone calls! He recognized that these two factors were *required* in any other business. And here, they're such rarities that people are impressed.

I think good taste is on the wane. Really. We went to see *Alegria* tonight; the current version of the Cirque de Soleil.

A major disappointment.

A Vegas show directed by Fellini.

We saw the original Cirque, it was marvelous in every respect: talent, excitement, music, the works.

Now it is thinned out, the only good acts were by the same group of acrobats who performed three times.

A few of the minor thrills but—all in all—a letdown after what we expected.

But the audience cheered and applauded and yelled and clapped and waved their hands in the air. They thought it was great—and it was far less than great.

But they have the reputation now and audiences buy it.

Too bad.

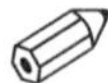

I have nothing to say today. So how do you go about filling a page when nothing fills my head?

Well, I can say this. Scott Hamilton got straight 6's on Style & Composition but Brian Boitano is still my favorite. He is so powerful and his landings are perfect. Real class—of course, Hamilton is to be admired. Thirty-six is hardly venerable (although the commentator—have Wylie?—spoke as though it is) but I guess the legs go in any sport but fencing and chess.

Well, my head still has nothing to emit. My wife asked me what I'm writing and I said nothing. She didn't (doesn't) know how true that is.

Communist China. (They love to smoke which makes R.J. Reynolds very happy.) *Margaret Thatcher* a representative for tobacco? My God, will sanity ever reign?

It is not much of a prediction to say that one day soon, everyone will look back at the centuries of smoking and wonder if men and women were insane or suicidal or both.

But then they will wonder whether our politics were insane or suicidal. Parties? Insanity. Unlimited tax expenditures? Insanity. Exclusively negative advertising? Ditto. Poor U.S., and we started so good, too.

Clinton is becoming a major disappointment. He started out so well. He *has* accomplished much; he really has. But his image gets more corroded every month. Now, giving in to the GOP victory, he has declared his intent to go centrist—interpretation: please everybody at the same time, crawl down the middle of the road. How sad. He started out so *well*. At least, it seemed as though he did. Now, though—he seems more intent on '96 than on creating a new image for the government. Is he for the people (as he claims) or for himself? There is definitely something lacking in the man.

Can I get profound?

In the sector of growing aptitudes, is it feasible that mankind's loss of innocence is predicated not—as we thought—upon a lesser connivance but, instead, on a wracking grossness which instead of engendering philosophical progress only decimates what we now know as "political" loss and surrender.

Profundity?

Of course not.

Absolute bullshit.

Well, this is a first; a hard one to write down.

I was turned down by an agent today.

He read two of my scripts—adaptations of two of my novels—and didn't care for them. He hemmed and hawed and tried to make some points but he didn't really. He just didn't like the scripts, period. I suggested that maybe he just didn't like the stories but that got me nowhere.

Well, who knows? Who cares?

11/27/94.

I have decided that, instead of *MUSINGS* (who cares about my damn musings?) I will write down everything I can remember about my life. Perhaps it will be of interest to my kids after I am gone. (Well, okay, not "gone" but "moved on.")

Where to begin?

I guess the thing to do is to go back as far as I can remember. I wish I was like certain people who seem to recall baby events, some of them (are they serious?) claim to remember womb consciousness.

Well, I don't go back that far. Not consciously at any rate. The first thing I seem to remember is attending (*being brought to* would be a more accurate phrase) a play being given in the cellar of Tante Evelyn and Uncle Tolleffi's house in Marine Basin, I think it was. Avenue M? Perhaps. My cousin Francis (Franny) and his sister Vivian lived there too, of course.

I recall the house—I think. Facing west, on the south side. Two stories, with a cellar; an outside entrance to it. A sun porch in front, I think the road was dirt. Across the way lived Billy McAndrew who liked Vivian but it was discouraged—because he was Catholic? I don't know—but that is another story.

I remember going down to the cellar—dirt floor, smelling of dirt; as I recall, an actual stump for chopping wood for the furnace. Did my brother tell me it was my father who paid their rent? This had to be right after the '29 crash, I think. My father ran three speakeasies in Manhattan—but I digress again.

Okay, my cousin Franny gave me what I thought was a bun. I bit into it. It was filled with cotton? Did Franny laugh? Did I cry? Probably. I cried a lot, I think. I was a cry baby. I recall a time—again, I was very young (five? six?) and my birthday cake (as I recall) was banana short cake (I always liked banana short cake) and when I started to eat mine, it toppled over. I cried, at which one then all of my relatives knocked over their cake slices to comfort me. Poor Dickey-bird, as Vivian used to call me.

What else do I remember about that house?

I remember a tent they had in the backyard. I remember talking (or whatever) my cousin Lily into removing her bathing suit. Could I have been sexually aware at such an early age? five? six? Anyway, I was so young that I couldn't help her get the bathing suit back on. That's *young*. So what did I do? Probably cried.

I remember being pushed in a wooden car that Franny built. A two-by-four beam with a cross strut in front for the bicycle wheels (small)—a loose bolt (several heavy metal washers?) so the axle could be turned from side to side by a rope fastened at each end of the strut, which rope I held and twisted to change directions. In the back was some kind of seating arrangement. Did it have a backrest? Don't know. But we always won, I think—our main opponents as I recall were the Naylor brothers—because Franny ran fast, pushing the car with a length of wood; and I was very light in weight. He called me Shadow.

I remember Thanksgiving at that house. Or was it pre-Thanksgiving?

No one even believes me on this (as they really don't believe me—I can tell—when I tell them that the first book I ever borrowed from the library on Linden Blvd. was *PINOCCHIO IN AFRICA*, swear it. Did Collodi write it? Dunno.) but we dressed in old clothes—did I cross-dress? Seems like it. Anyway, we went to people's houses and knocked on the doors and said, "Anything for Thanksgiving?" and asked in candy stores, as well.

Do I hallucinate? I recall Halloween there but I wasn't allowed to participate. Kids soaped windows and put wooden gates (removed from their hinges) on roofs. I don't ever recall them Trick or Treating first, just starting right out with the pranks. While no one was looking, of course.

My first words (I don't remember this, my mother told me) came at sunset. I was just a baby, what, two? Not much older. I looked at the sunset and said, "Look at the 'ky." Cute? My mother wrote it down in her baby book. Where is that book today? Is she back? Interesting if one met one's own mother reincarnated. Another story I won't write.

Enough for now.

RICHARD MATHESON

Continuing.

I don't remember anything more about Franny's house (in Marine Basin?).

The next place I recall was an apartment house; I think it was off Ave. L or M. It was three or four stories high, made of brick, and we lived on the top floor. No elevators in those days and my little legs got very tired going up and down those steps. I guess I was about six because I hadn't started school yet—I started at seven.

Not too many memories about this apartment. I don't even know if the five of us—Mom, Pop, Bob, Gladys, and me lived together. I think the schism between my mother and father began soon after I was born—maybe before.

I recall the flat roof with a kind of tarpaper surface. I remember us (not me, I'm sure) setting up folding beach chairs to sit in the sun. Did we have a radio up there? Was there a plug?

Of all things, I remember a game I got, probably for my birthday; maybe it was for Christmas.

It had two sides to it. It was shaped like this (I should have drawn the wooden car instead of trying to describe it). Anyway, the game looked like this: From above:

(Diagram of game)

From the side:

(Diagram of game)

A "gun" at each end which shot rings. (Diagram of ring.) You shot them at three or four slots in the middle. You tried to get your rings in all four (three?) openings at the same time. The other person tried to shoot his rings against yours and knock them out, thus placing his (or her) ring in the slot. Exciting? I must have liked it since I still remember it.

I really don't remember Jamaica where I had to stay at my Tante Lise's house because my mother and sister both worked, my mother in Namm's, my sister in A&S. I lived with my aunt and, I presume, my Uncle Johnny and their three children: Helen, Ethel and Buddy (Albert). I think I remember that Ethel was mean to me. I remember talking to a little girl across the alley, each of us in our own room. I suppose I was in bed to sleep. Ethel didn't like it, I guess, because she washed out my mouth with soap. (Is that why I identify with that scene in *A Christmas Story*?) And did my talking across the alley with that little girl cause me to respond to the scene in *OUR TOWN* where the two talk across the way? Of course, we were much younger.

I know I remember my mother coming to see me on the weekends and me crying (I think that crying was justified) bitterly when she left to go home; I guess she came on Sunday afternoon, went home on Sunday evening. No doubt that struck a chord in me when Ruth Ann and I used to see Tina in her foster home as we left, Tina cried and cried. Reflections.

I guess the house I remember first in any detail was on 39th Street off Avenue M (or thereabouts). A block or so from Flatbush Avenue. A two-story house, we rented the upstairs apartment (I bet the rent was in the $20's) and a family with two boys (Red and Don, Red the younger) lived downstairs.

A veritable cascade of disjointed memories in this place.

Me sneaking off to a birthday party at someone's house *on the other side* of Flatbush Avenue. (I know how *I* would have felt as a parent about that, a six- or seven-year-old going that distance alone? Leaving no message. My God.) I brought as a gift a little printing set I'd gotten as a gift earlier. Did I even wrap it? I doubt it.

My mother's reaction was not too good when I returned. She never spanked me but I must have sat in the corner (my usual form of punishment at that age) for a long time. She must have been terrified, wondering where I was. Children.

Other memories of 1282, E. 39th St? Is that the address? I know I remember others but so *early*? Well, the school was P.S. 119. But more on that later.

What other "events" do I recall? A good word. Calling back. Recalling. Bid time return. Commercial.

Continuing again with multiple memories.

Well, first, I might mention my birth. Apparently (according to my sister) my mother got tuberculosis and was in a sanitarium. Then she became a Christian Scientist (in the sanitarium? I don't know) and decided she wanted to have another child, so I was conceived. I had always thought my conception was an accident, Pop coming home one night under the influence and claiming his husbandly rights—but I guess not. She wanted me. I was twelve years younger than my brother, thirteen younger than my sister.

But to return to 1282, E. 39th Street—I think that was the address; good memory.

I won't try to put these things in chronological order. I couldn't anyway, they are all disconnected in my mind.

I remember falling down the stairs. A dim stairway. I was carrying a wooden box (as I recall) when I fell. I don't recall if I was going up or down, but I do remember blood coming out of my nose like water from a faucet.

I'm not sure if this is the time I dislocated my shoulder bone. The pain must have been excruciating; I have blanked it out actually. No doctor called. Never saw a doctor until I went in the Army. My mother called a C.S. practitioner. I was screaming with pain. I don't know what the practitioner said but she (he?) held out a toy for me, I reached for it and the collar bone *snapped* back into place; bet *that* hurt.

What else do I remember? I remember planting a peach pit in the front yard (not much of a yard) so a peach tree would grow there. How old was I? Seven? Eight? Not old enough to be very smart about growing trees. It's been—what?—about sixty years. Has that peach tree grown there yet? I doubt it.

I remember something else; an odd memory. A bird—probably a sparrow—on the front porch rail. It didn't fly away. It let me come right up to it, talk to it, even—this is the oddest part of the memory—pet it on the head with one finger. A transcendent moment? Couldn't say, maybe the little bugger was dying. But when I went upstairs to get it something to eat—a slice of white bread, no doubt (Silvercup? Tastee?)—he took off. Left a little token of his visit on the railing. I did not have it bronzed.

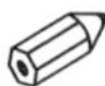

I remember all the sports I played when we lived at 1282.

Punch ball, for one. I had a sneaky way of punching the ball up over the trees—which covered the street. By the time the ball bounced down through the branches, I was home. Not exactly honest but it worked.

We also played stickball—in the street and in the yard of P.S. 119 which was right across the street at the end of the block—there was 1282, then an apartment house (red brick), then the corner. We played a lot of sports in the street and in the schoolyard—did I mention that the street was unpaved?

We played softball. We played football (touch) with full-size footballs and those little miniature ones. Red and Donny played. Odd but I only remember them.

And we played baseball but in an empty lot down the street the other way—across from the corner. Years later—seven, eight?—Bob and Mary had an apartment on the second floor of a house on—God, I remember its name!—Hubbard Place. The twins were born when they were there.

Where was I?

We also played stoopball. You threw the ball against the porch steps. There was an "infielder" and an "outfielder" on the other team. (I put the positions in quotes because it was hardly baseball, although I do recall now that we called it baseball against the steps—I think.)

You tried to bounce the ball in front of the infielder. One bounce—a single, two bounces, a double, and so on. You tried, of course, to hit the point of the step (the edge) and knock it over the head of the outfielder for a home run—but that was rare.

Then there were all the "novelty" items we played with. They were seasonal as I recall.

Certainly in the winter it was the chestnut on a string. You took turns hitting the opponent's chestnut with yours. The idea was to smash his chestnut to bits and off the string. You strung them by—I think—heating a needle and poking a hole through the nut, then pushing through the string and knotting its end. We enjoyed it, I guess. Seems silly now.

Then there were the picture cards. World War One Flying Aces. Indians. Came with a penny game. You flipped for them, sometimes one at a time, sometimes up to five as I recall. There were two different ways—well, actually, there were a lot of variations—but the two basic ones were flipping it forward and flipping it backward, that is, palm up and palm down. You tried to make it a science so you could match your opponent's card, face for face or back for back. Some guys were really good at it, they had the thick clumps of won cards with a rubber band around them, clumps that could barely fit in their pants pockets.

There was the yo-yo period. Some of the boys were experts—cat's cradle, etc. Sometimes I could get it to spin near the ground before I tugged it up or I could throw it up in the air. Not much. Other guys could use both hands, manipulating the string; was that the cat's cradle? I don't recall this period as lasting too long.

There was the paddle with the small brownish solid rubber ball attached to the center of the paddle with a long rubber band. Of course, the point of the thing was to keep hitting the ball as long as possible, keeping it in the air. What pointless endeavors these all were basically—but we enjoyed them, I guess.

Any other "fads?" Well, there were the strips with the little pictures on them that you wet and put on the back of your hand and rubbed it so that you had a "tattoo" on your skin. Just remembered that.

The "little" football was a periodic interest, too.

I guess baseball cards came into vogue when I was a kid. I don't recall collecting them. I did have a glove with "Goose" Goslin's signature stamped on it. I preferred a light .34 bat. I could bat from both sides of the plate—but maybe that happened later. I couldn't have been much of a baseball player at that time.

Then there was school—P.S. 139—or was it 119? *No*. I wasn't enrolled until I was 7 years old. Why? I wonder. So instead of beginning school in kindergarten, I started in 1-B.

What do I remember about it?

Very little.

I remember an accident that happened when I had first begun school.

When one wanted to go to the bathroom one had to raise the right hand and ask to be excused to "leave the room." Simple?

Not for me.

Obviously (or apparently?) I was unable to do this. What a poor little simp I must have been. The idea of raising my hand and calling attention to myself was beyond my comprehension. To actually have the teacher acknowledge my raised hand gesture and say "Yes, Richard?" or "Yes?" and have to say *aloud* (my God, *aloud*!) "May I leave the room?" was more than I could conceive of doing. Have the other boys and girls *look* at me (actually *look* at me!) while I was confessing my need to pee? My God! Unthinkable!

So what did I do, poor little Dickie Matheson?

Sat there. Suffered. I guess hoping recess would come before my little bladder gave way.

In vain. It *did* give way and my bladder emptied and I wet my pants and created a puddle of pee around my shoes and desk.

Can you imagine my shame? Me, who couldn't even *mention* my need to urinate in the presence of my classmates (*mates*?) actually *peeing* in their presence?

My face must have turned beet red. They noticed, of course, and the boys snickered and the little girls rubbed the bottom of one index finger over the top of their other index finger in the traditional, mocking gesture of "Shame, Shame." (Nya-nya-nya.)

I was humiliated, I'm sure I must have cried. I guess the teacher came and led me out of the room. Maybe I was allowed to go home. Surely, I couldn't have returned to class with soaking wet trousers. (Shorts?) By the way, I wonder who mopped up the puddle.

Poor Dickie bird.

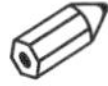

Any other memories of P.S.—I don't know *what* the correct number is, actually. 119 is, I think, the one—no, that's not right—numbers are jumping through my head. 139 *is* the one I graduated from. The first one may be 119 after all. The one in Flatbush? Something in the 90's? 92? Who knows. Not important—82? 81? (That "sounds" right, somehow.)

All right, I'll say that the final one *was* 119. Gory further memories? None as vivid as wetting my pants, of course, but I *do* recall a day when I went to some little girl's house. I'm not sure but it may have been that my mother wasn't home. It seems in retrospect as though the little girl's house was miles and miles away. Actually, it was probably a block or a street.

I remember that I had a stomachache. Did I throw up in the little girl's bushes? Can't be certain. But I do recall two things vividly. Sitting next to her on her porch step and her holding my hand and calling me "honey." The other thing I remember is her name, Ruth Woods. Amazingly close to Ruth Woodson, my guess who? (Her maiden name.)

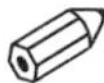

Another memory: nothing very vital. I remember seeing a Rin-Tin-Tin movie in school. I presume it was a sound picture. Maybe it wasn't. I don't recall any details of the film. All I do remember is receiving a green glass pen at the conclusion of the show. This was, of course, in the days before fountain pens—or, at least, cheap fountain pens. And eons before ball pointers. Each desk had an inkwell in it. No doubt this is where the apocryphal story began of the mean little boy dipping the pigtails of the little girl in front of him into the inkwell. I presume it must have actually happened at some point in history.

Paddleball, that's what it was (is) called. Just occurred to me. Interesting how memory works.

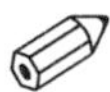

Anything else I remember from that period of 1282 E. 39th St?

Something I didn't experience but which I recall. Apparently, the entire family was living together at this time because, on a summer day, when Mom, Gladys and I went to Jacob Riis Park to try the Atlantic Ocean. My father left a note for my brother—in his meticulous penmanship—boy, was his handwriting grand.

The note informed my brother that we had gone to "bathe our bodies" in the Atlantic and, since he "knew" that my brother (Bob) was not acquainted with cooking methods, he was putting pink ribbons on the stove knob to assist him in his preparation of the evening meal. It was a very dry letter, very funny.

My brother wrote a return letter which described the events that took place when he attempted to follow my father's instructions. A fire had ensued which destroyed the apartment, leaving him sitting on the front lawn downstairs with our cat. My description obviously fails to capture the whimsy of his letter.

Which reminds me that we must have first acquired Professor (our cat) during this time, the cat was so-named because of the "wise" look on its (his?) face. As crazy a cat as ever lived. But then the poor creature was a tom and was *never* let out of the apartment. No wonder the animal was mad. If I remember, I'll describe how mad later.

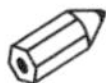

To get to Riis Park was virtually a day-long journey. First, we had to take a trolley car to the end of the line. Then a bus to the end of *that* line. Then a ferry across a channel. Then a mile walk (it seemed like a mile to my little legs, anyway) to the beach itself—not exactly a developed facility.

Later on, they built a bridge across that channel so one could drive all the way.

The beach was very clean, I recall. It should have been. Only a few adventurers would have traveled that far to reach the ocean.

I remember how blazing hot the sand was; white sand. So hot that one danced and hopped to the water instead of walking. And back to the blanket.

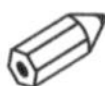

Anything else about that time?

I remember going to a candy store down on Flatbush Avenue to buy gum cards. What a useless memory.

All right—onward. Where did we move next?

No, wait. I remember something else. Uncle Sven lived down the street on Hubbard Place, almost in the same house Bob & Mary lived in.

I remember playing Hide and Seek one afternoon with my cousin Lily and some neighborhood kids.

I found a great spot in the kitchen—behind the big wood-burning stove. I pulled boxes around me and remained quiet.

No one could find me. I recall hearing their voices moving all over the house. They simply had no idea where I was. I should have called and let them know but I didn't. I don't know how long I hid there. I could be there to this day—a little boy skeleton—if I hadn't finally decided to come out.

I wonder if told them where I was—or did I want to save that hiding place for future use?

Well, that's really all I remember about that place. I would have been about eight or nine, I guess, before we moved.

I'd guess that we moved to 2258 E. 63rd St. in Marine Basin. How *do* I remember those addresses? Crazy. (It could be wrong, too—the 2258 part.)

I may be wrong but I *think* we moved there from 1282. If I'm wrong, I literally can't recall where else we might have moved. All the others came later. East 38th Street, Flatbush Avenue, Bedford Avenue. So I'll guess it was E. 63rd St.

I have many memories about that house. None of them are chronological. I will try to ignore that and merely notate them as I recall them.

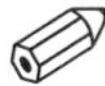

I remember the huge field of sand across the street. There was a sea of reeds beyond the sand. I remember some boys (Eddie Duyer?) building a house of reeds. I kept seeing boys go inside but couldn't talk myself into doing it. Finally, one day, I did.

Maybe I was claustrophobic but I remember not liking it and leaving soon. Also, I didn't like the big yellow spiders that frequented the reeds.

I remember (I think) us cooking potatoes—or "spuds"—in hot coals. One day, I saw what looked like an iron rod in the ground. I picked it up. It had been in a fire and was burning hot. I had big blisters all over my right palm. Very painful. I suppose my mother put butter on the burns. That was common practice in those days. How odd. Now to realize that cold water was the best solution. Or—later—something like butesin picrate, really a marvelous anti-burn ointment.

MUSINGS

In the winter, the reeds all died and came down. It all froze over and there was a huge field of ice. Many skaters in that period. We used to have sleds and fold up big pieces of cardboard like sails so that the wind propelled us for long distances across the ice. Fun, I imagine.

I remember a group of us stealing (borrowing) a rowboat and taking it out into Marine Basin. In the dead of winter, yet. All of us in our thick overcoats, and the other boys, chortling, rocking the boat from side to side. I don't know what I did. Pleaded at them to stop, I hope. My God, my mother would have had a heart attack had she known. If *my* kid did that and I knew about it, *I'd* have a heart attack. Four little boys in heavy overcoats. The water too cold. We'd have gone down like stones. I guess it wasn't our time.

I remember once going to the Basin in the summer with my father. I had a rubber tire tube around my waist. I jumped off the dock and right out of the tube. Down I went. Up. Down. I would have drowned if my father hadn't jumped in and carried me up. I was always afraid of water after that. I dreamed that I could swim for many years. It wasn't until I taught myself to swim that the dreams tapered off.

I think the school was P.S. 181. I think there were two sisters I liked—the Coulter sisters (Margaret and -?). They never knew. I could never tell them.

I recall the look of the place. It was red brick, near 59th Street, I think. I don't remember the teachers or the classes, all I remember is going to a special day with 35¢ in my pocket for sandwiches and cakes and milk. The teacher looked at me and told me I had a rash. I was humiliated. Did they take me to the school nurse? Don't recall. I know they let me take a sandwich and, I think, a piece of cake (no charge).

My mother (an ardent Christian Scientist, remember) poo-pooed the affliction—German Measles. She let me go outside and play, ignoring it. To tell the truth, I was never uncomfortable. I couldn't even see the rash when I looked in the mirror. Hysterical Blindness?

Random memories about that location.

There was a boy named Eddie Duyer who lived up the block. His father was an executive at Abraham & Straus Department Store where my sister worked.

Eddie was rich—at least to me he was. He always had the most advanced of toys. Guns. Cars. Everything. I think he even had a movie projector. I would go there to play—and admire, no doubt. And envy.

Fourth of July, he had a full assortment of firecrackers and rockets. There was no law against them at that time—1935, 36? I remember Red Devils. They were like—can't think of a comparison. Several inches in diameter, round, colored dark red, ½ inch thick. You ground them under the rear heel of your shoe and they made loud crackling, sputtering noises—minor (very minor) explosions. Poppings, really.

I have a visual memory of my father holding a one-inch firecracker in his right hand (lit) and letting it explode. Why did he *do* that? It must have scared me. Was he drunk? I don't recall that.

There was a Southern family a few doors down from us—toward the Marine Basin. The brother was probably thirteen or fourteen, his sister a little less.

They took me into their parent's bedroom and showed me a dirty comic book—Popeye and Mae West. I don't remember any specific pictures but they were vivid to me although (at the time) not stimulating. The main thrust of the story (if I may inadvertently pun) had to do with the gargantuan size of Popeye's organ and the difficulty—but pleasure—Mae West endured in receiving it.

When I went home, the little girl called after me, "Don't forget! Popeye and Mae West!" My mother inquired as to what that meant. "I don't know," I replied (rep-lied), "It's just something she's been saying."

Did she believe that? If she didn't, I'm sure she wouldn't have known how to pursue the subject, anyway.

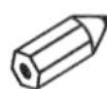

A brief entry, nothing to do with my past; in a way.

It is now 1995.

A new year, or not really. As I pointed out to Ruth Ann this morning, it is not really a new anything. It is an arbitrary breakdown, a choice made with some small logic based as it is on the revolution of the Earth around the Sun. Still, the psychological aspect of it is what counts and another cycle of the Earth around the Sun doesn't really affect that. Except as we choose to say it does.

All right, then. A "new" year, a new opportunity to change, to improve. That has a value to it, of course. Maybe that's why the "new year" idea became so popular. Who knows?

So why—or *what*—does it mean to me? My three-way resolve—instruction, walk, diet. I must try to read my instruction aloud in the A.M.—take a walk before breakfast—finally to stick to my Dr. Dulin diet—I *have* to do this to lower my cholesterol level, my SDL-HDL ratio, my triglycerides level.

Hope I can do it—see it through.

Back to memories. I recall a show given in a cellar, was it the same Southern brother and sister? The promise—or *offer*—was that we were going to see a movie. We didn't. It turned out that they (whoever they were) were going to buy a projector when they got enough admissions to raise the needed sum.

Ridiculous. What did we pay? 2¢, 3¢, a *nickel* even? We'd still be paying for that damned projector.

I think the girl sang and danced for us, her audience. Then they served refreshments, banana sandwiches. Never had I run across such a thing in my life and I never did again and Thank God for that. Sliced bananas between bread slices? Ugh.

It was in that house that we let Professor out for the first time. Or he *got* out. Have I already discussed what a weird cat he was? But understandable, for God's sake. He was a big tomcat and he wasn't fixed and he had been kept in for years on end. Jeez, he must have sprayed the ceiling.

Anyway, he got out on East 63rd Street and had a hell of a time, I suspect. Looked like hell. Got an ear ripped asunder. But got his rocks off, too, I hope.

There was also a chow dog I found. A nice dog, very friendly. We didn't know who it belonged to. We (my mother actually) let it sleep in the cellar where it was warm in the winter.

The chow dog mooed like a cow down there. Strange sound. A dog sounding like a cow. Down in the cellar.

Don't remember what happened to that dog. We didn't keep him, though.

A few more memories of E. 63rd Street. I wonder why there aren't more.

I learned to roller skate there.

I remember finding coins on the sidewalk.

I remember going swimming with my father. We were on a float. I had a rubber inner tube around my middle but I jumped right out of it and sank like a stone, rose to the surface, sank again. My father jumped in and held my head above the water. Saved again. (I *said* this already!)

It was a long trolley ride to get from there to church in Flatbush. Or anywhere.

My friend Norman lived nearby. What street was it? East 59th Street? That seems to ring a bell. Did that mean I could walk four or five blocks to his house? I don't remember doing it. (I don't think I'd met him yet.)

Well, I can't remember anything else about that house; why not? Seems like a blank, maybe more will occur to me later.

So I guess I'll go to the next place which—I can't remember any other place—was 962 Flatbush Avenue. There should be many recollections about that place. We'll see.

When we moved into the apartment on Flatbush Avenue, the cat (Professor) got lost. Did I say that we called him Professor because he usually had a "wise" look on his face? Well, that's why he was so named. I *did* mention it.

The apartment was on the third floor of the building, the

trolley tracks running by. On the final floor was a store, I forgot what it was. The only first-floor building I recall was several doors to the right as you faced the building.

It was a pancake restaurant—or coffee shop—or café; take your choice.

In its front window was a wondrous machine the like of which I had never seen before and have never seen since.

A pancake machine.

It had a round turntable—it was all stainless steel—at least it looked like it.

As you watched, a squishy white batter came down in a measured quantity. (I think they had to keep refilling the batter well.) These squirts came down in a regular pattern onto the slowly revolving turntable which was obviously a griddle. Equal distance from each other.

As soon as the batter hit this slowly turning griddle, bubbles would start to form on the top of the batter which miraculously (to me; it was probably just following the law of physics) formed itself into a perfectly round, perfectly sized, perfectly thick (after it rose a little) pancake.

Bubbles kept forming on top of the developing pancake—more and more. (I mean one could watch this process endlessly entranced.)

At exactly the halfway mark of its revolution, a spatula slid under the pancake (automatically, of course) and flipped it over, revealing the side that had been on the turning griddle—*perfectly brown*.

The pancake(s) kept turning until, at the finish line, another spatula snaked out of nowhere and picked up the finished pancakes—one—two—three of them—and deposited them on the platter for the waitress to serve.

Remarkable. I loved to watch it happen. It was a show.

My needs were simpler in those days.

But back to the apartment at 962 Flatbush Avenue.

On the second floor was a tuxedo rental business.

On the third floor, as noted, was our new apartment; which they called a "railroad" apartment because the rooms were all in a row.

You entered near the kitchen. To the right was—what?—a dining room? A family room? (No, there were no such things as family rooms in those—ancient?—days.) It had a mantelpiece with a mirror over it. There were windows that looked out over the Third Church of Christ Scientist where we went.

I remember (side-story) listening in that room, to the Joe Louis-Billy Conn fight (on the radio). It seemed as though Billy Conn was going to win. He out-boxed Louis for fourteen rounds. Then he got over-confident and thought he could knock out Louis. Mistake. Louis KO'd him in the fifteenth.

All right, back to the apartment. Next to the back room was my room; it had a window in it. One night, while I was sleeping in there and the family—my mother, sister, brother(?), father(?), anyway, "they" were in there when I started to make drumming sounds in my sleep—Bddirum—bddirum—bddirum—bum—bum!, etc. I don't know why I did it. Hardly a thrilling anecdote—but it *did* happen.

Next to my room was the room where my mother and sister slept. They had a yellow bedroom set—two beds, two end tables, two bureaus.

Also the upright piano was kept in that room—I think.

In the front room—the living room—the windows looked out on Flatbush Avenue. We had maple furniture with arms that folded down. A sofa and two chairs.

To the right of the living room, my brother had his room, a big bed and, I guess, a bureau. I think there was another door to the hallway in that room.

I said the cat was lost when we moved in. Well, we

found her—or rather the tuxedo rental place found *him*—he was a male, a tom—cowering under their tuxedo racks.

Professor Redux.

There are so many things I remember about those years at 962. No point trying to recount them chronologically, I'll just put them down as they pop up in my memory—like those little answer chips that popped up in that black "crystal ball" game—or novelty. You turned it over, no—set it upright, asking a question—and the answer floated up to the top. *Chances are good. You may be surprised*—and so on. Maybe that was where I first acquired the basic notion of The Nick of Time, my *Twilight Zone* with Bill Shatner & Pat Breslin.

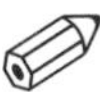

I remember the foods I bought and ate at 962.

There was a food store where I bought my bread (Pechter's) for 11¢ and small brown pumpernickels for 9¢. Corn rye (huge and delicious looking) cost 19¢ so we never bought them, as I recall; too expensive.

I remember when milk was on sale because of a strike. A nickel a quart! Wow! And, of course, there were bottles, I think—or maybe containers had just started appearing; can't remember that. No homogenization. The cream was at the top.

I do remember going to a grocery store on the corner of Bedford Avenue and, I believe, Albemarle Road. I brought, with me, a metal container with a tightly fitting top. They would take the milk from a *barrel* with a scoop and fill the can. Amazing. No one worried about sanitation and if the mild ever made anyone sick, I never heard about it. I did this for my aunt, Tante Evelyn.

MUSINGS

I remember buying bacon ends in Merkel's Meat Market. I think it was 29¢ a pound or close to it. All big chunks, some of them very meaty. I loved them. I actually took fried bacon on wheat toast sandwiches to high school. Cold bacon and cold toast, some mayonnaise, and I loved it! But that was much later.

I remember going to the fruit and vegetable market and buying a nickel's worth of "soup greens." They filled a big paper sack with turnips and celery and cabbage and carrots and so on. For a *nickel*, for God's sake! Need I add, "Them days is gone forever."

I remember a malted milk place across the way. Again, 5¢ for a malted. Mostly air and foam, of course, but tasty.

There was a candy store on the corner of Bedford and—can't remember (*Snyder Ave.- 1/30/98*) but the police station was on it—also The Edison Company. I remember there was a sale there in which we got a radio (*Emerson*), an iron, a toaster, and another appliance (I forget what), all for $29.95!

Pretty soon I'm going to start babbling about walking to school in the snow in my bare feet. But hell, these *were* the prices.

Anyway, in that candy store, they sold a cone-like ice cream from which they pulled the side paper, leaving, on the top, a round piece of paper which they held as they turned up the ice cream cone and pushed down on it, the cake cone or whatever you call it, and then peeled off the round piece of paper. I always got strawberry. Why did I always prefer that flavor? Anyway, the ice cream cone cost a nickel. Called Gobs. Sailor oriented, I think.

The most expensive ice cream, for some reason, was the Good Humor pop—delicious chocolate over equally as delicious ice cream - 20¢.

Any other food prices recalled?

Penny candy. One of my favorites—I was always frugal (probably because of the way we lived)—was called (I wince) *Dusky Dan*. The A.C.L.U. was obviously not in full swing in these days—or existent at all. On the wrapper was the charicaturish face of a "blackie"—big frizzy hair, dancing eyes, thick lips parted in a jolly, grimacing smile. ("Yessuh! Yessuh, boss!" he seemed to be saying.)

Anyway, I guess it was some kind of caramel; I don't know. If there hadn't been any rain, they could have erected buildings from them, they were so damned *hard*. On several occasions—in later years—we (my mother, sister and I) would walk *miles* from church to home and those *Dusky Dans* (2 for a penny) would last me the whole damn way! For the first half-mile or so, the best you could do was suck on it. If you had tried to bite into it, your teeth would have shattered.

Gradually, however, the warmth of your mouth softened the block (about 1 ½" x 1" and ¾" thick) to something vaguely malleable. In time—with patience, much mouth heat and an occasional judicious bite, the block would become chewable. It was an enduring piece of candy, that. Amazing value for a *penny*. I'm amazed that all that sugar didn't destroy my teeth.

Then again! Maybe it did. Our dentist, on the other side of Albemarle Road (around the corner from the church) *didn't believe in fillings*. My God. His name was Kaufman.

Enough about food. Except for one dessert we shared—my mother, sister, brother and me. A pint package with a layer of frozen strawberries and one of vanilla ice cream. Loft's Candy was the place.

The pint served all four of us. Thinking back on how much us kids ate ice cream, I can hardly believe it served all four of us.

I think it cost 29¢. Maybe 39¢. Very little though.

Well, I can't get away from food without mentioning the meals my mother made.

MUSINGS

Until Ruth Ann and I went to Epcot a few years ago and had a meal at the Norwegian Pavilion, I thought that everything my mother prepared for our meals was her own creation—except maybe *Fiskeboller*, which is fish balls and *Baakles*, a Christmas delicacy made with lots of butter, cream and flour, cut into shapes like this: (diagram) with a slit in the middle that one pointed end was inserted into so that the whole thing was folded over. Oh, and maybe *Lefse*, a kind of Norske tortilla. But I believe that all the main dishes were also Norwegian.

I remember in particular a soup she made with meatballs in it. It was for this soup that I went and got a nickel's worth of soup greens. I never liked that soup although I think I would now. I used to wait until the next day and scoop out the meatballs, slice them and make myself a meatball sandwich on rye.

I remember, too, one Saturday a.m.—a midday—when I had nine (9!) slices of pumpernickel with a slice of American cheese on each—all of which I ate white I read an illustrated volume of *ROBINSON CRUSOE*. The first time I read it, I think.

Food. Food.

My mother made a kind of chow mein with lamb that I liked a lot. Also a paprika with lamb and rice that was good. Something called *Lobscouse*, I think it's spelled, really just mashed potatoes with some steaks of cooked beef in it. Corned beef and cabbage, too—all that salt!—which, of course, I did not think was Norwegian.

Page 52—Obscured by writing on the other side with *dark*, wet pen.

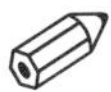

The Astor Theater was on the next block, across the street, next to Erasmus High School (at the time I didn't know who Erasmus was; I'm still not sure I do).

The Astor showed foreign films. It had *great* seats that could be pushed back into a reclining position—well, almost reclining, and the row you were in was so wide you could stretch your legs out all the way. I loved going there. No popcorn, of course; a candy machine, probably—which was all that *any* theater had—even the Loew's Kings. Did I mention the Loew's Kings on an earlier page? I forget.

Anyway, the film I remember most vividly from The Astor was a Russian version of *GULLIVER'S TRAVELS*—I must have seen it three-four-five times. And *never once* did I have the slightest suspicion that the film was Communist propaganda. So much for warping the minds of the young. How can you warp their minds if they don't even know you're doing it?

Only later did I realize that there were two types of Lilliputians—the intolerant monarchy and the hard-working (oppressed) laborers. (Did they work in *mines*? I'm not sure.)

But guess who won? Guess who The Big Guy *helped* to win?

There was a bookstore across the way. And once I was idiotic enough to take all the books I'd gotten as presents over the years—*HEIDI*, *LITTLE MEN*, *THE JUNGLE BOOK*, etc. and *sell* them to the store for *peanuts*!

My mother was very unhappy about that. I don't blame her. She said that *she* would have bought them if I didn't want them.

MUSINGS

What an idiot. Beautiful editions. And I got $7 or a little more, bought some other books, not exactly a good deal.

The *ROBINSON CRUSOE* I mentioned reading was not my book but from the library.

(Don't use this black pen anymore! It obscures the opposite page. Gleeps! As some cartoon characters said in those days.)

Onward—

The theaters in that area. Did I already describe them? I don't think so.

Closest was The Albemarle, almost across the street from our apartment. (Sidetrack—I remember when they started running "streamlined" trolley cars on Flatbush Avenue. Very attractive and quiet—sort of grey in appearance.)

Down the street was the Loew's Kings. Does it still exist? I don't know.

I remember seeing a program on PBS about the Loew's Kings. It was so wonderfully ornate, a true movie "palace" of the day.

There was a time when they had matrons in white (nurse's) uniforms with flashlights who saw to it that young'uns sat in the children's section.

I hated that. I remember going to see *THE THEIF OF BAGDAD* with Sabu and sitting in the adult's section, sitting as erect and tall and adult as I could.

No good. The matron came and shone her damn flashlight at me and asked how old I was. I should have lied but I guess I told the truth—which was about thirteen. (Jesus, now really *rough* films are classified PG-13!)

So, anyway, she escorted me to the children's section where I sat, offended and in high dudgeon.

I remember seeing *THE FIREFLY* there with Allen Jones and Jeanette MacDonald. I still remember the damn lyrics of that song Jack Jones' daddy sang—or at least the climax of them. "*Senorita donkey sita, not so fleet as a mosquito, but so sweet like my Chiquita, you're the one for me!*"

Many a film seen there. No popcorn stands of course. One candy machine. My Tante Evelyn used to send my cousins Vivian and Francis and me to the *Kings* with paper sacks of food—sandwiches, cookies, even oranges—I remember the pungent spray as I peeled the orange in the darkness, certain that someone would complain and have me ejected forthwith.

Down the street, further, on the same side (North, I think) of Flatbush Avenue was The Rialto. Part of the same chain as The Albeemarle—there was also The Parkside, The Patio, The Farragut, The Marine, so *many* movie houses—that was an important part of my childhood and adolescence. All those plots still swimming around in my psyche. *GONE WITH THE WIND, THE CAT PEOPLE, THE GUNFIGHTER, THE JUNGLE BOOK, FOUR FEATHERS* (loved that one), etc.

My mother wouldn't let me see scary pictures—*or* listen to scary programs on the radio; amusing to consider that. I used to listen to *Let's Pretend* (Nila Mack's, I think) and those stories were really scary—I remember Blue Beard's former wives groaning as they hung on hooks in the Secret Room, that the heroine was NEVER supposed to open. (Yeah, sure.)

But no *Lone Ranger*, no *Gang Busters*, no nothing else like them. Amusing.

I remember talking her once into taking me to see *THE WEREWOLF OF LONDON* with Henry Hull. (I should have told him about this when I met him on the set of *MASTER OF THE WORLD*.) When Henry started sprouting hair and fangs, I flopped down into the aisle and crawled out of the theater; *Lord*, I was sensitive. Saw no more of it.

Needless to say, Mums was piqued by this.

Down the street from The Farragut was The Glenwood Theater, a part of no chain (no self-respecting chain would have deigned to operate it). A true disaster of a theater that showed only long-used films, i.e. once they had a big sign outside that said BUCK BENNY RIDES AGAIN—which was surprising since that film was playing first-run, in the New York Paramount. (Later, I'll speak about the movies and other items—in Manhattan.) Upon approaching, one could see that what the "poster" actually said was *Jack* BUCK BENNY RIDES AGAIN *in "ARTISTS AND MODELS*." The ruse did not work.

The theater was a true wreck. Ready for the junk heap. I remember one particular Saturday matinee when they had a stage show—a magician. The thing is, there was no stage as such but only a ledge about 18" wide on which this pathetic magician was trying to prestidigitate and, at the same time, try to keep himself from toppling off the ledge onto the first-row laps of bored boys.

Then, too, the seats were all rotting. While viewing the ancient films, one would idly pluck tufts of straw stuffing from the seats.

Once, when my mother and I went there, we had to move because it was raining outside and, where we were sitting, it was *also* raining. The Glenwood roof was not in the best condition.

Then, of course, up the block the other way was The Astor, and on the next street (I forget its name, I shouldn't. *Church Avenue*?) was The RKO Kenmore to the left, The Flatbush Theater to the right.

The Flatbush was later converted to a legitimate theater house and was pretty good as I recall—in my teen years, I saw *JASON* with Charles Bickford, *HARVEY* with Frank Fay, *BROOKLYN, USA* (a gangster melodrama—I vividly remember an ice pick murder in a barber shop scene).

But when I first went to The Flatbush it was not too much higher in the esteem than The Glenwood.

The one film I remember most seeing there (because it caused a book in my head) was *DRACULA*. I guess I was sixteen. And I remember thinking, "If one vampire is scary, what if the whole world was *filled* with vampires?"—The birth of *I AM LEGEND*.

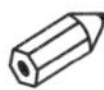

My sister Gladys saw a lot of movies back then—pre-marriage and motherhood, of course.

Often, after Sunday school for me (Rhoda Wynick), I remember my teacher speaking despairingly of the Catholics, saying, "They're walking *in* darkness, boys. *Darkness*." And her, Jewish! Funny, I *said* this. And church for my sister and mother. Gladys often took us to one of the two cafeterias around the corner and we'd have lunch. One of the cafeterias was named Bickford's; I forget what the other one was called.

After lunch, Gladys would take us to The Kenmore and we saw such films as *LITTLE MISS MARKER* and *WEE WILLIE WINKIE* and so on—it was Shirley Temple's heyday.

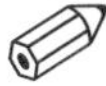

While we lived at 962 Flatbush Avenue, I went to two public schools.

MUSINGS

The first one was P.S. 89(?) 81? 18? It was on the corner of Bedford and Church Avenue. It was an old brick building with a bathroom out in back.

What do I remember about it?

Not much. Mostly *The Quill*. The first "newspaper" I ever worked on. I have one of them somewhere. The student who wrote the most articles on any given week got to keep that issue.

I got to keep the biggest issue we ever put out. It was about 82 pages long (now that I think about it, I think the school *was* P.S. 81) and each page was inked individually.

I think I was some kind of editor on it. I think the editor was a short kid named Harold Hempling, a dynamo. The sports editor was George Jackson, a black boy. I well remember his editorial which exhorted us readers to make sure we put out our cigars when we were finished with them. (The teacher must have had great trouble stifling her hilarity for our sakes.)

I did the cover for that issue—a quill pen in a holder—naturally.

We copied stories (none of them important) from newspapers, magazines, etc. How old was I then? Eleven? Something like that. Ten maybe.

I began to write around the time I was eight. I had little poems and stories published in *The Brooklyn Eagle*. There was a kid's page called Aunt Jean's Column—or Page, I don't recall.

Payment was in stars that you could add up and exchange for various gifts.

Somewhere in the void of the cosmos are my stars, floating about eternally uncashed.

There used to be pictures with no details. The details you cut out separately and pasted on the picture.

For example, there was a house front and lawn and you cut out the furniture for the porch, the window curtains, the flower banks, etc. I pasted the welcome mat on the roof, why I don't know. That amused my mother.

I had a poem about Columbus printed on Aunt Jean's Page.

> When Columbus sailed
> He said "At least
> I'll find
> A short route to the East."

Not exactly T.S. Eliot, but okay. It also had lines like:

> They sailed and sailed across the sea
> 'til the lookout said "I see the branch of a tree!"

And about our cat, Professor (I mentioned her before I think):

> She's just a ball of mischief and always full of fun
> But still we love him dearly when all is said and done

Well, not too bad for a kid. It was a start, anyway.

Up on Bedford Avenue, off Snyder Avenue, at (I believe) 2258, was the house of my aunt and uncle—Uncle Tollef and Tante Evelyn, my cousin Francis and my cousin Vivian.

MUSINGS

There are so many memories about that house, they tumble through my mind and I hope I can recollect them all.

First of all, the shape of it. There was a porch in front on which summer furniture was kept. Actually, the front of the property which was on the sidewalk of Bedford Avenue had some high bushes and a picket fence. I helped Uncle Tom (the Americanization of Tollef) build it. Well, of course, I merely assisted as best I could; he was a carpenter by profession. I could scarcely drive a nail. I suppose I held the pickets for him. Maybe I sawed a little. He must have planed down the picket tops by *eye*; amazing.

So anyway, the porch steps were on the left and the front door was on the porch. The house was two stories high with an overhanging roof providing the porch "ceiling."

In the front hall, the stairs of the second floor were to the left, the wall on the left. To the right of the staircase was a hallway leading to the dining room which, today, would be called the family room.

To the right was the entrance to the living room—or parlor. (I didn't mention that the front entrance had double doors with windows in them, curtains in the window.)

The living room had two windows which overlooked the porch. There was an upright piano in there, I think to the left. Also to the left was another entrance into the dining room.

I remember the round heavy table in the dining room, a fringed hanging lamp above it. There must have been at least six chairs around it.

To the right was one window which overlooked the alley—a narrow walk. I would say there was a fireplace to the left of the window but there were no fireplaces then. I suspect there was some kind of mantel, though, and to the left of that was Uncle Tom's chair, brown leather upholstery (cracked as I recall) and a wooden frame. Flat arm tops and on the right (or was it the left?) a button that you could depress so that the back of the chair leaned back—an early (*very* early) recliner. Next to the chair, to its right, was a window that overlooked the backyard.

The dining room led to the kitchen which was a step down. I remember them bathing their dogs there and making something they called "Calorie Balls" out of dog food and bread and what other ingredients I *don't* remember.

Their dogs were crazy about them, though. Whenever they said "Calorie Balls!" the dogs would come out of their skins with excitement. They were *big*, too, the size of a very large matzo ball. Not the dogs.

Their dogs were as follows; in the beginning of memory:

Boots belonged to Tante Evelyn (and Uncle Tom, I guess). She was a terrier of some kind, like our dog Katy. But *very fat*! They would let her sit at the table in a kind of high chair. Her rear end was so capacious she could sit up. She wore a bib—or a napkin—around her neck and they fed her by hand. It seemed okay to me at the time. Now it seems a little weird, after having two dogs in *our* lives.

Paddy belonged to Vivian. She was like a small, brown English Setter (I don't suppose any of them were breeds) and quiet, sort of pleasant.

Franny had a little dog named Snubb. I do mean little, not much bigger than a large Chihuahua. God knows what breed (or breeds) she was derived from. I remember that her lower jaw protruded a little in front so that her tiny teeth showed. She was a feisty animal, often attacking larger dogs.

All of them were females, of course. I'm sure they weren't fixed, either, or even taken to a vet. My sister had a dog that died of—what?—Epilepsy? No, some other common—and terrible dog affliction. She never took it to the vet. Bad news—our vet bills were sky high but they were *our dogs*, our *family*, we would not have done otherwise.

Later, Franny got (after the war) a Belgian Sheppard. I forget what he called her; it may come to me one day. A sweet dog.

But back to (approximately) 1936 or '37.

There was a backyard to the house. It was about—I guess—twenty-feet wide and forty-feet deep, ending in the brick wall of a building. On the left side of it was another brick wall of another building.

On the right side was a fence with a grape vine (vines?) growing on it. Purple grapes. I remember all of us picking them and Tante and Mom and Vivian cooking them up and then bottling jam they made from it, sealing them with wax.

There are things that we did in that yard. It was our playground.

There was a house next door in which The Mulroys lived. Their son was George, their daughter Mary, a pretty Colleen. Franny had a crush on her. It was one of the many heartaches in his life then and to come in the ensuing years. But more on that later.

I remember—much later but I'll mention it now—playing "Desert Island" with George (we weren't very good at games without Francis). We were "shipwrecked" and had adventures and planted fruit and vegetables for ourselves to subsist on. The food was made of some kind of pottery or something. They came from refrigerator displays at the Sears Roebuck several blocks away. How Franny's folks got hold of them I have no idea. This included roast chicken. George and I planted them, as well. It was remarkable soil. It grew chickens already roasted.

By the way, that Sears used to give variety shows on Saturday nights. I remember going to them with The Nelsons;

I was over there a *lot*. As a matter of fact, all our social lives consisted of seeing each other exclusively, The Nelsons, Mom, Gladys and me (and sometimes brother Bob) and Lily and her dad, Uncle Sven (Svenningsen). The adults played Bridge on Friday nights in a group Tante Evelyn called "The Ha-Ha Club." While they played, I read the "funnies," stacks of newspaper comics which my aunt never threw away.

While I read them (sitting in my uncle's chair), I nibbled from a plate of groceries my aunt always prepared for me. I recall *Milky Ways* sliced up like a little chocolate bread. Cookies too, I guess. Fruit? I wonder. Did we *ever* eat anything nutritious?

That was, of course, when I wasn't doing something with my cousin Francis—I always called him Franny.

More on that backyard and my memories of it.

First the "obstacle" course Franny and Bill McAndrew (I mentioned him earlier, in the Marine Basin house section) built against the brick wall on the left side of the yard.

It was very elaborate, a true maze that ran pretty much along the entire length of the wall. It consisted of rooms and tunnels and overhead exits, etc. One tried to get through the maze as fast as possible fighting the clock—or watch that someone else held. In through the top, around corners, over walls, through tunnels, and through the roof, down in again, whoom, whoom, whoom. It was fun.

Then there was the summer house. It was—or had been—an exhibit in a travel office. I guess Uncle and Tante cleaned there. Now that I recall, they did a lot of office and building cleaning. Obviously, making a living during the Depression was not an easy task; they probably had to do a number of jobs to get by.

Anyway, Uncle rebuilt the house in the back of the yard. It was very cute. The lower part had been redone so there was a bench on each side, a table between them. We had many a Sunday early "dinner" out there—usually, as I recall, cold cuts and rye bread and pickles and potato salad—oh, that deli potato salad was good. It was all from the deli, of course. Also lettuce & tomato, I'm sure.

Upstairs—or, at least, on the second level was a small, enclosed room the floor of which was, of course, the ceiling of the floor below.

Franny used this room as his clubhouse or something, I can't say. You went up a ladder to get to it and had to crawl on knees inside, hunched over like a beetle (it was a sweatbox in the summer). I don't know what we did up there, held conspiratorial meetings, perhaps. It *was* the site of a highly dramatic moment many years later. I may as well describe it now although I don't think it took place until 1930 or '40.

Franny owned a pistol that was the marvel of our trio—him, George and me. It couldn't have been as great as we all thought but it was our idol. I don't know where he got it, maybe he saved so many B-O Oatmeal tops that he could send for it—probably fifty or a hundred. Bobby Benson was the name of the show he listened to on the radio; his Indian companion was named Harka—what useless memories.

Anyway, we played cowboy games and other shoot-'em-up games and naturally Francis always won them because he was years older than we were. (I'll speak about the attic games later.) But one day when George and I showed up after school, it was to find a note tacked to the back door. It was from Franny and he explained that he felt he was too old now for guns and accordingly (he didn't use the word "accordingly," of course) he had destroyed his priceless gun.

George and I were stunned. We couldn't believe it. As a matter of fact, it was following this traumatic incident that he and I attempted to play games together. Failing totally, of course.

So, following the instructions of Franny's note, we went out to the Summer House, up the ladder, and into Franny's secret room where we found the Wonder Pistol in fragments—he had broken it to pieces with a hammer, maybe on a chopping block (more on the cellar later, too).

George and I hunkered, aghast, over the pieces of Franny's pistol. I don't remember if we spoke. Perhaps we were too choked up, hard to say.

Of such moments are made up the melodrama of growing up.

Nothing more about the backyard I can remember. This is a five-subject notebook and I seem to be coming to the end of the first subject. As arbitrary a division as that on the clock or calendar.

There is much more to be said about the house, which I will do next time I write. My accident in the cellar, the upstairs, Franny's room in particular—and the attic.

Well, that concludes Subject One, whatever it was—71 pages of penned comment and remembrances.

Onward.

There was a cellar in my aunt and uncle's house, too. A real, old-fashioned, honest-to-God cellar. (Interesting how much that house is featured in my memory; probably because we never had a house, not really.)

The cellar had a dirt floor, a very steep, almost ladder-like set of steps down to it from the kitchen, a low ceiling.

I'm sure my uncle must have done carpentry work there but I remember mostly the chopping block. The furnace must have been wood-burning. I don't associate anything uneasy about the chopping block—undoubtedly a tree trunk part with an axe-scarred top.

I remember my cousin Lily and I having a duel with two sticks. Unhappily, the stick she used had, near its end, a nail sticking through it and, in taking a swipe at me, Lily (with amazing ease, it seems) knocked the nail *right through the thumb* of my right hand. Ugh! The memory gives me a twinge, I must have screamed—how old was I, ten? Eleven?—and my aunt came down—or we went up; I forget.

My aunt took it out—pulled it out of my thumb!—and bandaged the thumb. No doctor used. No tetanus shot. Just wrapped a clean bandage around it. Amazingly, I never got infected or lockjaw. Good health? Good heredity? Christian Science protection? Who knows?

On another occasion, in that same cellar, I stepped on a board with a nail in it and the nail went right through my sneaker and into my foot by an inch or so. Another scream. My uncle, this time—I think—pulling out the nail and my aunt bandaging the foot. Again, no doctors' visit—we were, after all, Christian Scientists and never saw the inside of the doctor's office—no tetanus shot, not even disinfectant on the foot. I suppose my aunt washed it with soap and water. But, again, *no* infection, *no* lockjaw. Was everyone's belief that I wouldn't get infected prevent—or help to prevent—that infection? Power of the mind? After all, the cellar floor was hardly sanitized.

Then there was the upstairs. Odd that I used that house as the pattern for the hero's childhood house in my novel—as yet unpublished (1995)—*THE LINK*. It is a haunted house. Do I believe that house to be haunted? It probably isn't even there anymore.

But the house, in my memory, *is* haunted, of course. But it isn't unpleasantly haunted. To be haunted merely means that "something" remains, resides, not necessarily unpleasant. And my memories of that house are primarily pleasant.

The upstairs.

Odd that I remember so little of it.

It seems, in my recollection, that I never went into my cousin Vivian's room. She was always reclusive, stayed there by herself often, even ate there. Kept the door closed.

And I don't recall ever going into my aunt and uncle's room. Odd that my aunt I remember only as Tante—which I presume is "aunt" in Norwegian, maybe in Scandinavian. But it is *Uncle* Tom. Was there no Scandinavian word for uncle?

I *must* have looked in their bedroom but I just don't ever remember doing it. The only two rooms I recall were Franny's room and the attic, which you reached by going up a staircase as steep as a ladder; well, almost.

Franny's room was very small. I would have to say no larger than seven foot by nine. There was his small bed, his tiny desk. I don't think there was much floor space at all.

I recall being in there on an evening with Franny, Cousin Lily and Snubs. We were watching a Mickey Mouse movie on the wall, the projector cranked. The entire room was filled with us.

It is June 2, 1995. I bought a book last weekend entitled *FLATBUSH ODYSSEY*. I wish I hadn't now. So sad. At first, it brought on nostalgic smiles. But then the author—who had travelled through Flatbush today—described the changes.

Small ones, of course. I quote:

"Now only The Kenmore [I think I wrote about it earlier] remained in business, sliced into quadrants. [Four theaters, I add to explain.] The Farragut Theater was The YMCA. The Albemarle belonged to the waitresses. The Flatbush Theater was [is] a furniture store. The Rialto was [is] the grandest of the multiple Eglises de Dieu of the Haitian Pentecostals; its 1500 seats were intact but its stage had become a pulpit and, in place of the silver screen, was a mural of a domed and spired city, set in a peaceful glade called 'The New Jerusalem.' And the Loew's Kings, the Versailles of the Wooded Flat, was locked up and dead."

All my old theater hangouts, Kaput. I'm sorry I found out. The only theater he missed was the old Astor Theater, the wide-rowed, comfortable seat theater that showed foreign films, where I saw the Russian *THE NEW GULLIVER*.

More later, a trip *into* the locked-up Loew's Kings. And I saw a program on PBS (or was it AMC) about how The Loew's Kings had become a national—or state—landmark! No longer.

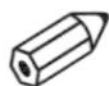

More on the attic. I hope I haven't already written about this. Maybe it's because its "written" in my mind, always. So it seems already done.

Anyway, I was a spoiled kid and Franny preferred the deferential quietude of George Mulroy in our elaborate games—all evolved by Franny; all of them.

He built an airplane section against the left wall as you entered the attic up those steep, steep stairs. It had a cabin inside with two seats, a windshield, steering wheels, instrument panel, even a special water bottle.

Franny and George were the pilots, Franny actually the pilot and George the co-pilot. I was jealous, I think, but no way was I permitted to "fly" in that craft—which even had the contour of an airplane; a wonderful pretend ship.

For me there was a cabin boat on the other side of the narrow attic. Inside there was even a stove with knobs made out of L-shaped hooks. But I didn't know how to play the games of intrigue on my own. While Franny and George were ensconced in that wonderful cabin, I was either slumped in *my* cabin, turning the gas stove off and on, or sitting on the "deck" in back of the cabin, staring at the attic. Not too evocative. You would think the future writer would come up with something. I didn't. Franny did it all and he and his co-pilot were cut off from me. Who did I portray, anyway? The bad guy? Some schnook in a boat? Who knows?

We also created—Franny and I, I don't recall George being a part of it—an entire world in which we each had a flying group, a corps. Of course, Franny was the source; he always was. His great imagination and talent makes the story of his life all the more tragic. But, as formerly noted, more on that later.

Franny subscribed to—at least purchased regularly, a magazine called, as I recall, *Bill Barnes Air Trails (Adventures?)*.

Bill Barnes had a group of flyers who he led. They became involved in all sorts of adventures; I wonder why no one ever filmed them. He had a modern plane, with a huge pontoon base with wheels, called The Snorter. Later, he had an even more elaborate plane with two pontoons, called The Silver Streak.

So Franny and I made up our own crew of variegated heroes. His leader was Kent Grayson (later, Franny made Kent his middle name). Funny, I can't remember the name of my leader, although it's on the tip of my mind. We had faces (James Ramsey? Possible) for each of our flyers that we cut from the Sears Roebuck catalogue. Regular dossiers with description.

Moreover, we had our own model airplane for our men! Franny built them all; he was marvelous at that, too; God what talent! I tried to build my own but they were dross, absolutely dross. I remember a Fokker Tri-wing WWI plane, Richthofen's plane. It was perfect, painted red and everything. Franny built it.

And the body was carved from a plain piece of balsa, with no pre-shaping at all, as model planes later had more and more. I recall how clever and gifted my cousin Francis was.

That house holds many memories for me. I may repeat, Franny and me and my cousin Lily all crammed into his little bedroom, cranking a little "movie" camera—I think it was mine—and laughing as a Mickey Mouse movie cartoon was projected onto—what? A sheet? The wall? And did we laugh at the movie, or at the absurdity of the three of us crammed into that tiny bedroom, watching a movie. Snubbs was there, too!

I remember Vivian's Sweet Sixteen birthday party. It was like a highlight of our family experience. I have thought, at times, of writing a play about that party because, in a way, it was the high point, the peak. The immigrant family at its zenith. Everyone was there, even my father, as I recall. All the kids. All the Ha-Ha Club, everyone. Vivian happy, her life ahead of her. Laughter. Joy. Everyone's lives ahead of them. But we didn't know, of course, what *was* ahead in our lives. Tragedy, mostly. My father dying of pneumonia because of his drinking. My aunt destined to die of a heart attack. My uncle Sven doomed to drink again and die of a heart attack. My brother never able to throw off his alcoholism, finally dying of colon cancer which, I believe, was caused by his drinking. Vivian doomed to grossly overweight spinsterhood, lonely last days. Franny doomed to a period of total alcoholism before his premature death. Uncle Tom drinking again, never a happy man. Lily drinking to excess, I was told by my brother, losing her husband to suicide. I don't know who else was there—Albert? I don't know if he was present, or what happened to him consequently. (Have I spoken about him and "Greasy" picking up Franny and I to play baseball? If not, I will.) His brother Eddy, a professional Army man, was an alcoholic. God, what a family legacy! I'll never write that play because, while the centerpiece of it—the party—would be (or *could* be, anyway) quite funny, all the character "realizations" would be totally tragic. Never; never.

I remember standing on a board—how old was I—ten, eleven, twelve? Don't remember, but I was blindfolded, lifted up and up, told to hold my balance or I would fall. They told me how high I was. I could feel the *ceiling* over my head! I guess I lost my balance and fell, and was caught—no more than a few *inches* from the floor. The board was barely lifted, another board held over my head for the "ceiling." Laughter. I was duped.

How can I recall those parties? The decorations on the table. Party hats. Laughter. There was always laughter in my family, I recall.

Until the laughter ended in sadness.

Well, I forgot. Gladys was there. I hope her life was happy. Bob's wife Mary—I think they were just keeping company at that time—was there. She and Bob had both been drinkers but she stopped after motherhood came—although later drank beer regularly—in a champagne glass; what did that signify? She always referred to me as Bob's "big-shot Hollywood brother." Did she dislike me a lot? I know she thought I was spoiled when I was a kid. I'm sure she was right.

I may go back to that house in memory but I should return to 962 Flatbush Avenue and see what else I remember.

P.S. 139, I'll try to recall some of that.

But first I recall my father and mother's 30th Anniversary party. I think they were given a set of silver-plated tableware; the 30th is the silver anniversary, of course.

Lily and I were the watch guards. My father had taken my mother to The Kenmore Theater to get her out of the house while the decorations were set up. We sat in the darkest living room, looking down to the left. The Kenmore was on Church Avenue, a long block away. In order for my father to not forget, he brought a little blue table alarm clock. He didn't have a watch.

Lily and I amused ourselves by playing the (age-old?) game of "My Car—Your Car." To do this, the one "up" would say something like, "The next car coming is my fancy weekend car." Then if a small wreck of a car appeared, we had a good laugh.

My father fell asleep at the movies. I think he did that a lot. In the quiet of the film, the alarm clock went off. At first, he didn't even wake up. My mother had, I believe, to retrieve the alarm clock from my father's coat pocket and push in the knob to shut it up; most embarrassing for her, I'm sure.

Anyway, we spotted them coming and gave the word to the guests—family, actually, and it was "Happy Anniversary!" as they entered.

I can't believe that my mother didn't suspect that something was going on.

A memory in the mist.

All right, P.S. 139.

It was on Cortelyou Road. There was an electric bus that ran on Cortelyou. Very comfortable—leather seats—and *quiet*. I rode it when it rained, I'm sure. It was quite a walk, actually. I think I went there for two years, ages twelve & thirteen.

The principal's name, I seem to recall, was Nathan Dickler. He was bald; I remember. He is probably with his ancestors. I'm sure he must be or he'd be over 100 years old.

There was also Kane. He was seventeen. Consequently, he always won the races on Field Day.

He also slugged the shop teacher, a maintenal named Mr. Dannerberg, also gone from the world, I'm sure. I believe Kane knocked him across a workbench. Dannerberg used to rap kids on the knuckles with a metal ruler. I escaped it. Kane obviously didn't—to Dannerberg's surprise.

I never knew if Kane was ousted for it.

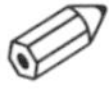

We took cooking classes in that shop room. Ridiculous recipes.

The only one I remember is a cheese sauce that tasted so bad, we poured it out the window when the teacher wasn't looking. On those below? I hope not.

MUSINGS

My memories are very fragmentary regarding P.S. 139.

I remember Richard Greene and his incredible maps of the United States he made. I suspect he traced them. They were too perfect.

What we did was draw an outline of the United States, then put capsules of various matter—corn, wheat, sugar, etc. on the appropriate spots on the map—agricultural, obviously.

I remember a drug store fountain we went to on—I think—Mondays at lunchtime. Some of the boys ordered a cream soda to go with their bag lunch, I suppose I brought milk but I don't recall that, and I wonder to this day why the server let us use the back room for such little return.

I remember Betty Hecht, who taught us Grammar (I never understood it and don't to this day) and Music Appreciation. I remember her teaching us the *Andante Cantabile* by Tchaikovsky. We had to sing it "This is the *Andante Cantabile* by Peter Ilyich Tchaikovsky." But it stuck with me anyway.

I had my first taste of popcorn at P.S. 139. It was at a class party. Maybe it was Halloween. For some reason, I always thought of Crackerjacks when I thought of popcorn. I could actually watch them making the popcorn with butter and salt and still visualize it as tasting like the sickly sweet caramel flavor of Crackerjacks. How fascinating. (Not really.)

At the party, I tried some anyway and fell in love with popcorn. Of course, it was the only time I ever had it until I was in basic training in Georgia and they sold it in the town theaters and, I believe, in the post theaters. And, of course, at college, all the theaters in Columbia served popcorn.

One little theater there had an old man (I think he was old) who popped corn in the lobby. I always felt that he used the popping machine as a social aid. He only made a little

Brooklyn Tech, on the other hand, was *way* down town, past Prospect Park, around the circle, all the way down through Brooklyn Heights to Atlantic Avenue, then a long walk to the school on Fort Greene Place.

A long trolley ride, five days a week. Less sleep. Late hours, doing homework. (I'll describe my jobs at Merit Farms later.) Weariness.

Idiot.

1940's

I had begun to worry about the difficulty of trying to organize this account. Tell it properly—in the correct sequence.

Then I decided it was unimportant and would hamstring me. So the key with it—I'll just remember items as they come to me. If it fouls up chronological accuracy, so be it. The memories are more important than the accuracy.

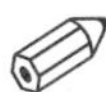

Third Church of Christ Scientist.

Around the corner from 962. As I think I mentioned, I could see the back of the church from the back window of our railroad apartment.

I went to Sunday school there during this period.

I met my long time friend Norman Kennelly there. (So, obviously, I could not have known him when I lived on E. 63rd St. in Mill Basin; I hadn't met him yet.)

Amazingly enough, I can remember his telephone number! Esplanade 7—6947, what keeps such a memory in the brain?

Like the fragments of W.S. Gilbert lyrics from a song in—I believe—*IOLANTHE*—or maybe *THE GONDOLIERS*.

When you're lying awake
with a dismal headache

and repose is tabooed
by anxiety
I suppose you may use
any language you choose
to indulge in
without impropriety
if your head is on fire
your bedclothes conspire
of usual slumber to plunder your first
your counterpart goes
and uncovers your toes
they your sheet slips demurely
from under you

and the conclusion:

You're a regular wreck
with a crick in your neck
and no wonder you snore
you're head's on the floor
you've needles and pins
from your soles to your shins
and some fluff in your lungs
and a feverish tongue
and a thirst that's intense
and a general sense
that you haven't been sleeping on clover!

Something like that. A lot of words ensconced in the bean with no value whatever. W.S. Gilbert—what a lyricist!

One of my teachers in Third Church was Rhoda Wynick. She was Jewish by heritage, a lot of Jewish people decided to "become" Christian (and escape prejudice? Who knows?) by joining the C.S. church.

It didn't always work.

I had a young "formerly" Jewish boy in my class.

His uncle—a Rabbi—had "torn the vest" and declared the boy dead.

A bit harsh on a kid.

Another teacher I had was Mr. Feeney—I think it was in this class for older teenagers (but not co-educational; the girls had their own classes) that I met Norman.

Mr. Feeney was a tough old guy as I recall. He worked for the FBI, I think. A no-nonsense Christian Scientist. Never said to persevere with science if you weren't up for it. Call a doctor instead. Not that science might not work—it *did* work. But only that if you didn't feel up to the challenge, don't grit your teeth and die. Or let you *child* die...as some of the C.S. folks have done.

Fanaticism is an evil thing. Especially when *imposed* on others. *Children*? Terrible!

Rhoda Wynick used to wail about the Catholics.

"They're walking in darkness, boys," she told us. I alread mentioned that.

Very educational.

I remember learning about Pearl Harbor on Sunday, December 7, 1941. Most people do remember that—of my generation, that is. People remember those things. Like the day President Kennedy was assassinated.

Anyway, we were not listening to the football game—the NY Giants?—but the concert from, I imagine, Carnegie Hall. I don't remember the composition they were playing or who the conductor was—Bruno Walter? The NY Philharmonic? Possibly?

The next day, a shop class in Brooklyn Tech was interrupted so we could listen to Roosevelt's "Day of Infamy" speech. (I wonder how many Americans knew what "infamy" meant. A derivation, I suppose, of "infamous.")

Brooklyn Tech.

Clearly, I started attending in the fall of 1939—I graduated in June, 1943. Ages thirteen-seventeen.

It was while I was in Tech that I "achieved" my height. When I graduated from P.S. 139 I was taller than 5'7 or so; a little plump, too, I think.

I don't remember too many details of my first year.

I recall wood shop. I was lousy at it. Especially waxing fillets at sheet edges.

I remember Strength of Materials. A *very* expensive lab. Extremely intricate machinery to test—what?—when a piece of paper would tear; when a piece of metal would rupture. Fascinating.

English was not emphasized.

I was good at algebra so that helped. After all, it was a math test that got me into the damn school in the first place. Would that I had just failed that test and just taken general high school courses—English, a language, etc. at Erasmus, *across the street* from our apartment!

Instead, coming, was forge classes, sheet metal shop, machine shop, ship building, et al. Spot welding, rivet guns, oxyacetylene torches. Jesus. And I wanted to write, compose, and be an "artiste." Yeah, yeah.

RICHARD MATHESON

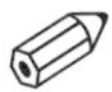

I don't suppose I'd be able to fit in all things chronologically, so I'd better stick to what I've started and put down everything I can remember about Brooklyn Tech, my days and months and years there. (One page a night will do this if I persist!)

So 1939—1943, high school.

In the second year, there was sheet metal shop, to begin with.

First we had to use mechanical drawing to put down the plans for a lamp. As it would be if opened up and spread out.

I couldn't get it right. The teacher kept having me redo it and redo it.

Finally, he accepted it reluctantly and I began on the piece of sheet metal. First, lay out on its surface the design we'd drawn on paper. I remember tapping in small holes, then joining the holes (connecting the dots?) with lines. Then using these big machines to feed the metal until it could form the lamp, which we spot-welded together. In the process, I sliced my fingertips to shreds on the sharp metal edges.

I think we made a shade for the lamp, too. I don't recall for sure. All I do recall is the teachers examining the lamp, under-grading it—and with a scornful look, tossing the lamp into a wastebasket.

I didn't have the nerve to take it out so I could keep it.

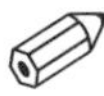

Forge shop. I was *really* bad at that. (What was I *doing* in that school?!)

I remember the teacher. A big, overweight man, out of his time. He used to tell us that we saw more in magazines at that time than he did in burlesque shows when he was young.

I spent a good deal of time trying—in vain—to make a chain link. You got a round piece of iron about 6—7" long, put it in the hot coals and got it reddish-white, then worked it on the anvil until it was the right circumference. Then you got each end reddish-white in the coals and flattened them—hitting it with a hammer on the anvil caused a shower of sparks.

The tricky part came then. You had to bend the rod around into a link form by heating it again in the fire. Then you were supposed to get the ends white and, somehow, weld them together by hitting the ends expeditiously with the hammer.

I never got it. The two ends never clung to each other. The old teacher would hit the "link" once and it would promptly fly apart. I'm sure I failed that course. Can you believe me spending time trying to weld two damn round bar ends into a chain link? Insane.

Almost as crazy as me trying to make that sheet metal lamp.

Or work in the machine shop.

I have failed to write in this book for more than a year. Terrible discipline. But I'll try to continue now. 1/31/98. From '94?!

More on my shop experiences at Brooklyn Tech. I will lump them all together in one section because, if I try to tell my story (does anyone care about "my" story?) in chronological order, I will surely forget items which will pop to the surface if I confine myself to one area at a time. That's my lazy theory, anyway. I have no true writing discipline. I have told people this for many years. I am more likely a compulsive obsessive as a writer. When I put together novels, I did it obsessively. Case in point: *BID TIME RETURN*, or as it's more "popularly" known, *SOMEWHERE IN TIME*.

Truly an obsession.

From the moment I saw Maude Adam's photograph 'til I finished writing the novel, I was totally caught up in the venture.

I remember going to book stores, searching for material on Maude Adams, intrigued by her—so much so that I was going to call the novel *THE MAN WHO LOVED MAUDE ADAMS*. But I didn't.

Odd, too, that only two photographs of her really "reached" me—the one in the opera house in Virginia City and one from, I believe, a biography of her by—Robbins? I don't remember. But the photo was haunting to me. She sat in a high-backed chair with a dark dress on and with an expression of such infallible sadness that I could almost—and *did*—imagine that she had lost the man she loved as Elise McKenna did in my novel.

The fact that, later, it was intimated (where I don't remember) that she may have been a lesbian (was it the astrological reading I had done on her?) didn't help. But that was later.

And when I discovered that the *very year* I had chosen for my heroine to have undergone a radical personality change (because she lost the man she loved), Maude Adams *also* underwent a radical personality change...well...writers thrive on moments like that.

And like the memory I had of an old woman staring at me at a party at Stephens College in Columbia, MO.

And learning, later, when I did my research, that Maude Adams was teaching drama at Stephens College at that time...well—wham, bam, hairs standing on end time!

But I was totally fascinated by the project.

And when Ruth and I were at the Coronado Hotel (recommended by Bill Idelson) having a drink, I knew I'd found the ideal place for a novel. If I was living in Michigan, I would undoubtedly have set the novel on Mackinac Island at The Grand Hotel as the film did.

I cannot imagine, now, (age?) doing what I did (obsessively) at that time—the 70's—to actually *become* my major character, to drive, as he did, to end up at The Coronado, to find research books on time travel as he did, to totally immerse myself (in San Diego) in the illusion (delusion?) that I was Richard Collier, that I was experiencing what he was experiencing—or, rather, vice-versa. It was a wonderful experience, equaled (well, *approached* anyway) by the experience of seeing Elise McKenna come alive and speak my lines in the shooting of the film.

Well, there is more I could say but, jeez God, I *was* about to talk about my shop experiences at Brooklyn Technical High School on Fort Greene Place in the years 1939—'43. So I will.

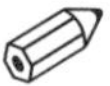

In the third (or fourth?) term I took machine shop.

More interesting than forge or sheet metal. By far.

Interesting machines. Funnel lathes. Machine lathes. Drills. Presses.

I actually made a hammer which I have to this day (1/98). Gladys' husband Bernie (Bernard Stocker) mounted it on a board with a tiny plate identifying when and where I made it. It hangs on the wall in our family room.

The most interesting—and horrendous as well—shop occurred in my junior and senior years—structural shop. As

I said earlier, we were building a goddamn ship, for heaven's sake!

I remember having to do a three-dimensional type drawing of a ship, a cut-away view. I didn't get a good grade on it but I look at it today and think, Holy *Moses*, how did I *do* that? None of our kids had to do anything *remotely* as complex.

And good 'ol P.J. Trosello gave me a lovely passing grade.

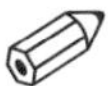

I did riveting in that shop. Can you imagine? An air-powered rivet gun that vibrated in your hands like a damn machine gun. I was barely able to do the *round* rivet heads where, at least, the "thing" (don't know what it's called) on the end had a rounded indentation to form the rivet head. The ones that were killers were the *flat* rivet heads, where the "thing" you pounded against the rivet heads (mine, anyway) looked like—I don't know what, but definitely *not* like rivet heads. I smashed and mushed them into something damn near unrecognizable.

J.P. didn't like them.

He was a stolid, unsmiling, bleak man. The only time we ever saw him smile was when he told us how a friend of his had missed a thrown red-hot rivet with his cup and it had fallen down his pants. A true comic was J.P. Trosello.

Can't remember anything more about the shops.

No cooking classes, for sure.

I remember years and years of mechanical drawing (drafting). Actually, I wasn't too bad at it, I remember clearly the roll of brownish tape we had to buy (to fasten down the corners of the paper sheets), in addition to S-curves (think that's what they were called, anyway), these plastic doo-hickeys (not a technical term) we used to scribe curves, etc. And, of course, a small lead case with a compass in it and pens in which you put the black ink—that had a screw on the end so you could draw lines of varied thickness.

I remember using the compass to make a three-dimensional figure.

Very valuable to me in my later years.

However, learning to letter well has always stayed with me. I can address a package when I mail it with really nice lettering and numbering.

Four years of technical training for *that*?

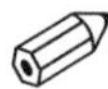

Well, also a little of the algebra stayed with me.

I can pre-calculate the number of pages a novel or screenplay will have based on what I have at any given time—by use of—hell, what are they called? You know… *equations*! (Just came to me.)

Mathematics in "Tech" (as we called it) was variable in enjoyment.

I liked Algebra and did reasonably well in it—actually got a 90 grade in my third term. Because the stuff made *sense*. But *Geometry*?

Oy.

I hated it. Memorizing all those bloody theorems. Agony. I never *did* figure out what good the stuff is. I was failing the course with a 55 average. Then I cram-studied for the NY State Regents test and got a 98 and managed to pass the course with a 65.

Now, Technical Trigonometry—that was okay. That made a lot of sense, was very practical.

RICHARD MATHESON

Thank God I never had to take Advanced Geometry—Solid Geometry, is it called? Plain Geometry was enough to do me in as it was.

Speaking of the NY State Regents—I was reprieved by the Physics test, as well.

My teacher—a little guy who dressed rattily, forget his name at the moment, (*Cohen*?) used to say to me, "You don't know your physics, Matheson!" and he was perfectly correct. I *didn't* know it but, again, I cram-studied, and since I have a photographic memory (at least I *did* have it at the time) I was able to get a 96 on the Regents test. I remember drawing a picture of some electric armature (correct word?), anyway it had brushes and coils and all sorts of stuff—and I was able to draw it *exactly* as it looked in the textbook.

I wonder now if the guys who marked my test thought I'd managed to sneak a textbook in with me to the test and was copying the picture out of it.

What else about those years at Tech?

Not too much.

I remember writing an English composition (I'm surprised they even bothered to have English courses since all they were preparing us for was technical stuff).

Anyway, my composition was told in first person by a telephone pole.

Seems rather an odd notion to me, even now. I recall that the pole remembered gangsters speeding past, shooting at each other, and lodging bullets into the pole.

I even hinted (however obversely, I don't recall) about a dog taking a pee (or *dogs*) on the pole! A wondrous commencement to my writing career.

But I've said nothing about my writing in those days.

What do I recall?

After the *Brooklyn Eagle* "triumphs" I wrote some more little poems and even a little story about an eagle named Rega-Willie (how come I remember that?) who did some sort of good deed, helped some little kid—the details are murky in my head. No triumph of literary accomplishment.

Anyway, my mother liked the story. I doubt if it's publishable. Or even readable. I don't know where these mini-manuscripts of mine are—or were. I'm sure my mother left them in a "treasure" box. But after she passed on (I'm glad that the phrase comes automatically to me now—instead of "died") they were all disposed of, I imagine. Unless, in some dusty attic or cellar corner, my brother kept them and they are there to this day. But I doubt it.

Along with the little stories and poems were my "comic strips." I drew panel tales about a Tarzan-like character and his pet elephant Tantar. I can't remember the Jungle Lord's moniker. These are no doubt somewhere in the atmosphere as ash floating about. Maybe.

I don't remember doing any "serious" writing until I was a teenager.

I wrote a story called "The Tinsel Monster" about a Christmas tree that killed people. What a lovely yuletide sentiment. My mind was warping even then.

I think I mentioned how my mother forbade me to listen to "The Lone Ranger" or anything of its "violent" ilk. I *could* listen to Nila Mack's "Let's Pretend" which, at that time, had stories as grotesque as those on "The Inner Sanctum." Did I mention one I remember particularly? Probably I did. Anyway, it was Bluebeard and I vividly recall his latest wife opening a door she was told *not* to open. (Where would gothic literature be without bone-headed heroines who never did what they were told?) Inside the room were the ex-wives of Mr. Bluebeard. Hanging on *hooks* like sides of beef and groaning in pain; I don't wonder.

Well, mama didn't hear that one or, no doubt, Nila Mack's "Let's Pretend" would have been auditory off-limits as well.

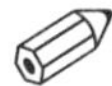

When I was (fourteen) sixteen I wrote my first novel—if you can call it that.

It was entitled *THE YEARS STOOD STILL*. I got the idea from—of all places—Mary Baker Eddy in *Science and Health/With a Key to The Scriptures*. An odd place to get an idea from.

Anyway, she spoke of a girl of sixteen who fell down a flight of stairs and bopped herself good on the head (not Mary Baker's way of describing it) and for the next thirty-forty years, did not age one day.

So I wrote this novel (it took place in England which, of course, I knew all about at fourteen-sixteen, living in Flatbush). My heroine fell in love with a no-good rogue who had to take it on the run for some crime. As I recall, he swam out to some ship and climbed (clambered more like it) aboard only to discover the ship totally empty because—yikes!—it had been quarantined for—what?—the plague? Something like that. End of no-good rogue.

The heroine promptly fell down a flight of stairs—or had some kind of accident which bopped her on the head.

And she stayed young-looking. I don't remember how I got 167 pages out of this. All I *do* remember is that the story began in the mid-1890's and concluded during the WWII "Blitz."

By then, some old rové had taken a fancy to our lovely heroine and married her. While in their nuptial bed (did I write sex scenes then? I doubt it), a bombing raid by the Germans took place and the shock undid our girl's brain and suddenly the old rové was in bed with something of a hag. He promptly went mad and ran out of the house (I think) and got blown to bits. I may be elaborating the story out of ill-conceived memory but the basics are correct. Good Harlequin title, unpublishable book.

I have, as a matter of fact, written many unpublishable (at any rate, unpublished) novels in my time.

I wrote a good deal of material on a novel called *ISLAND OF THE ANIMALS* (sorry, H.G., I knew not what I was doing).

I wrote a lot of material on a novel entitled *ZOO BREAK* about some nut releasing a bunch of wild animals from Central Park Zoo and what happened to them. The only story of the lot I recall is about some disillusioned heavyweight boxer who is confronted in an alley by a gorilla and fights him to the finish, ultimately (unbelievably) knocking out the gorilla and regaining his confidence. Sterling notion. A bit unfeasible.

If the rest of the novel was this bad...well, the word "unpublishable" takes on true significance.

I supposed there were other ill-conceived, aborted literary efforts as well but I don't remember them.

One I *do* recall—how could I forget it?—I wrote it after I graduated from college. It was called *HUNGER AND THIRST*—a true Russky title if I ever saw one. It told the story of a disillusioned (I must have been disillusioned at that time) young guy who holds up a pawnshop. As he exits, the owner of the pawnshop gets off a shot which hits our "hero" in the back.

He makes it to his furnished room where he promptly collapses on his back on the bed and something "gives" in his back so that he's totally—well, almost—paralyzed.

I then proceed to describe how he dies of hunger and thirst over the next few days, during which he recalls his past—his childhood, his experience in WWII as an infantry soldier (I later used much of this material in a novel that *did* get published; *THE BEARDLESS WARRIORS*), his college days and deterioration after graduation. (I used much of that in a shorter novel called *LEAVE YESTERDAY ALONE* which was—you guessed it—unpublished.)

So the guy dies at the end of a 900-page epic and an agent I'd gotten after publishing my first short story in print—*Born of Man and Woman*—told me that *HUNGER AND THIRST* was from hunger—I'm sure he said it more politely, but no less hurtfully.

In later years, Henry Kultner read *HUNGER AND THIRST* and wrote me—quote—"Your agent is a goddamned fool." Whether he really was or not, I left him after writing *A STIR OF ECHOES* and having him tell me that it would "hurt his reputation" to submit it. I showed it (courtesy of Charles Beaumont's aid) to Don Congdon who promptly sold it.

My former agent, when he finally saw the book in print, opined that "Matheson must have done a *massive* re-write."

The book was published exactly as it was when he spat upon it.

But even Congdon couldn't sell *HUNGER AND THIRST*.

One more comment about my writing and then I'll go back to high school days and the general chronology of my life.

MUSINGS

I have always had virtually zilch confidence in my work.

I could—and *have*—worked for *years* on a novel and, when one (count that, *one*) editor frowned on it, I *stopped* the project. I find that incredible now. I'm convinced that if I had ignored the one editor and finished the novel(s) on my own, they would have eventually sold. But I didn't and they didn't. So I have cabinets of unfinished novels and finished unpublished novels and I'm sure they aren't worth publishing.

Except for *THE LINK*...which began as a proposed project for ABC—to be a twenty-hour mini-series. For which I worked a year and a half (approximately) on the *outline*—which ended up at 800+ pages—and scared the living bejesus out of Brandon Stoddard at ABC. When the project was reduced to seven hours and I was, none-the-less, asked to add *two other stories* to it, I should have said no. I didn't and—no surprise—it didn't work out.

Later, I acquired the novel rights from ABC and began to write it. I grew restive at 800+ pages—which was only part of *Part One*—and submitted it to Don Congdon—who informed me that, if I completed the book as it was going, it was likely to be 2000+ pages and have to sell—at that time—for $45. Now it would cost $75.

So (no surprise considering my track record), I dropped *years* of work. Like a true idiot—if only—if only—if *only*—I'd had the balls to complete the book, 2000 pages or not, I think it would eventually have been published by some courageous editor. I mean, the damn thing had everything to do with the psychic world. The history of the field from the Fox sisters in 1840 to the present. All the current (at that time) work being done in parapsychology. Three separate stories, one about a writer who must invariably accept his psychic gifts—this story with a love interest and, ultimately, with an epic-like approach to the ultimate source of things psychic—including (appropriate for the period I wrote the book) a trip to Russia to examine *their* psychic investigations, and a trip to England and the investigations of a badly haunted house.

PLUS individual psychic experiences by many different people, a full account of a psychic incident that dealt with the sinking of The Titanic, and a full account of a Brighton psychic who actually identified Jack the Ripper.

Plus a second story about a young girl blessed with psychic ability and cursed with a mother who, having suffered herself with a Spiritualist mother, does all she can to thwart her daughter's gift to the point of physical cruelty.

And the story of a mother who approaches a psychic to help her locate her kidnapped daughter.

All of these stories eventually *melding* into one. Jesus, what a job of plotting! Walls covered in corkboards all filled with full cards. An immense undertaking. Which I dropped. Oy. Idiot.

Congdon suggested I try to make it into three novels. But as carefully as it was plotted, that was impossible. It was designed to be and would have been *one*, seamless story.

So goodbye to *THE LINK*.

I took out some of the historical material and put together a book entitled *MEDIUMS RARE*. That hasn't sold, either.

Three strikes. Out.

One more comment (self-negating) about my writing—this in the area of script writing.

If I had written novels instead of all these unproduced scripts, my "oeuvre" would be substantial. Instead, I have full drawers and cabinets and shelves filled with scripts no one will ever see in theaters or on the TV screen. Thank God (or someone) that many of these are based on published novels, which is exactly my point, of course. The novels will always be available to read. Even for films made from them which stank.

MUSINGS

To quote the old anecdote about Raymond Chandler, when someone commiserated with him as to how a certain film had "ruined" his book, Chandler calmly took his novel off its shelf and replied, "They haven't ruined it. Here it still is." Something like that—point made, anyway.

Shall I list—can I remember them all?—the scripts I've written which were never filmed?

1. *THE FANTASTIC LITTLE GIRL*—sequel to you-know-what. Scott's wife starts shrinking and ultimately joining him in the microscopic world.

2. *GULLIVER'S TRAVELS*—a little boy is Gulliver. Later, Cantinflas & David Niven—*sure*.

3. *BEING*—based on my novelette.

4. *SWEETHEARTS AND HORRORS*—to follow *A COMEDY OF TERRORS*, adding to that wonderful cast Tallulah Bankhead. They mostly died.

5. *PUBLIC PARTS, PRIVATE PLACES*—never made in England. Based on a novel about the porno business in London. I couldn't take it seriously and turned it into a black comedy.

6. *IMPLOSION*—England again—hired by American International. A somber tale of poisoned water sterilizing almost all women. Those who were not sterilized put in "breeding camps"—one of these the wife of a high British cabinet member.

7. *I AM LEGEND*—for Hammer. Turned down by the censor. Made (badly) in this country (in Italy, actually) with a bad re-write—not by me.

8. Can't remember the title. About a UFO that lands in the west, buries itself, and the investigation of it. Excellent script—for Tony Bill. Ulu Grosbard was going to direct it.

SIDE COMMENT—why do producers give a writer really *dark* stories and then expect them to "lighten" them up? I have always accepted the premise of a novel or story, assuming (naïvely, of course) that this premise was what interested the producers in the first place. And if the premise is dark, the honest presentation of this premise is—big surprise, Mr. Producer!—*also* going to be dark. In this case, honesty is not the best policy. Not if you want to work for these guys again.

9. A *perfect* example. Three years spent on a six-hour mini-series based on Philip Wylie's *THE DISAPPEARANCE*. *Inevitably* dark. Idea: for some inexplicable reason, the world "divides." In one world is only men, in the other only women. It is—I respect—*inevitable* that the man's world would ultimately go all to hell as it does in the novel. The women's world is no picnic either but they do better despite jealousies and some violence attendant to same. But the *men's* world—whoa! A disaster. Hell on earth, eventually. Technologically maintained—psychologically fouled up almost beyond recognition. It has a happy ending—but too late. Dark. Dark. ABC was probably thinking—oh, boy, oh, boy, women sleeping with women, men sleeping with men, yahoo! Instead, they got a grim, *grim* (*honest*) picture of what would really happen (according to Philip Wylie anyway), sex included. I worked with Peter Strauss those three years—his hey-day. Hope I didn't end his career.

10. *THE LINK*—of course.

11. *THE LOST WORLD*. Conan Doyle. A really dandy script. I was told that Universal was just starting *JURASSIC PARK* and didn't want another dinosaur film. They were probably lying.

12. A John Saul novel—can't remember the title (*CREATURE*—1999). Modern medical technology creating a super college football team—which, of course, backfires. Universal liked the script so much they hired the director of *THE LADY IN WHITE*, who re-wrote it into a *gothic* story! Not filmed. The idea of going back to my script obviously never occurred to them.

13. *JOURNAL OF THE GUN YEARS* from my novel. Ian Curtis loved it. I love it. TNT said no. ABC loved it, said no. Strange world out here.

14. *SHIFTER*—with Richard. Would have made a neat film. Killed by Lauren Schuler Downer.

15. *LOOSE CANNONS*—with Richard. Our story: hockey all-star commits serial murders with an antique ice-skate. Bob Clark's story: Neo-Nazis vie with porno group for porno films of Hitler. Slight re-write. I regard this as unmade even though there is something they show on TV which contains two or three lines of ours.

16. My script for *EARTHBOUND*—unsold.

17. My script for *7 STEPS TO MIDNIGHT*—unsold.

18. My script for *SHADOW ON THE SUN*—ditto.

Oh, there are more but I've forgotten them—no doubt on purpose. Some bomb squad film, too.

Back to high school and thereafter—less complex (in most ways) than now and here.

Where was I? In my latter two years at Brooklyn Technical High School. It remains a wonderment to me that I attended that school. Me, who wanted to be a writer or a composer. Riveting. Machine shop lathing. Drawing ship's lines. An astrologer told me once that, until I was 38, I was mostly drifting with the tide, not thinking for myself. I can believe it. Except am I thinking for myself yet? Who knows?

Did I mention going into Fort Greene Park in the winter and being a transit? Sort of fun. We could look all the way down town at the girls walking around.

They told me I couldn't graduate if I couldn't swim—do the length of the pool. I responded, "I can swim [I couldn't] but I can't do that." Rejoined the teacher, "Then you can't swim." He was right. But I graduated anyway.

I don't believe I've described my years at the YMCA. Have I? If so, I'll now proceed to repeat myself.

I guess I was about fourteen when my mother enrolled me in the Summer Y. It was a good program. Many athletics. Trips galore. I met guys I knew for years.

When summer ended, I joined the winter program. That was even better. There was a marionette club I belonged to. We made the marionettes ourselves (with instruction, of course), then performed the plays with them.

I remember being Rip Van Winkle. Standing above the stage, manipulating the marionette. I even recall a line gaffe—Rip (me) telling Mrs. R, "Go down to the food and get me some more store." Giggles on my own part. I'm not sure if the kid audience even noticed.

I remember narrating a play in which I had to say, "The Jolly Roger was rolling scuppers under in the ocean swell." I had no idea whatever what "scuppers under" meant. I still don't, come to think of it.

The YMCA was a beautiful old mansion, converted. It had a bowling alley in the basement and a complete log cabin interior. In the attic was a marvelous miniature train set-up, landscape and all.

Well, the memory of the Y is painful because it burned down and I was, at least, a witness to its cause. Very painful. I don't think I'll write about it. I remember "Pop," the athletics coach and Phil Breux and Les Finlayson. A very sad memory, all in all. Not to be a revelation in this journal.

And the boys I knew: Harry Pierice, Ken _______, Johnny Exposito, Gilbert Gingold (who picked on me mercilessly, until I snapped and bloodied his nose, and we were "pals" after that. The male animal).

Later on, I became a "leader" at the Y because my mother saw me wasting away a summer and asked them to help me. They were very kind and even paid me a little for being in charge of the younger boys on excursions.

I'm getting tired of recounting my life. Maybe I can find a more valid area for discussion.

MUSINGS

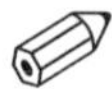

Odds and ends memories about Brooklyn Tech.

The cafeteria. It was very modern. I always brought my lunch because, I guess, we couldn't afford to buy me a hot meal every day—it cost 25¢! I usually brought a *cold* bacon on cold whole-wheat toast sandwich. I can't imagine why I liked that so much; it was my favorite lunch. I bought a container of milk to wash it down. Sometimes, in a fit of financial madness, I bought a bag of pretzel sticks - 5¢ or 10¢, I recall. I was able to eat during the afternoon classes without being detected. My mouth never moved as I chewed them. What a clever boy.

The cafeteria was run by a teacher named Mr. Sjogren. He was forever on the P.A. system, enjoining us to behave and not make noise—unwarranted noise, anyway. His favorite comment was as follows: "A noisy noise annoys a noisy oyster, boys. A word to the wise." I cannot believe that it ever did any good at all.

Any other memories? Mostly, how rotten I was in various shops. First term: wood shop. Little book ends. I could not, for the life of me, manage the wax fillets at the juncture of two pieces of wood.

I already described how crappy I was in forge shop and the utter contempt my teacher had for my sheet metal lamp. I *did* make a nice clamp in machine shop. I believe I mentioned the display of it Bernie Stocker made for me, my one evidence that I was not a total shop klutz.

So I graduated from Tech at the age of seventeen and got a job at Arma Engineering.

I am aghast at what they permitted a teenager to do—prepare really high-tech gear units for tracking tables on Navy vessels. Christ, how many ships did I send north instead of south?

First, you went and picked up the various pieces which were to be assembled into the unit. If memory served, there was a base, gear holders, gears of various size, etc. First, one had to drill holes in the bars to—okay, this is boring! Suffice to say, it took about a week to put the damn thing together, and the "play" between the gear teeth could be no more than three or four *thousands* of an inch! By week's end, it was painted black and the gears were all polished and shiny and God help the poor Navy folk who had to depend on it even though we *did* have inspectors who would turn it back if it didn't come up to snuff. There was some old duffer (he was probably in his 40's) who used to solve "one's play" between the gears by walloping the gear holders with a rubber mallet until the proper "play" was achieved. It's a wonder we won the war.

For all this, I got 70¢ an hour. That was standard pay for the time. The "old timers" got 90¢ an hour. That was high pay then.

Well, it was obvious that I was going to be drafted, so I enlisted in the ASTRP program to avoid the draft and was sent to Cornell University to study pre-Engineering.

I don't have to detail any of this because somewhere in my belongings is a day-by-day (almost) account of the entire experience. If you want to find it and read it, please do.

Anyway, the program was shut down about halfway through the term, and we merely goofed around the remainder of the term, knowing that we were going to end up in the infantry. Was it all a ploy to get us in the infantry? Who knows?

MUSINGS

I took basic training at Camp Wheeler, Georgia. I was eighteen, barely, and weighed, at the end of the training, 169 pounds. Gaunt, I was.

Memories of basic training are sketchy.

Marches, of course. I mean hikes. Firing the Garand M-41 (?) on the range. In the beginning, even though I held the rifle tightly with the leather sling, my shoulder turned black and blue from the recoil. By the time we had finished divisional training, I could fire the rifle *without* the sling.

I think I scored something like 137—barely qualifying as a "marksman."

I was particularly good with the smaller rifle carried by the officers—I forget its name (*Carbine-1999*). I scored very high on that.

I remember the food. Pretty awful. Actually, the food was probably great. It was the preparation of it that was dreadful. Very often, I didn't even eat dinner. I showered, raced to the PX, bought a box of chocolate snaps and a big milk and had that for supper, then went to the Post Theater to see a first-run movie—I remember *LADY IN THE DARK*—and had a box of popcorn and a Coke. Great nutrition. I was first introduced to popcorn in movies at that time. Theaters didn't have anything but a lone candy machine in back. In Flatbush, anyway.

I recall K.P. Wonderful experience. I remember defeathering chickens and/or turkeys in the tubs of hot water. My fingers cracked open along the fingerprint lines. Very painful.

Lectures. Movies. More hikes. Exercise sessions. Learning to strip the Garand, clean the parts, and re-assemble it—fast. Could I do it today? I doubt it. 122 9310—that was my ID #!

I remember the obstacle courses. Firing at figures (cardboard) that popped up from the ground. I recall one course in particular. It was 120° in the shade. I sweat buckets. I didn't take any salt tablets. Later, when we got back to the barracks, we had to shower fast, put on ground uniforms, and go to stand at attention for some reason. We had our bayonets fixed. Everything started to go black on me. I started falling forward. If a friend had not caught me, I might well have fallen right on the bayonet blade and probably been out of the war if not out of life itself.

When I came to, I was lying on the grass. A charming memory.

I recall sitting in foxholes all day on a rifle range, holding up a round marker if anyone hit the target. I never knew if anyone hit it, I just waggled the marker in the air periodically to show them I was still alive.

What else? The east hike—twenty miles with rifle and full field pack. Two pairs of socks. A real ordeal.

The sergeant didn't like me, until I became friends with a tall Irish kid name O'Shea. The sergeant liked him so he came to accept me.

Went into Macon once during the entire eighteen weeks. Nothing much.

Never thought about what it all meant: That I was being prepared for combat.

Had my ten-day leave. I remember sleeping on a chair in the club car. Woke up and tried to put on my shoes. No way. Jesus, my feet have ballooned overnight! Alarm! Then I discovered I was trying to put on the shoes of the little soldier sitting next to me.

MUSINGS

Visiting my family. Everyone came to Gladys and Bernie's house. Franny and Vivian and Uncle and Tante Evelyn. Mom, of course, and Bob and Mary. Uncle Sven and Lily. She tried to teach me the Lindy. Nice—but I guess I always knew that I was still going to war.

Fort Jackson, South Carolina. The 87th (Acorn) division. More training. More hikes. More shooting ranges. Still bad food. Films on sex education. "Hubba, Hubba, use a rubber! Prophylaxis beats the Axis!" (I can't imagine how.)

Went into town there. Went to a Christian Science household for dinner. Cordial southern hospitality. But I remember them telling us when we were going overseas. I sometimes wondered if they were Christian Science Nazi spies.

Went to a USO once. Saw *JANE EYRE* with Orson Welles. Danced once with a girl. Too shy to speak. I was SHY.

Soon enough, we were out of there and on our way to New Jersey, to go overseas. I had a book I was reading called *QUEEN OF THE FLATTOPS*. I mentioned it in a U-mail home. The censor blacked it (or cut it) out, obviously thinking I was being very sly, letting my mother know I was going overseas on the *Queen Elizabeth*.

The entire division (20,000 "strong") on one boat. What a coup for a Nazi sub. Fortunately, the *Queen Elizabeth* went 35 knots and we were ahoy—no convoy because we were going too fast.

Six of us in a cabin. Bunkers three high. I took baths in hot water—salt water. Special soap to use. Food okay, I guess. I was keeping a journal. I was going to call it (named after a French town or city) Mars Letour—"*The Gateway to War*." It was taken from me after we went into combat. Burned? I wish I still had it.

We landed in England and got on a train, I'm sure. Rode it to somewhere in England—we'd debarked from the *Queen Elizabeth* at South Hampton. After the train ride came either a truck ride or a hike, I don't remember which. We ended up at what they told us was the former estate of a well-known tennis player. I remember little about it. There was a gate house where we all stood guard around the clock—to make sure the Nazis did not make a surprise attack on the estate, no doubt.

We slept in a long stable converted into a dormitory. As I indicated, my memories of this estate stay are sparse indeed. I do recall standing guard at the front gate house—ever alert lest those damn Nastys showed up. Very spooky standing guard in the early morning mist. Dracula country. I was primed to see him gliding across the meadow in his full dress suit. Why did he dress like that? And who dry-cleaned his suits? They must have had bad earth stains on the back of them. Maybe—although Bram (short for Abraham, I learned recently)—Dracula was like Little Orphan Annie and had dozens of suits, all identical. As I started to say, Bram Stoker never mentioned Dracula's wardrobe arrangements. But you'd think he'd have a jumpsuit or two—or maybe a leisure suit. Wearing that damn dress suit all the time must have been a drag. (Dragula.)

Anyway, my imagination was enhanced (not the appropriate word. Enlarged? Who knows. Inflamed?) by the fact that I read a novel while there entitled *THERE WERE NO ASPER LADIES*, a vampire tale, of course.

I recall, vaguely, a visit to the nearby town; I don't remember its name.

I had fish and chips—which sounds a hell of a lot more appetizing than it really was. Soggy, deep-fried potatoes and bready, deep-fried fish wrapped up in a piece of newspaper, which was soaked in oil. Grand gourmet delicacy.

I recall seeing a circus film starring, I believe, Ben Lyon and Bebe Daniels. The villain was a (must have been) young Herbert Lom, who I thought was reminiscent of Charles Boyer.

There was a song the soldiers sang; the main repeated phrase of which was, "Roll me over, lay me down, and do it again." It told of an entire sexual relationship all the way through to eight—"the doctor's gate"—nine "the baby's doing fine" and ten (the concluding phrase)—"and we're doing it again." Of such patriotic visions, the war was won.

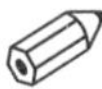

I don't think we quartered in the tennis player's estate for even a month, maybe a month. But, soon enough, we filled our backpacks—I don't know what happened to our main ("diddy?") bags with all our clothes in it. Anyway, we left the estate and trucked—or trained—to the English Channel and boated over to Le Havre. D-Day was long past—this was December '44—so there were no pillboxes blocking our entrance.

Another long train ride across France—with occasional rest stops. (Those who couldn't wait were held out of the open box car door so they could relieve themselves—what a sight that must have been. And fortuitous that, while they were occupied in their waste removal process, another train didn't come from the opposite direction and knock off their butts.)

We got off at Metz, which is near the German border. Most of the details of this story are written down in *THE BEARDLESS WARRIORS* so I won't repeat. Years (many years) later, we attended a film festival in Metz and they took me to the church we stayed in. At least they said it had to be that church since it was the only one standing at that time.

I will by-pass entry into combat. Most of the details—slightly enlarged—are in *THE BEARDLESS WARRIORS*. But the morning I left the lines (because some idiot—or idiots—had ordered us to remove our overshoes before we moved into combat, then marched us through streams into a meadow where 88's compelled us to "dig in" for a few days. It rained the whole time. Our feet suffered. We ended up being called "The Trench Foot Division").

At any rate, I went to an aid station and managed to peel off my shoes. At which point my feet blew up into blue balloon-like entities. And *I* had a "moderate" case of Trench Foot. Some men lost their feet entirely.

To another, larger aid station—and ultimately to a hospital in Paris where I experienced my first visit to that fabled city, lying in a hospital bed; at least I could see the Eiffel Tower through the window of my room.

In addition to the Trench Foot condition (later, I referred to it as "frost-bitten" feet because it sounded more "romantic"), I had, like all the others, gotten my drinking water by scooping it out of puddle shell holes and dropping chlorine tablets in my canteen. Obviously, the tablets had a limited effect because I ended up peeing constantly, with a burning sensation accompanying said pee. So I had to keep calling for a "duck"—a portable urinal. A German prisoner was the ward boy. He was a happy soul. (Who could blame him? He was out of the war.) "Ja, ja, duck!" we would cry, laughing merrily. My earliest memory of romantic Paris.

Re-crossed the channel on an English (hospital?) ship on which what they referred to as bacon and eggs defies my ability as a writer to describe adequately.

I ended up in an English (no, it must have been American) hospital, where I received thirty penicillin shots (I kept a list on my bedside table so I could alternate arms). The nurse I liked threw the hypodermic needles (into my left or right arm) like darts. No pain whatever.

Once, she wasn't there and a different nurse *slowly* slid the needle into my arm, making me cry. The pain was so intense.

The "good" nurse would give us all alcohol rubs, and half the men—I don't recall if I was one of them—(I wasn't a man anyway, I was a kid) were in love with her.

I also read Westerns. Armed Forces editions. (They were *great*. Whatever happened to them, anyway?) I read two Westerns a day for a month or more. This had to be where I got my taste for them (in addition to Hollywood Westerns). I don't recall the authors but Louie L'Amour was one of them. Very good writers, though. Luke Short was one of them; a pseudonym, of course. Probably why I wrote five Westerns in later years, to get the Old West out of my system. Of course, I only skirted the surface—as most Westerns do. The gunman, the outlaw, the sheriff, the marshal, fast-draws, "show downs," etc. If I had continued in the Westerns genre (never a possibility) I would have had to examine the lives the majority of people lived in the Old West—in towns, anyway. Raising families, going to church, running businesses, etc. I forgot to add "Indian trouble" to my list before. But that is an entire subject on its own. Some wonderful books have been written about the Indians.

Fast forward (I seem to get farther and farther away from recuperation after combat; but I'll get back to it).

I had an offer once to write a sequel to *SHANE*. Bantam offered me $100,000 to write it. I prepared an outline which they liked; entitled *SHANE LIVES*. Mrs. Schaefer, who was first all for the project, reneged, and that was that. For which I will always remain grateful. Write a sequel to a classic? Impossible. A no-win situation. *MOBY DICK RETURNS*? *RETURN TO VANITY FAIR*? *PEACE AND WAR*? Yes, as a rule, sequels are a *bad* idea. Witness the sequel to *GONE WITH THE WIND*. Abominable. Took place mostly in *Ireland*, for Chrissake.

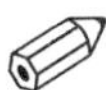

Our good nurse kissed us all goodbye affectionately and we left the hospital after about three months there.

I shouldn't but I'll describe what happened to my feet while I was there. They went back to normal size but the outer layer of skin—*several* layers, I think, it was so *thick*—dried up and turned black (especially my right foot which, to this day—September '99—remains the lesser of the two, getting cold easily). Anyway, they turned black and *crispy*, like the surface of a well-done pork roast. Fortunately, my compulsion to crack it off was allowable. I broke off big chunks of black, crispy, dead-as-a-doornail skin, to reveal, beneath, baby-pink skin, *very tender*.

So, at any rate, we left the hospital and were (trained, I presume) back to South Hampton, where we boarded the *George Washington*, the ship (we were told) that Wilson returned to the states on after his attempt at The League of Nations.

A pleasant—if occasionally nausea-inducing—voyage home. Excellent cuisine. Read a lot, I don't remember *what*. I discovered that seasickness could be diminished by consciously setting yourself to a motion *counter* to the roll of the ship. If you went *with* the motion—got caught up by it—upchucking time. So I did rather well in that department.

We ended up in a hospital on Staten Island (much later, I discovered that Nick Perito was there at the same time, entertaining; he played the accordion).

Naturally, the first thing I did was telephone my sister's number because my mother was living with her at the time. Knowing now what it feels like to be a parent, I can imagine the ecstatic joy she must have felt, hearing my voice. Because, as far as she knew, I was still in England. I'm sure I corresponded with her during my hospital stay.

I went home on a few day's leave and was greeted by the entire family. A happier ending to the tale than that of too many soldiers.

I remained in the Staten Island hospital for a while. Good food. Reading. Movies (I remember seeing *SISTER KENNY* with Rosalind Russell). Resting.

Then we were shipped to North Carolina to rehabilitate some more. I must have still had the whim-whams from being shelled in combat because I slept completely under the blankets, never seeing the light. I remember waking up once on a Sunday to find it was mid-afternoon! (We didn't have to follow any schedule.) I was shocked.

In a later year, out of curiosity, I tried to sleep completely covered head to toe as I'd been at that camp. I felt as though I was smothering, had to stop.

I took a typing course there. I played softball. I remember a spectacular catch I made—I was the center fielder.

Then came the discharge and the train ride home. June, '45. I got a 50% disability check each month.

I think I lived with my sister and her husband. I got a job at Petty & Wherry, stocking and shipping big fly wheels (not car wheels, ones used with belts in industry). I took a course of Intermediate Algebra at Brooklyn Tech (God knows why). I investigated colleges. I went to a wonderful vocational advisor named John Roberts. With enormous skill, he convinced the government that I was going to segue my high school degree in Structural Engineering into a Journalism degree at the University of Missouri, in order to become a technical writer, the last, *last* thing in the world I cared to do.

They bought it, though, and I was authorized (under the G.I. Bill, Public Law 16) to attend the University of Missouri where—because I had no language at Brooklyn Tech, I would have to take three terms of French, no three *years*.

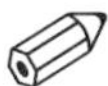

Happily, my good friend Norman Kennelly (to his mother, Helen Kennelly, it was her "third" son) chose to attend the University of Missouri, too, not to earn a degree in Journalism, but one in English in the College of the Arts and Sciences.

Did I speak of how I met Norman in Sunday school in the Third Church of Christ Scientist and remained a friend until his unfortunate death? (I wrote a letter to the Manhattan hospital he was in. I got the letter back with the chilling "pat. exp."—patient expired—jotted on the envelope.) Horrible.

Norman and I arrived in Columbia, Missouri, on an evening in the early Fall of 1946. I presume we took a cab to our places of residence—me in a room in the apartment of Ada Smith, the aged Christian Science practitioner, and Norman around the corner. I shared my room with a young man named Joe. Norman was in a cellar room with three other students. The only one I remember is Raymond Rushefsky who, each morning, rolled to a sitting position on his cot, eyes still closed, and requested gutturally, "*Butt* me." When someone inserted a cigarette between his lips and ignited it, Raymond would draw in a deep lungful of smoke, blow it out, then open his eyes, ready for a new day. (I think Raymond must have died a long time ago, smoking like that. Sept. '99)

I was "in the chips" since I received $90 a month, having had a medical discharge from the Army. The rest got $65 a month. (Why didn't Norman get $90, now that I think about it, he had a medical discharge too, from the Navy, an intestinal infection.) I guess it was because his condition was cured, mine never could be entirely.

At any rate, I paid $15 a month for the room and allowed myself $1.05 per day (how I came up with that figure I'll never know) for food. Breakfast was usually a hot roll and coffee (20-25¢). Lunch was God knows what for a bit more, leaving the munificent sum of 60-70¢ for supper. At one point, we ate in a boarding house for about $30 or so a month and ate well. Later, Norman and I worked in the kitchen of a male student dormitory, washing food trays in a steamer. The food was good. The work was not so good.

RICHARD MATHESON

GO TO THE END OF THIS SECTION—*OR* THE BEGINNING OF THE *NEW* SECTION; I'LL EXPLAIN WHY. →

To my shame, I must admit that—as I scrawl this—it is *2003*! I have not written in this journal for *years*! Why? I have no idea. Well, yes I do. I lost interest. Why? For one reason, because, although Chris suggested that I write all this down so that my four children—TINA, RICHARD, ALI and CHRIS will learn—or, at least, know—about the life of their father. I am still—after all these years—unconvinced that *anyone* would be interested in my life. The same modesty (false?) or conviction that my work, and therefore my life, would be of zilch interest to anyone. I am usually surprised (*honestly*) to discover that I am respected as a writer. So the same incredulity about the public's (at least a *small* portion of it) acceptance, even admiration of my writing carries over into my estimation (which I never indulge in anyway) of my personal life. I'm just another Joe who does some scrubbing. Believe me when I say that this is *not* false modesty. I really *don't* regard myself as anything special. Where this strange appraisal (or non-appraisal) of my career came from I don't know. My family treated me well, I look back at nothing but kindness and love from all of them. Was it because it was a matriarchy? Because little was expected from the males in the family but earning enough money to provide bed and board for wife and children?

As a result (I am beginning a new paragraph even though my thought runs on in a straight line.) But as a writer, I *am* aware of the need for a page of writing (or, more likely, *printing*) to have a certain *visible* credence (or, rather, *attractiveness*) to it. A page—or pages—of solid print is disconcerting (or *boring*) to a reader. "Daunting" is the word I want. (I have not really written anything in some time and words do not pop into my consciousness as they once did.) (About which more a little later.)

So, anyway, that is a hell of a long-winded explanation of why I started a new paragraph and just started *another* one! Visibility is a strange concomitant (well, *that* word popped into my head) of printed words, but it *is* a genuine one to be considered. I imagine (I have not imagined much lately) that is why the screenplay form is so easy to read (except for some). So the idiot readers or producers can deal with them mentally. Play form is slightly more demanding but not much. The worst is non-fiction books which often have wall-to-wall printed words that put the reader to potential sleep. I did that, for *THE PATH*, restructuring the *look* of Percival's writing (the way it was printed, that is) to make it look more visibly appetizing. I didn't change a word of it—what idiocy would prompt me to do that since the writing is perfect for what he has to say? But visually…daunting; there, I'm repeating a word—not a good sign (for me anyway).

Anyway, where the hell was I?

Well, I may as well plunge (limitedly and unsatisfactorily, I suspect) into my current (April 12, 2003) feeling or attitude—or confused state—or casual acceptance of my feeling about the fact that I have not written anything for some time, and interestingly (at least to me), my total lack of *desire* to write anything. Short stories? I gave them up in the early 1970's. Not with any feeling (or belief or conviction or whatever) that I had mastered the form. For God's sake, *hardly*. I would be mentally defective to think that. Oh, sure, I've written some interesting short stories and/or novelettes. But *mastered* the form? Whoa, Nellie, don't even dream that. Ray (Bradbury) is still working at mastering the form (in his 80's!) and he has written *hundreds* and *hundreds* of short stories in his remarkable career. I have not even written a hundred—a *single hundred*. So I am not a master of the form. Not at all. I diddled with the form for about twenty years, then called it day. I don't know why, I just *did*. I think a few of my stories are excellent (oh, my God, I'm *praising* myself?) but that's *it*. *No mas*, as "Iron Fist" said when he stopped (voluntarily) the fight with Sugar Ray (not the original) Leonard—a remarkable boxer and fighter—and what baser element exists in me—or at least *did*—that allowed me to get excited and involved in great boxing matches. I don't feel that way now (age?) but definitely did when I was younger. Even paying Pay-Per-View rates to see some of them. Ye Gods (and little fishes; I believe the phrase goes).

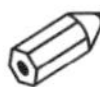

A break in the page—and a new question in my mind.

Where was I?

Okay, continuing.

Novels? I wrote a few decent ones, some I like better than others. Allowing myself the grandiose estimation of secret appraisal I can say I think I wrote two classic Science-Fantasy novels—*I AM LEGEND* and *THE SHRINKING MAN*. (I am amazed at how good my writing was when I was in my twenties and thirties. I even re-read the novel I wrote, starting it at the age of—*gulp*—*fourteen*! and was astonished at how passible it *was* for a novel written by a callow *teenager*, for God's sake. Multiple characters (which I never attempted again except, limitedly, in *HELL HOUSE*), "exotic" locations—London in the 1890's, the World War I trench warfare, South Africa for God's sake! What did I know about *any* of those things? NOTHING. But did that stop me from reeling off page after page of description and character analysis? Strange little Dickie Bird (what my cousin Vivian called me) to simply ignore his total ignorance of those subjects and blandly (more likely *blindly*) forging into each new aspect of the story. Remarkably enough, Barry Hoffman of Gauntlet Publications (bless him!) is going to *publish* it—as part of an enlarged book by Mark Rathbun entitled (I blush) *HE IS LEGEND*, which was (oh, my, my, next crossed out word!) what he and his collaborator whose name I (shamefully) do not remember called a short "book" written many years ago that included a number of items, one of them an article written by Bob Bloch (and *bless* him, too). If I remember I'll speak about my afternoon with him on the day he died (*Dick*, for Pete's sake, after doing several metaphysical books, you *still* say "died" instead of "passed on." Which really *is* the better description of what happens when we shed our physical bodies like the removal of an overcoat—a story I have planned to write but haven't yet—and "move on" with our *true* selves. Hopefully, "move on," that is—some, I fear, "hang around"—"earthbounds," not even knowing they have passed on. Possible ghosts. I have also thought of trying to "reduce" Percival's remarkable book *GHOSTS* but haven't yet.

Oh, here we go again.

Where am I?

Oh, yes. Okay. Novels. I did a few, some I like better than others.

I continue to believe that *BID TIME RETURN*—logically changed to *SOMEWHERE IN TIME* is the best written novel I've done. (Being—that is having been written almost as a living journal—in my imagination, anyway.)

I think *WHAT DREAMS MAY COME* is my most "important" novel. A novel which has (most happily to me) altered the belief systems of a number of readers. I have, somewhere, letters written to me which recount how their mothers or fathers, fearful of imminent death, found comfort from the book. In truth, I suppose if I had done nothing but that one book and caused nothing but that effect, my writing career could be adjudged a success. Partial.

Anyway, I never achieved the public enthusiasm achieved by Stephen King or Dean Koontz because I simply could not remain in the horror-terror-suspense genre. A book or two and I became bored and had to move on to another genre, then another—and another.

I wanted to write *I AM LEGEND*, *THE SHRINKING MAN*, *HELL HOUSE* and *A STIR OF ECHOES*. Then I had to do "something else."

I wanted to write a war novel so, partly for that reason, and partly to "do" a "straight" novel at the same time as Chuck (Beaumont) was doing his straight novel *THE INTRUDER*, I wrote *THE BEARDLESS WARRIORS*—the reaction to which I had only refamiliarized myself with recently when the novel was re-issued (by, was it TOR or GAUNTLET, I don't recall) and I had to select some past reviews of it. To my astonishment (and, of course, pleasure) I read that the book was one of the best novels about World War II ever written, compared (favorably) to *THE RED BADGE OF COURAGE*! (So how come my ego is not more sizable about my work? Because my estimation of it is that I was expected to bring home enough money to pay board and bread for my wife and four children and did so with my writing, and that's all that mattered anyway? Ugh. Repeat. Ugh.) I should have a smidgen more ego than *that*. *Shouldn't* I?

So I wrote my war novel and it got published.

So I wanted to write a haunted house novel and I did. *HELL HOUSE*. Well received. "Possibly the best [or was it *scariest*?] haunted house novel ever written." Blurb by Stephen King—who, incidentally (or *not* incidentally), has always been very generous in his praise of my work.

So I wanted to write a love story and I did—*BID TIME RETURN*—slash—*SOMEWHERE IN TIME*, the film of which has generated an amazing amount of effects on people—a news letter INSITE still being published *years* after its inception by Bill Shepard and a yearly weekend at The Grand Hotel on Mackinac Island—always a sellout.

So I wanted to write a love story about life after death and I did. *WHAT DREAMS MAY COME*, the less said about the film version, the better. Thought I must add that I can't really blame Steve Simon (who was Steve Deutsch when he produced *SOMEWHERE IN TIME*). He stuck it out with my script for a long time, even turning down Wolfgang Peterson, who wanted (I gather) a major revision of my script. There are others—who shall remain nameless—I can blame for the fact that *WHAT DREAMS MAY COME* was a (brutally declared) lousy film. A small consolation to me was the remark of Tom Pollack (once the head of Universal Pictures) to me that "they should have filmed your book." He may actually have said "shot" your book but I don't believe he meant "put a bullet in its head."

So I wanted to write a children's novel and I wrote *ABU AND THE 7 MARVELS*, *beautifully* published by Barry Hoffman of Gauntlet with superb artwork by Bill Stout. A truly gorgeous book. And, I think, a very funny and exciting story, too. Why no one has chosen to film it, I don't know, or maybe I do. When Don Loze (of whom I'll write more later) took me to some well-known organization to discuss possibly having them do the artwork (this was before Bill Stout became a part of the project), the head of the organization—I apologize for not remembering his name—said that, when he read my story, he felt that it must have been *already* filmed. Which, in retrospect, may have meant that the story was dated. Which it *is*. If it had been filmed (or, more likely, *animated*) in the 1950's it would have been fresh. Because I wrote the damn thing in the 60's! Or the 50's, I don't recall. But it is definitely *not* contemporary in its outlook.

So I wanted to write a Western and I did. *JOURNAL OF THE GUN YEARS*, which was fantastically received. One of the writers in the field (why can't I remember names?) said that "with *one* novel" I had become one of the leading Western writers in that field.

It won the Silver Spur Award for the Best Western Novel of the Year.

Perhaps overwhelmed by this praise, I published four *more* Western novels—thanks to my editor at the time, Gary Goldstein. Oddly enough, all of them—save one—were already written—more in my slush pile of unpublished novels. There was one which, incredibly—I mean really *incredibly*—I had *forgotten* that I'd written.

The only "excuse" for this amazing lapse of memory (forgetting that you wrote *an entire novel?!*) was because I had shown it, years and years before, to my friend and established writer, Bill Cox (William R.) and he suggested that we make a screenplay out of it. Which we did. Which was never purchased. (Oh, where have I heard *that* before?) So, I forgot—literally *forgot*—about the novel. When, looking through my file cabinet drawers, I ran across the novel—completely written, I was amazed that I'd forgotten I'd wrote it. So I sent the ms. to Gary Goldstein and *that* was published.

Next came a collection of short stories and one novelette that had been published in various Western "pulp" magazines. (I had obviously, I realized then, been more intrigued by the Western genre than I thought.)

So that was published.

Next came *SHADOW ON THE SUN*, which (part of which) had been written in 1956 or '57. I had suffered a slipped disc in England while there to write the screenplay of *I AM LEGEND*. I mean the "groundwork" for the slipped disc had taken place in England when, staying at my producer's (Tony Hinds) cottage for the weekend, I smacked my head not once but twice on a beam probably centuries hardened. So when I got home and was (I recall) in the act of making love to my wife, the disc popped out. I was bed-ridden for a long time, living on codeine. And when I reached the point where I could, at least, sit up at my desk, I typed up half the novel in one sitting (bettering my record of writing *FURY ON SUNDAY* in *three days*). Then I let it grow fallow (is that the proper phrase?). Anyway, I didn't finish it even though I had a detailed plot line for the remainder of the story, and finished it at Gary Goldstein's request. He published it.

Finally, novelizing a screenplay (need I ad *unsold*?) about Wild Bill Hickok which I called *THE MEMOIRS OF WILD BILL HICKOK*, it was published as well. I like the novel (I think it's amusing) but I imagine (or *know*) that it went over with a great THUD with Western readers since the premise of my novel (not entirely illogical) is that Hickok had been a coward, albeit one with a developed sense of humor. But you don't besmirch an icon, I guess. I know.

So that was it with Westerns.

So I wanted to write (prepare, as it turned out) a metaphysical book and I did. *THE PATH*. Which I didn't truly write so much as organize. I took from Harold W. Percival's *magnificent* tome, *THINKING AND DESTINY*, some of its simpler (to me) concepts and cast them in the form of a conversation between a man (really, *me*) and a stranger who bestows on the man the wonderful concepts about life in Percival's book.

At first, no one wanted to publish it. (Surprise.) Then a man in Santa Barbara published it (very attractively, too) and, later, TOR published it in—also—a very attractive form.

Later, I recorded (with dismal dramatic effect, I later came to realize) a CD called *REALITY* which encapsulated much of *THE PATH*'s observation.

Then, later (much later), I compiled and edited a small book entitled *A PRIMER OF REALITY* which presents my complete metaphysical belief system. And in a suspense novel I wrote and had printed by TOR in 2002 (they called it *HUNTED PAST REASON*, a lousy title which they imposed on my novel against my wishes—a *first*) I called it *TO LIVE*. Anyway, it contained the bottom line of my metaphysical beliefs (in addition to, I hope, a suspenseful story). I guess it's an okay book because *Publisher's Weekly* called it my "masterpiece."

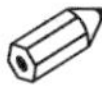

So, anyway, it is not surprising (to me, any longer) that I have no desire whatsoever to write anything else. I've said what I had to say. Period.

Also, I became interested in writing for the theatre and, as this is written, there is definite interest (by a number of highly-ranked theatre people—i.e. Peter Larkin and Jules Fisher—in producing it). My producer—friend Don Loze—has been working tirelessly on the play's behalf for years now and a goodly number of highly-ranked theatre people in London seem determined to set it on the stage there.

If it gets produced and is successful—as it should be, it's a dandy suspense- comedy play—there is the book I've written for a musical play of *SOMEWHERE IN TIME* and another suspense play, already completed, which I, personally, believe could be quite successful.

So I hope (I hope, I hope, I hope; what comedian said that? Joe Renner?) to be involved in theatre for the next decade. At which point I'll be 87 and probably ready to sit on a sun-lit porch somewhere dribbling Cream of Wheat down my chin. Or maybe not. Maybe I'll just go back to short stories! Wouldn't that be a kick?

I'll stop for now, having written sixteen of these scrabbled pages in one afternoon's sitting. (Minus toilet visits.)

Later, I guess I'll try to analyze a little further my desire *not* to write anything (creative, that is) at the moment.

Also, I have to (well, I don't have to, but I will) return to the continuing saga of my life. I believe I had just reached college in 1946. '47? Who knows?

Anyway, I'll point out that much of my life story is in pieces and fragments in my stories and novels. So no point in rehashing *that* info.

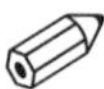

To discuss (briefly) my current lack of desire to write *anything*—although, for a while, I *did* do a lot of work on a play meant to be like *THE LION IN WINTER* or *A MAN FOR ALL SEASONS* or *ANNE OF A THOUSAND DAYS*—replete with ornate and colorful—and hopefully *telling*—speeches and soliloquies. Its plot was created ages ago (when Gene Kelly did *THE THREE MUSKETEERS*!). When I wanted—sort of desperately as I recall—to write a swashbuckler. So I plotted out a very action-filled and "tricky" story for him (I doubt if he ever got it—I mean *received* it, not understood it) and nothing ever came of it.

Later, when I started writing plays (and will *NOW YOU SEE IT ever* get produced in London?!), I acquired—or, rather, developed—an inner craving to do something I had done only on occasion in short stories—worked diligently at creating really outstanding prose. This was sort of stepped on when all the critics spoke admiringly of my "less is more" style—so I rarely tried to create truly *rich* prose. I decided I might try it, however, in a play. So that became my ambition and I have it all plotted, the characters all created (in my mind, if not in flesh-and-blood creation—there are a goodly number of them and I believe that, if I can write the play correctly, it will be a fitting companion to the three plays I mentioned—with wonderful dialogue and even more wonderful soliloquies—I aspire to match, or at least approach, the magnificent word-creation of Shakespeare—can't fault me for low aspiration). It may never work but I'll give it a shot. It's about the only kind of writing I've never attempted. Except, of course, for poetry. But then, in iambic pentameter, my soliloquies, at least, should *approach* poetry.

I did write what I think is an excellent poem in *YOUR MUSEUM MY MUSEUM*. Also in *THE JAZZ MACHINE*. I don't know if I ever wrote how I did *THE JAZZ MACHINE* using virtually all the colorful phrases from Mezz Mezzrow's book (*REALLY THE BLUES*?), putting them in a short story that was so *thick* with colorful language that no self-respecting editor would buy it. Then, one day, I had a brainstorm (it used to storm regularly in my brain, a lot more than it does now) and re-cast the story into poetry form—at which it sold immediately.

Another sort of poem is a very amusing (I think) song lyric entitled *I WANT A BARBARIAN*, supposed to be sung by an older woman (like Bea Arthur), in which she laments the lack of men in her life and her desire for a barbaric lover to "break the bed right under me." I even have a melody for it, too. Another impossible venture which Michael said to his father in *THE GODFATHER*: I don't recall the Italian phrase. Something like, "Another _____?_____, Pop."

Well, anyway, I will write that play someday. Especially if I get established in the theatre before I get senile and talk to trees.

Creativity. A strange bird. I believe that we are born with the productivity. But of course we have to work in it to make anything of it. It's there but can just "flab" away if we don't life creative weights every day and muscle-up our minds.

It is also a free form potential. By that I mean (and I *believe*) that it can manifest itself in any number of ways. As I believe I said in some interviews, if my family was a family of artists and I was exposed to art and there was enough money to buy me expensive art equipment, I might well have become an artist. The potential was there. The means for developing it were not.

Or if my family was one of musicians and/or composers, conductors, etc. I might have become a musician and/or composer. I *did* study piano at college (after having been taught the rudiments of music and playing by my mother). I got quite good at it, too. I played—not too badly, either, (I believe it's called) The Second Rhapsody by Brahms. Not a simple piece to play.

And, in later years, I played, too—piano music with writer/friend Jerry Sohl. We got *very* good, too. Played music by Brahams based on a theme by Paganini. I played the "alto" part, Jerry the tenor (?) part—the *upper* part of the piece.

And I composed, a *lot*. From my teenage years to just recently. I wrote many (*many*) songs with words and music. Provided part of the songs from The "J" Show (at the University of Missouri) *When Knights Were Bold* and all the songs from the play Norman Kennelly and I wrote called *The Eyes Have It*. Sort of proving my point. We were *not* well-to-do. We *could* afford a second-hand upright piano. So my creativity went into writing because all I needed was my Smith-Corona portable (which my brother and his then lady friend Mary gave me for Christmas when I was thirteen) and some paper. Later, a set of scripts pencils when I started writing in longhand rather than directly on the typewriter.

Proving my point again, I *think* I was *born* with a creative urge. Economics determined which area of creativity I went into. 1. An upright piano and some music manuscript. 2. A portable typewriter and some paper. Dictating which "branch" of creativity I was to climb out on.

I think I could have been a very good actor, too. I have the "feel" for it. But not the aggressive personality needed to pursue that elusive quarry. So I had the equipment there—my body, my voice, and my looks. But no psychological equipment.

What else? A creative photographer? Equipment too expensive. A dancer. Lack of drive—and maybe rhythm, who knows?

No, I'm glad that economics led me, primarily, into writing. Because I think it's the branch of creativity which allows one to comment on society, to develop all manner of thought processes et al. Creativity on the cheap but more satisfying in the long run. Oh, I would like to finish that *Symphony in the Style of Tischler*, for which I have about thirty to forty minutes of written composition (not *orchestration*, of course). Another "passemavantic." Pop! Was that it? Sg lk ta—my most often used speedwriting phrase: it stands for "something like that."

I took a correspondence course in speedwriting when I lived in Brooklyn—before I went to college, after I was discharged (with a medical discharge) from the Army in WWII. Is *that* speedwriting? WWII?

It's a very helpful shorthand method. I.e I z ab t tl u ab my flg ab war. (I was about to tell you all about my feelings for war.) Good stuff. I still use it *60 years* after I took that correspondence course! As I use algebra, left over from Brooklyn Technical High School in my teen years, mostly to estimate probable page count on an uncompleted ms.

At any rate, why has my creativity at this point (April, 2003) gone west? Or *has* it gone west? Is it just fermenting beneath the surface, preparing me for some other creative route to follow? I don't know. But, oddly enough, it disturbs me less and less, I find, and, of course, I *am* writing this "journal" with little difficulty. So I can still *write*; that's concerting (is that the opposite of disconcerting?). Is this where the word "concert" comes from? Is my inner system scheduling another kind of concert in my mind? Who's the conductor? Me? Or... *someone else*. What someone? Aye, there's the rub a dub dub, three thoughts (possibilities?) in a tub. Shut up, Dick, you're babbling.

But I really don't want to write anymore about short stories. I short-storied myself out in the 70's. I really *don't* want to write another novel—although I have most of the plot of another one. I can't say I really *don't* want to do another play since my toes are barely wet in this pond.

But I really don't desire to write another teleplay or screenplay. I've done so *many*—and so many that were never filmed. I have always regretted the fact that these unfilmed scripts—which I continue to believe *should* have been filmed—kept me from writing more short stories and more (especially) *novels*, which might have sold for films or—if nothing else—would have increased my body of work in the novel form. But, as I have always said, the big money came from script writing, and I had a wife and four children to support. And script writing got us into several nice houses and locations, especially the last one, in Hidden Hills. So I can't lament on that score. And several scripts were filmed, and filmed well. The *Twilight Zone* scripts, for instance. And the *Kolchak* scripts. And *SOMEWHERE IN TIME*. And *THE MORNING AFTER*. And *DUEL*. And some others like *THE DREAMER OF OZ*, and so on. The Poe films? Definitely *THE COMEDY OF TERRORS*.

RICHARD MATHESON

Well, I think I have dealt enough with my creativity and its curious abatement at this time. I really have said all I have to say (I hope that doesn't sound arrogant) but, still, it came upon me gradually but strangely—and leaves me wondering, "What's next?"

So now I'll return to my life story. If anyone cares.

I just got to college, as I recall. And, as indicated, much of my attitude—and actual experience—can be found in some of my stories (like *Mad House*) and in *HUNGER AND THIRST*. Those are, of course, fiction, but they do detail much of my life experience, especially at college. The searcher will have to determine which is reflected reality and which is fictional device. Certainly, the hero's (*hero*?!) relationship with Sally is very much like my relationship with Mary Bolton. Very *much* like it. The rest is pretty much fictional device. Especially in NY, after the hero graduates from college. The woman in the NY sequence was not in college but met in NY. And the character of the hero's friend is almost entirely fictional, the character is based (loosely) on a guy I knew at school named Bill Vaughn.

I think it best if I list every separate element of my years at the University of Missouri. For the simple reason that, although I would like (for dramatic emphasis—always the writer, you see) to present these years in chronological order. My memory of these years very much lacks chronology but consists of separate "shots" (movie talk) recalled, which jump all over in the spectrum of time.

So here goes. College memories.

1. Where I lived—1316 "J" (?) St. Memories of living there. The old lady in the back room. The *real* old lady in the front room. Cockroach. Description of room. "Time for Bankage!" Norman. *Me*.

2. Applying for classes. Waiting in lines. French teachers. Earl English and General Semantics. Aesthetics class. Summer school. Weather. David Silber in G.S. class. Piano lessons with Mr. Sheldon. Song his wife performed. Journalism classes. (Principles of —") Dean Mott, Music critic. Editing "disk" Teacher. Relationship. His home; harps. Suicide. Principles of Advertising. Hay ring caught.

3. Mo. Workshop. Rhynsburger. "Dear Ruth" try-out. Music for "Winterset." Bill Vaughn. Later on, FM station. Rita Saunders. Working on sets with Norman.

4. Stephens College. Dates. Elmo Tanner & "Heartaches" whistling. Barbara Cypiot. Girl whose father "owned Colorado's" Playa. John Cornell; later in soap opera.

5. Mary. *HUNGER AND THIRST*; already mentioned. Class in Modern Dance suggested by Rhynburger ("Abe Lincoln in Illinois"—between him and Massey). "Ezekial Saw The Wheel"—flinging ourselves on floor. Norman and me, neither did acting. But met Mary. Standing over me in tutu. Her body.

6. First "J" show. Met Goodman; he's brother of Mississippi's 3 Don—director. Fredna Parker. Stanley Niemstedt. (Later with him.) BMOC then "A Princess Has a Full-Time Job." Spencer Albert. Jack Flynn. Two sophisticated writers. "Sodie" number inappropriate. Song Cycle? Bill U directed. Two-piano music. My songs. Bad reviews. "Canard" sad fellow. Wish I had a film of it.

7. Leaving home for college experience—*good*!

8. Saturday night, study. Midnight shows. Guy who asked, "Butt me," yelling in theater. "Kennelly put your belly close to mine!" *DON JUAN* with Errol Flynn. Crush on Ava Gardner in *ONE TOUCH OF VENUS*. Small theater. Popcorn man (already mentioned).

9. Concerts. 176—orchestra—"Midsummer Vigil"—Mary's hand. Laurity Melchior. My award. Dean Mott's initiation. Claire Coci—organ—wink. Eugene Ormandy. James Melton. Stupid comment. Bill U. "Thanks a lot, kid."

10. Return in 2000 (?) Distress. *Okay*, '52, not changed that much. But 2000! Oy. Rickerby music building gone. New building.

Overall experience:

Enough memories to detail. I'm sure collateral memories (like *Collateral Damage*? Ugh! What a disgusting euphemism for blowing women and children to bits!) will occur. As they do, I will notate them. Why not say "write them down?" I don't know, "Hoity-toity," as my sister said? "Notate," I mean.

ALL RIGHT! College memories.

1. I have a photograph—in my limited photo book—of the front of the house. Steps up to the porch. Screen door. Front door on left. I guess there was an apartment on the right side of the building, too.

Entering, the living room was on the left. I'll try to remember to mention the photograph there. "Hoo Hoo, Miss Ada! I went to get up!"

Down a hall, as I recall, it was a long haul. My landlady, Miss Ada (I don't remember her last name—SMITH!), had her bedroom on the left, next to the old lady's room (and Joe's, then Norman's), on the left again. More hall, the kitchen on the left. Miss Ada, cook of my pork chops, so leanly spiced she couldn't eat them. Because of aging taste buds, of course. And all the way in back, the slightly less old woman who would call down the hall each evening, "Time for Bankage!" (sp?), a St. Louis newscaster that Miss Ada and she listened to on the radio. When Miss Ada couldn't do it, the old lady got cranky.

My room. A closet on the right and, further down the right wall, my "student's table," where I kept my textbooks and studied and wrote my term papers and/or compositions. I might add, which I remember to, that the manner in which I (was taught?) put together my term papers I used and continue to use to this day. 3"x5" index cards. Every item I can think of—plot, character analysis, dialogue, action sequences, et al—all jotted down on the cards. Then hanging cork boards (once in the room that transitioned from my office to Richard's room—covering all the walls and several *thousand* file cards! When I put together the story for the 20-hour mini-series about parapsychology for ABC in my garage book room and putting the file cards in some kind of order, then beginning to go through them as I wrote the story, the novel, the script, the outline, whatever. That it took me a year and a half (!) to complete the ABC outline (more than 800 pages) scared the hell out of Brandon Stoddard (the then-head of ABC Films) and they ended up electing for seven hours. I should have said, "Forget it! Impossible!" but like an idiot, I tried, even (at their request) adding *two more major stories* to the mix. It *was* impossible and the entire project tanked.

Later, I got their permission (I'm sure I'm repeating myself here) to make my whopper outline into a novel. Which I tried to do. And when Part One (*partial*!) was in excess of 800 pages, either my agent or an editor said that the book (estimated, by me, as 2000 pages long) would cost too much for a publisher to sell. It was suggested that I make it into three separate novels, but I just couldn't do it (creatively, I mean) because the story was conceived as one story and was not amenable to cutting it in thirds.

So goodbye to *THE NEXT STEP* or *THE LINK* or whatever it would have ended up being called. For aye, I believed. For dear old (he's not old) Barry Hoffman plans to publish my gigantic outline, which he feels "reads like" a novel. Well, at least, some of my readership (and public) will see what I had in my mind. As they did when Barry published one section of *COME FYGURES, COME SHADOWS*; an afterward by me explained (and apologized for) why the master plan for that novel (another gigantic project) never came to fruition.

At least *HUNGER AND THIRST* was entirely written. So Barry could publish an entire story for a change.

RICHARD MATHESON

I am (dismayed) by the side-tracking of my intention to describe my room at college. So I'll return to it. As I recall, I was still on the right wall and my student table, a window to the left of that (as you sat at the "desk"). I presume—I don't remember, exactly—that one other student table was on the left wall. Two cots or beds or whatever they were, were in between the desks. There was a second window on that side.

I have to go check on what I put down for step one.

I made a story point of this in *BID TIME RETURN* (*SOMEWHERE IN TIME*)—about the very old lady—blind and bed-ridden, her mind a vagary—crying out, periodically, as I said "Hoo Hoo, Miss Ada! I want to get up!" Of course, she couldn't get up. But Miss Ada (a sweet old lady herself) would toddle to the old lady's room to comfort her. Miss Ada was a Christian Science practitioner—which explains how I (and Joe, at first) got the room.

The story point I used was a "long ago" dredged-up memory from that time. I believe I was in the front room, making (with Miss Ada's permission) a telephone call. And while I made it, I saw on a nearby table, a photograph (portrait photo, actually) of this exquisitely beautiful young woman. And it was the very old lady in the front bedroom. And to sit there, look at this gorgeous face, and, at the very same moment, to hear her fragile cry about wanting to get up, created an intense emotional reaction; the mystery (and cruelty?) of time very vivid in my mind. Which later, of course, fitted perfectly my approach to time in my novel. And, once again, the disturbed human being is turned into the cold-blooded writer, who—in the name of creativity—*uses* the emotional disturbance to make a story point. Oh, we writers can be strangely *unemotional* constructors when it serves our purpose. Not that we do not, honestly, experience the distress, but that we *utilize* it for our "work." Strange creatures indeed.

What else about Step One?

The incident with Norman. Once again revealing the coldness in me at that time. Not creative. Just character flaw persona.

One night Norman came in late (I was going to say "stumbled" in but that would be fostering my ease, and there is—at least *now*—no way it *can* be fostered).

So Norman "came in" drunk and banged around noisily, waking me up and angering me. I don't recall if he apologized or not. He may well have. Even if he had, I would not have accepted it.

So from that night on, I did what my mother did to me—gave Norman the "silent" treatment. A *terrible* procedure. But I knew no better. It must have hurt him terribly as time passed (time again). We were working at that Frat house at that time, cleaning food trays (in great steamer cleaners) and it was a long (and extremely *early*) walk to the Frat house from our room (Norman had moved in after Joe left) and it was winter, as I recall, and we trudged along with breath steaming, me in dead (as icy as the weather) silence. It went on for days and days.

Finally, Norman could take no more and spoke up one morning as we walked side by side. I don't recall exactly what he said except for one phrase, which remains in my consciousness to the present moment. The phrase was, "Technically, I love you." I'm sure he added *technically* to protect himself from being too demonstrative.

At any rate, we made up and were "pals" again. But, to this day, I feel a sense of emotional pain to recall how badly I treated him, especially in light of what he said.

But then, I was definitely an incomplete, "unformed" human being in those days. And, when angered, I could withdraw and cover my behavior with an icy sheen, and how awful of me that was. For God's sake, to this moment, I feel guilty about the one time (one time!) I hit Bart on the backside when he was misbehaving on our deck. (Bart was our wonderful Lab.) He turned and gave me a look of such *pain* that, remembering it, can bring tears to my eyes right now.

So imagine how utterly lousy I feel about the way I treated my dear friend Norman. Terrible. Just terrible. Inexcusable. But that was me in those days. Sort of fun company until I felt emotionally crossed. Then turning into a speechless Mr. Hyde.

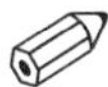

So...Step Two, more technical stuff. Waiting in line to apply for classes. I'd say that most students elected to get all their classes crammed together early in the morning and early in the week so they would have long weekends off.

Not me. I spread my classes out from Monday to Friday (and in the afternoons, if I could) so that my schedule wasn't too heavy. I remember how I *hated The Principles of Economics* (a required course, naturally—I would have never signed up for it otherwise). Not only was the subject matter staggeringly dull, but the text made it even *duller*; written, of course, by the teacher. They all augmented their salaries by writing the course textbook. And who can blame them?

But to top it all—all this was brainwashing dullness—the class took place at seven in the morning! So we had to get up at six in order to make the class. I developed the skill that all students (of early classes) *must* develop; the ability to shade the eyes with one hand, conveying the impression that one is "attending" the class while one is actually sleeping soundly. How I passed the damn course, I'll never know. If I got a *C*, I was lucky.

What next? (Check the list.)

French teachers? A minor memory. I had to take a year and a half of French because I'd had no language at good ol' Brooklyn Tech (I was too busy building a ship and learning to rivet and oxyacetylene torch welding). The first teacher I had I thought was really good, although, despite my work, I never got more than a *B* out of him.

The last half-year of French I took in summer school. The teacher was the head of the French Department and he made it so *easy*! And gave me an *A* with no trouble.

For a while, I became quite proficient at French, I even corresponded in French with David Silver! But now, all that remains is a scattering of phrases and a few song lyrics, i.e. "Elle fit un fromage, et non-non-non petit patapon! (?) Elle fit un fromage. Du lait du see mountain, non, non. Du lait du see mouton." Utterly useless. As are the opening words of "The Raven," which are implanted in my mind. As are the lyrics from a Gilbert & Sullivan song (from *THE GONDOLIERS*?) about not being able to go to sleep. "When you're lying awake—with a dismal headache—and repose is tabooed by anxiety, I suppose you may use—any language you choose—to indulge in without impropriety," etc. Ending with "You're a regular wreck with a crick in your neck and... "—so on. What makes us remember these things and not others? A couple or three of Uncle Don's songs (he was a kid's radio star when *I* was a kid) and some of Joe's "The Bells." "Hear the silver bells, how they tinkle-tinkle-tinkle in the icy air of night—while the stars that oversprinkle..."—etc. *Why*?

So that's it for French teachers—plus added recollections.

Earl English. He later became the Dean of the Journalism School. (Neal! That was the "J" school teacher's name—I'll use it when I come to that.) He taught the class that was my favorite course in my entire stay at the University of Missouri (M.V., as they called it).

General Semantics. Korzybski. Wonderful class. I met David Silver in that class. I believe, a History major and an English Literature minor.

We both loved General Semantics. Dr. English started us off telling us that he wanted us to keep a journal. That's all he said. Marvelous! Just—keep a journal. David and I loved that—relished it. I think some of the students were very perplexed by that "instruction." What kind of journal? How long? Including what? Etc. David and I bounced off and loved keeping our journals. And we got *A*'s without trouble. And I think Dr. English thought we were his favorite students. Because we never asked, we just did.

LEAVE YESTERDAY ALONE

~~~~~

A Novel

[Publisher's note: Written just before or right after HUNGER AND THIRST: Approximately 1949]
~~~~~

one.

Mostly he said it because he was drunk and had never been drunk.

"Self concern is a spawning bitch that whelps all manner of disfigurements. From its narrow, obscene womb crawl all the multiple inversions a man may destroy himself with. Selah."

He said it to Lynn Mace. It was April, night.

"It depends," Lynn said, "on which self of your many selves you're concerned with."

"Get me another drink," Erick said.

Lynn got up and went over to the counter. They were in the fraternity playroom, what was called the Rathskellar, what amended became the Rat Cellar. They were in one of the booths, those dimly lit booths that hold some sort of intangible capacity to loosen a person's tongue. Was it the intimacy of it? Or the liquor one did away with while one sat in the booth? Confessionals with beer. That's what Leo called them. But that was more than a year away.

Erick looked hazily around the room. It was filled with French-cuffed frat boys and their falsied dates. It was Lynn's fraternity. Erick lived in a room, alone. Lynn had invited him over that Saturday night to look the place over while they talked over plans for the show. Lynn said that Erick might have a few drinks and contemplate membership. Erick was having a few drinks.

"What in the hell," he inquired as Lynn set down the drinks and slid in across from him, "made you join this junior Bedlam?"

Lynn smiled.

"When I came to college," he said, "it seemed like a good idea. Now I'm used to it. I'm adjusted."

Lynn had come to the University from New York a year before Erick. With aspiration, effort and a good brain, he had piled up a straight *A* average his first two semesters. He joined the school scholarship society and was the very model of a superior student.

Then he saw it got him nowhere. Grades didn't make all the difference, he discovered. This, plus recognition of the string which all the threads of his life had been twisting themselves into caused him to slacken his storming of the academic walls.

He became active in campus affairs, was in touch with various business people who had long ago offered him jobs upon graduation. He was a casual intellectual now, with both feet firmly planted in the practical world. That he still pulled down frequent *A*'s at least proved that his brain could still put out.

Erick first met him while Lynn was editing the campus short story magazine. They printed one of Erick's stories and Lynn was so impressed
with it that he got in touch with Erick and they had been friends ever since.

"I am mildly blotto," Erick said. "I have never been blotto in my life to any degree. My dear mama would shriek out in horror if she could see her little boy mildly blotto. I shudder—shudder—to think of the added wrinkles I would bestow on that precious brow were she still alive today. I have despised liquor in my day. It struck my dear dead daddy a fell blow. And here I am, none-the-less, mildly blotto. Selah."

Lynn took a sip from his glass and pulled out a package of cigarettes from his side coat pocket. He flicked a finger against the bottom and one cigarette popped up. He inserted it between his thin lips and offered the pack to Erick.

"You know I don't smoke," Erick said. "Nor care for ladies that do."

Lynn opened the book of matches and hesitated a second as Erick asked, "We got a dancing director yet?"

Lynn shook his head. Then he struck the match and held the flame against the end of the cigarette. Smoke veiled his eyes.

"We start rehearsal in a week," Erick said.

"Quite true," Lynn said, picking the cigarette from his lips.

"What do we do?"

"Look for a dance director," Lynn said.

Then he raised his glass a trifle.

"To your first glandular debauch, baby," he said.

Erick looked at him. "Yes, ma," he said. They drank and, putting down his glass Erick rested on one bunched fist and looked around the room.

"See the people," he said. "See the funny people. What are they dreaming of?"

"Nothing," Lynn said. "They have no capacity for dreams."

"One would think it," Erick said. "To see them wander aimlessly, idly pressing groins together in the dance and giggling and chatting of baseball scores and thinly-veiled libido. What does it mean?"

"Nothing," Lynn said. "Absolutely nothing."

Erick turned to him, ran his eyes over Lynn's thin, ascetic face, peered into his shifting grey-blue eyes that moved like living things behind rimless glasses.

"You are consistent," Erick said, "if not prolix."

He turned his gaze then and did his own tour of eye duty around the smoky, noisy room, over the paneled booths crowded with college youth, over the columned floor where danced as many couples as could possibly crowd there and still leave room for the glowering juke box.

"I think it *is* prolix," Lynn said. "*Nothing* is the most complicated value there is. It entails everything canceling itself out. The good balanced by the bad, the intelligent by the doltish. All leaving a vacuum, a dead space of lethargic immobility."

He blew out a cloud of nicotined smoke and adjusted the bridge of his glasses.

"Look at them," he said. "Unreasoning animals. Ambulating evidence for the mechanical theory of life. Pitiful little summations of outer and inner influence, thoroughly incapable of dealing with themselves, much less others."

He looked a moment more.

"Advocates of the inordinate screw," he said slowly and coldly.

Erick chuckled without noise.

"Lynn," he said, "you would have given Jesus a hard time. You would have been the guy who carried the hammer."

Lynn smiled at him and Erick pretended not to see what he saw.

"Thumb me a woman," Lynn asked. It was a game they played, trying to characterize a woman entirely with one short sentence.

"She had fluff in her belly button," Erick said.

"Thumb me another," Lynn said, looking carefully at Erick.

Erick said, after a moment's thought,

"She was a man."

♦ ♦ ♦ ♦ ♦

She was with Felix Karis, one of the bulkiest quarterbacks in the annals of Midwestern college lore. They had been there all evening. Lynn had pointed out Felix as a prime example of the Neanderthal extant.

Erick hadn't noticed her.

Now, about eleven or so, Felix was pussy-footing it around the floor, two drinks mangled in his great paws, his big, trusting eyes searching for a place to park. She was following him.

Fate. Erick later guessed that was what he'd have to call it. The fact that Felix lived on the same floor of the fraternity that Lynn did and that as a result, they had a nodding acquaintance. Which Lynn made every effort to suppress.

There was Felix standing by the booth.

"Hiya, Mace," he said, smiling broadly.

Take your fat face away from here, Erick's mind requested on the spot. He and Lynn looked up mutually to examine the rills and ridges of Felix's broad Polish face.

It wasn't that Felix was ugly, they later decided. It was just that his features were too rough hewn, as though they had been axed out. There was too much of him, from the bushy top of his coarse black hair down to the two chins and including the vase handle ears. It was the sort of a face, Erick thought, that looked as if it were blasted out of a cliff.

"Hello," Lynn said with a tone that added, to Erick, anyway—Kindly thaw and resolve into a dew.

"Say, uh, look Mace," said Felix, fumbling the conversational ball, "could we, maybe, my date and me, that is, I mean, maybe share your booth? There's not any place to sit,"

Lynn's pained scrutiny moved for a moment to the girl, then back to Felix. Erick paid no more attention, occupying himself by jiggling ice cubes in his drink.

"Well, I..." Lynn started, unnaturally at a loss for words.

Erick turned his head then and looked the girl in the face.

She looked back and seemed to smile although her lips didn't move. First link. He didn't sense it exactly. But something made him extend his hand in the best hotel manager fashion.

"Sit down!" he said, with ersatz gusto. "Pray!"

Then he glanced over at Lynn with a smile, getting amusement at the expected ice in Lynn's eyes. For a brief moment, he felt like some teasing date who had successfully irritated Lynn, then the feeling drifted off into the cloudy wake in which all his thoughts mingled.

Felix and the girl hesitated, imagining that either Lynn or Erick would move to the other side of the booth and give them one half of it. But they didn't move. So Felix out down the drinks and gestured to her to sit next to Lynn. Erick felt Felix's bunchy shoulders as he slid in beside him.

Elation seemed to mist over him. The dizziness, the room spinning with colored lights, the vibrating dull glow of the drunken fancy. Touch of the fantastic, came the thought.

"Now," he said, "isn't this comfy, dears. Where were we? Oh, yes."

He turned blandly to Felix who was sipping his drink.

"I was telling you what an intellectual citizenry we would have if people only had the right books in the bathroom."

"What?" Felix said, his giant forehead sliding down over his skull.

"And the kiddies," Erick said, "how are they? Bless me, it seems like eons since I bounced little Muggins on my wooden leg!"

And in his mind he heard Felix saying—*What's he been drinking?*

Felix looked at Lynn, Lynn who had forgiven Erick, Lynn who was erecting a tributary smile at one end of his sensual and snobbish mouth.

"What's *he* been drinking?" Felix asked.

Lynn shrugged his shoulders, his eyebrows, as though he had just noticed Erick sitting there.

Felix let it go. He turned to his date. And Erick looked at her.

Her face was non-committing. There was no way to tell what emotion was bordering on it. Later, Erick grew to appreciate how rare such a look was on her face. It only happened, he discovered, when she was more or less mystified.

"Mace," Felix said, "I'd like you to meet Sally Birch."

Lynn turned his head and smiled politely. "Pleasure," he said. *No, it isn't*, Erick's mind observed.

"Hello," she said, smiling now. A smile that made Erick feel something, he didn't know what. It was the sweetest smile he'd ever seen.

"That's not your first name, is it?" she asked Lynn.

"Lynn," he said.

"Hello, Lynn."

Lynn turned back front. His eyes met Erick's. He pointed a well manicured finger at Erick.

"This, I am called upon to indicate," he said, "is Erick Linstrom."

"Oh!" she said. "The one whose show is being produced!"

She actually sounded awed. It set Erick off balance. Upset, flattered into startlement, he could do nothing but set aside mental dazzling and smile at her.

And she smiled back with such a lovely smile that it made his heartbeat catch. It absorbed him, her smile absorbed him.

"Hello, Erick," she said.

"Hello," he answered.

And the next moment found Felix getting socially acceptable revenge by reducing Erick's right hand to a pulp. Erick decided he could have gotten the same effect by putting his hand into a vise and turning the handle slowly until the bones snapped.

♦ ♦ ♦ ♦ ♦

"Gee, I think that's wonderful that they're putting on a show you wrote all by yourself."

He didn't write the music. He almost told her then decided not to. He basked in her attention. It was a new sensation and he liked it. He was the center and Felix didn't like it but Erick did. He leaned back against the booth and studied her through half-closed eyes. She noticed it but he had finished another drink and was just about past caring whether his surveillance was obvious or not.

"What's it about?" she asked.

He gave her a few hints as to the plot, always looking at her, appraising.

She had a coarse loveliness. There was no delicate precision of line to her features. All was molded roughly and no more. It was as though some potter had fingered out a general symmetry and then gone on to other work before he could refine.

Once, when she got up to dance with some boy who had stopped at the booth to ask her, Erick noticed her figure. It was fabulous. The dress seemed to sheathe her more than anything else. She was soft, swelling curves from shoulders to ankles.

"What did you say you did?" he asked her.

"I teach dancing."

"At the school?"

"That's right."

He looked at Lynn. "Our dance director?" he asked.

Lynn's face didn't change. But Erick saw warning in his eyes. In order that Erick be pacified, however, Lynn turned to her.

"Have you ever done any group work?" he asked politely.

"Oh, *yes*," she said, "I'm a co-director of the dance recital we give every spring. We're having one next week. Why don't you come and see it, it's free."

Erick smiled at the way she spoke, in such a headlong fashion, rushing from thought to thought without usual grammatical bridges or rests, as though she had so many things to say she must blurt them out eagerly before she forgot them.

Lynn smiled thinly at her invitation to the recital.

"Perhaps," he said.

"I think she'd be a good dance director," Erick said. He didn't look at Lynn. He already knew what Lynn's expression would be.

"Would you be interested?" Lynn said, getting tighter and tighter. Then, as she almost bubbled over with—Yes!—he added a dampening, "In trying out?"

She kept smiling although she couldn't hide the disappointment. Erick wanted to hit Lynn and hold her hand and say—there, there, the job is yours."

"I'd like to try out," she said, quietly.

Erick was conscious of Felix, restive at this side, being shoved aside in the conversation. He didn't care. She was looking at him and he wanted to kiss her. She looked superbly beautiful to him there in the dim light with his eyes half clouded by drinking.

"You'll be fine," he said, "Very fine."

Later. More drinks in him, a few of them. Lynn still dead sober, watching Erick like a detective searching for clues. Erick discoursing. To her.

"What a horror story I could write," he said, "about drab routine. Werewolves? Vampires? Monsters? Witches?" He raised a finger which weaved in front of his eyes. "Romance, ethereal delight, all of them. But *routine*? Ah! It is the very word horror, inescapable, harrowing and all-pervasive."

He took a swallow from his drink, feeling dryness in his throat. The cold wetness washed the membranes in a moment and he did not relinquish the floor, even though Felix tried to say something. He broke in.

"I feel a creeping dread of it," he went on, melodrama bound. "Like a child's fear of the darkness—unreasonable and irrational. But childish fears of the dark pass, as do all transient fears, but *this* remains—a blood-flecked monster that eats you from the inside out!"

At that he laughed out loud, *laugh number 3-A*, his mind said—*laughter at one's own extremes of expression without the negation of one's basic argument*.

Then he let it all go, letting the floods of fancy wash over the wall of his brain, conscious of Lynn watching him carefully, conscious of Felix being bored into rapid death. Conscious of her, rapt and mystified.

"Never," he said, "never shall I slide down into the still green waste of common life, letting the stench of uselessness close over my poor head.

Lynn's lips twitched a little, out of control. Erick didn't know what Felix was doing but Sally's face he saw—not registering amusement. She was taking it straight. He caught her eyes and they were almost vibrant with sympathy for him. It was a jolt to his equilibrium to have his obvious extremes taken as gospel. He began to know her then, the limits of her humor, but more, the powerful kindness in her.

And something else he wasn't conscious of, until later. That Sally was seeing underneath and knowing that, basically, in spite of bald exaggeration, Erick was saying the things he believed in. For it was his common ailment to coat over with humor those things which he believed yet could not help suspending.

"Finished?" Lynn asked.

"Finished?" Erick said, with pseudo-shock ringing in his voice. "I have not yet begun to fight, is this Paul Jones whiskey?"

Lynn smiled and Erick turned to Sally. He looked at her and something flickered between them, something happened to her eyes. He could never have described it but he felt it. She saw that, for she turned her eyes down suddenly and he saw a soft flush move across her temples. He saw her throat move, once.

"I think routine is necessary," she said, after a moment with an indefinite glance at him. "We couldn't get anything done without routine."

"Right!" he said, congressionally. "However, ninety percent of the populace makes of routine not a slave but a god. True, if we mold it and place it where we will then it is a benefaction, a mechanical aid to accomplishment, but!..."

"Sally, we…" Felix started to say.

"But! When it becomes our master, then are we truly lost," he said, feeling a sudden tightening in realizing that he was drunk and out of order even if it was only with Felix Karis. He went on stubbornly even though he began to feel ill.

"When it becomes our master," he said, "then are we truly lost. We are no better than clay. We are driftwood in a terrible, devitalizing current. We are dead before death. Selah."

"Hymn number 307," said Lynn.

"Pass the plate," Erick said.

Sally smiled, a healthy, honest smile.

"I'm glad you're only joking," she said. "It would be awful if you really felt that way."

And they all sat in silence for a moment while Lynn smiled and pushed his cigarette into an ash tray.

"Sally, let's dance," Felix blurted quickly, wedging in his request.

She smiled at Felix, his date once more.

"All right," she said happily.

Erick felt a sudden iciness coursing him. He'd known all along that she was with Felix, that he was once a stranger, but he was drunk and he wanted to be more to her. And now this coldness came, spoiling his little bubble, upsetting the dream boat, and he felt lonely and disgruntled.

"I want her for dance director," he said sullenly as Sally and Felix moved off into the crowd, swallowed up in a maw of hips and stuck-out arms.

Lynn looked patient. He lit another cigarette.

"Lynn," he said, with rising impatience.

"For Christ's sake," Lynn said, "will you give these things a little thought? Don't go embracing the first dance director you meet."

"You talk as if they grow on trees out here!" Erick said sharply. "What the hell do you want—Agnes De Mille to fly out from New York?"

Lynn's mouth took on the lines of patient disgust Erick knew so well.

"Let's sit on it, shall we baby?" he said.

"Oh...horse manure."

Erick leaned back and looked out in dull belligerence at the floor. He saw them dancing. She was looking over Felix's shoulder at him but she turned the other way quickly.

"Pretty," Erick said softly.

"What?" Lynn asked.

"I said she's pretty," he said, knowing it would irritate Lynn.

"In a rather obvious way," Lynn said.

"How's that, kiddo?" Erick said.

"I mean," Lynn said, ignoring the tone of Erick's voice, "there's no subtlety to her. She's uncomplicated, a prototype of the dull-thinking American woman. Legs and breasts and possessiveness."

"Horse manure."

"That's a fine answer," Lynn said, and Erick had to go on.

"If you dwell on visceral detail," he said, "all girls are alike. Otherwise they're all different."

"In making woman," Lynn said, "a rib was taken away from man. Since then, woman has devoted herself to taking away everything else, too."

"Unquote—Erick Linstrom," said Erick, "and you're still wrong."

"Perhaps," Lynn said. "I doubt it."

Bored voice, argument ended. Erick let it go. He slumped back drunkenly irritable and looked out into the room without seeing any of it. He felt an urge to write so he could see how his handwriting and intelligibility showed up in the morning light.

He had never before experienced the odd sensations that being drunk made possible. The strange fuzziness in his head, the feeling that the circumference of his mental circle was coated over with some sort of numbing insulator which left the core intact and hyper-brilliant. The loss of balance, the feeling that the center of gravity in himself and others and everything around him was constantly shifting, that his gyroscope was out of order. Yet all without the slightest loss of acuity. He knew he was drunk and he was doing and saying silly things. He fully appreciated just how silly they were and he could think—I'll stop them if they get too silly.

But they never seemed to.

And all this fuzziness which was, moments before, pleasant had now become a black fuzziness. He felt disgusted with Lynn, with Lynn's smugness and detached arrogance. He wanted to punch Lynn right in the nose. He didn't feel like summoning up any intellectual body blows. There were times when all he wanted to do was hit out and hurt. All he could think of definitely was that Sally would be dance director or he'd take back the script. Mutely truculent, he sat there, watching his own thoughts fight it out among themselves.

♦ ♦ ♦ ♦ ♦

When they returned, someone came up to Felix. Erick didn't hear exactly what was said, something about football team and little meeting upstairs and rah rah rah. Erick didn't hear because he was staring quite frankly at Sally's large, firmly arched breasts. He didn't know whether she noticed it at first. But Lynn did. And for some reason it gave Erick a perverse pleasure to see the look of wordless warning that Lynn gave him.

Felix asked her if it was all right, he'd only be gone a few minutes. Stag stuff. He kept using the phrase until Erick felt like holding Felix's hand in his and gently vomiting on it. Sally told him it was perfectly all right, she understood.

"Sit here by me," Erick said, when Felix was gone. "While the cat's away, the mouses will play."

She hesitated, then slid in beside him and their eyes met a moment. He could smell the perfume her body breathed. It surrounded him.

"Is he as bad as he pretends?" she asked Lynn.

Lynn's mouth twitched, then he said, "He's pretty awful."

He looked at Erick.

"He's ignoble," he said.

"Oh my God," Erick said, "am I ignoble?"

Elation returning, slowly. Felix gone, her next to him. Lynn the only dampening factor. It seemed odd that whenever he was with Lynn and a girl he wanted Lynn to go away.

"Yes," Lynn said, "you are ignoble." And he meant it.

Erick put his hand on Sally's arm. The flesh was warm and soft. His fingers felt sandpapered, like a safecracker's fingers, he could feel the delicate hairs on her arms.

"Do you think I'm ignoble?" he asked, looking into her eyes. *Lynn get out of here!* his mind yelled.

She looked back at him. She looked inside, then she smiled and he saw her throat move again.

"I don't know," she said. "I don't know what you are."

"A man," Erick said.

Lynn snickered. *I'll punch you right in the nose*, Erick's mind said, slowly and calculatingly.

"You're pretty," he said, trying to ignore Lynn.

"Thank you," she murmured.

"Now what were we talking about?" Erick asked.

"Nothing," Lynn said, pulling the cigarette case from his coat pocket. He offered it to Sally. "Cigarette, Sally?" he asked casually.

"No, thank you," Sally said, with a smile.

"You mean you don't smoke?" Erick asked.

"No," she said.

Erick leaned back, a smile raising him lips, his hand still on her arm. He caressed it and she said not to with her eyes so he stopped.

"It's incredible," he said, "You're the first girl I've met in a coon's age who doesn't smoke. Why don't you?"

"It's not healthy," she said, a little nervous under his steady gaze. She glanced toward the door.

"Felix is making an end run," Erick said. "You must not disturb him.

She looked back at him, this time without pleasure.

"He's a nice boy," she said firmly.

Erick glanced away at Lynn. Lynn was bored, looking at the table, poking one slender finger in the wet circles his glass had made. Then abruptly, he slid out of the booth and stood up, a far-away look in his eye.

"Excuse me," he said flatly and walked away.

"We're alone," Erick said. "Doesn't that excite you?"

She was watching Lynn walk away. Erick watched her profile and had a strong desire to press his lips against her warm, ruddy cheek.

The she took his hand off her arm. She got up and sat on the other side of the booth. They looked at each other. Her face was not recriminating yet it was neither the warm face it had been before. The whole room seemed to fade away, sight and sound, as they looked at each other. It was like looking into a crystal ball, he thought, in the darkness, all surroundings disappearing.

Finally she smiled, unable to frown any longer.

"She has a well-proportioned face," Erick said, "full in all features."

"Who?" she asked.

"You," he said. "There is nothing thin or lacking. It is healthy in its entirety."

She leaned back and clasped her hands on the edge of the table.

"Clasp your hands on the desk, children," he said.

She didn't say anything, she didn't smile. She didn't have to. She was still searching, he saw, so he kept on talking.

"It is as though," he said, "the molder of her features had said—Here we will hold no effort but give richly to each particular. To eyes a wide space of separation. Full pupils, tinted evenly with warm brown hue. Long even lashes to—to *brush* her magic with or," he waved a finger and gazed into his own conception, "or to hold glistening tears like dew drops on a downy wing—a sight which well may touch the heart."

He paused. She was looking intently at him. *Fall in love with me!* his mind cried out in its secret place. *Fall in love with me terribly, I want to break your heart!*

He took a heavy breath and felt a sudden wildness pass into him. He leaned forward and rested his chin on both hands. He stared at her and kept on talking, the words tumbling out in unkempt bundles from his whirring brain. There was no one in the world but her.

"Wide brows," he said. "Not thin or pinched but full and dark and of elliptical excellence. A high brow to prove the store of ken within. Healthy chestnut hair which may fall long in tangled locks upon her round, her soft-fleshed shoulders."

He let the last words of the sentence roll off his tongue like Barrymore intoning a Shakespearian oath. She pressed her lips together and forced back a smile.

"Don't smile," he said. "Your face might crack."

She couldn't hold it. It beamed out on him like Spring and was a silent blessing.

"Don't stop," she said.

So he went on. *I'm weaving my golden web*, he thought, the little boy in him chuckling. *I'm throwing my net over your head and you know it not.*

"A nose, not thin, with only excellence of fragile architecture. Full nostrils, a broad ridge, straightly cut which is in keeping with all. And lips..."

He pushed forward a little, saw her swallow convulsively, saw the color in her temples again. He leaned forward more as if he meant to kiss her with his words.

"Lips," he said, almost fiercely. "A mouth wide enough to preclude the irksome Cupid's bow or irritable little girls. Wide enough to shape a smile which could be nothing but the warmest of smiles. Full-fleshed lips of every scarlet, each shaped alike, not tiny dips of flesh but cushions of glistening plenty. Warm. *Soft*. And always inviting the touch of...*other* lips..."

She took in a sudden breath.

Sounds flooded in around them. Something had broken. The spell was gone, excess had broken the trance. She smiled, nervously now, and looked around the room.

"Well, I..." she started, then stopped. He held her with his eyes. You're going to fall in love with me, the little boy commanded, you going to fall terribly in love with me.

"Well, you what?" he asked and, as she picked up her glass, he noticed that her hand shook.

"Nothing," she said lightly, and her voice shook enough to show him it was forced lightness.

"Shall I go on?" he said with no intention of going on.

"You'd better not," she said, "now that we're down to the chin line."

"Tradition," he said. "Rank wind in the garden of life."

They were apart now. She wasn't at ease and he didn't care anymore, she had lost her attraction for him.

"Here comes your fullback or whatever the hell he is," he said.

Her head turned quickly and she smiled broadly as Felix came up to the table. Erick felt a twinge of anger that she should waste such a smile.

"We're invited to another frat party," Felix said.

Good, Erick thought, *get the hell out of here and take your breasty bitch with you! Leave a poor drunkard alone*. That idea appealed to him suddenly. He decided he was doomed to be a drunkard. Like father, like son, some moral debility leaking from generation to generation.

Sally got up. Felix asked where Lynn was and Sally didn't know. He glanced at Erick but Erick didn't even look up.

"Goodnight, Erick," Sally said. "I'm so glad I met you. Good luck on your show."

"Goodnight," he said, offhandedly.

They left and he watched them disappear and felt a terrible sinking depression in his stomach. He wanted to break something violently. All the excitements were gone. He emptied the glass with one swallow and the drink was cold and tasteless in his mouth. He closed his eyes.

"Have they gone?" Lynn asked when he came back.

"No, they've acquired invisibility," Erick answered.

Lynn sat down, then got up again and got two more drinks. When he came back they sat in silence a while. Then Erick said, impulsively,

"You're right, she's nothing. Absolutely nothing."

"Oh?" said Lynn.

That was how Sally became the dance director.

two.

She was waiting for him on the porch steps of the music building.

"Hi," she smiled.

She was dressed in a light cotton dress whose pattern had pink elephants sporting delphically over her lithe body.

"Hello," he said, and they went into the building.

She walked close to him. It was the third time he'd seen her. The second time was in the dramatics office where all those concerned with the production met to discuss general plans. It was there she asked him to meet her on the porch so she could sit with him tryouts.

"Good turn out," he commented, glancing around at the girls singing to themselves in corners, some boys and some girls taking practice turns on the creaking floor.

Lynn looked up from his front row seat as they came down the aisle. He nodded to them. Sally said hello, then she said, "Let's sit over here" and they moved into the third row and sat down.

"What's the notebook for?" he asked her.

"So I can take notes."

He stuck out his lower lip. "Logical," he said.

He smiled at her and then glanced down at her knee where the dress had slid over it.

"Where did you get the scrape?" he asked.

"Practicing for our recital."

"Still practicing?"

"Un-huh. Coming to see me dance?"

"Maybe," he said.

Impulsively she took his hand and put it on her knee. He started.

"Just touch it and it will be all right," she said, almost childlike. He caressed the warm skin a moment. Then, as two girls came down the aisle, he drew back.

"A most seemly knee," he said, pretending aloofness. When he looked at her, her eyes seemed to draw him in. Her lips pursed slightly and a heavy breath made her shoulders quiver.

"I have goose pimples," she said.

"Goose pimples?"

"Yes," she said. "That's what you do to me."

He looked at her questioningly. A girl had never spoken to him that way before. It was only the third time they were together, they hadn't held hands, they hadn't walked together, had a date, done any of the things that were accredited as going together. Yet she said that.

The evening went fast, a quick round of watching people dance, hearing them sing, listening to them attempt pseudo-comical dialogues.

Erick kept looking at Sally during the evening as she took notes busily. But never too busily not to stop and give him a warm smile as though, for a moment, all the world would have to stop so she could smile at him.

Before the night was over, he'd walked her to the bus and, after she pointedly mentioned a concert by the University orchestra that Sunday and how much she wanted to hear it, he had asked her to go with him.

♦ ♦ ♦ ♦ ♦

He was supposed to call for her about three, the concert started at four. He spent the morning reading a book on comparative religion, having several months before given up church-going completely after making the rounds of every church in town looking for one that satisfied him.

After reading, he went out for dinner, then came back and napped until two-fifteen. He got up, went to the bathroom and cleaned up, washing out his sleep-ridden eyes.

Back in the room he sat down and checked the time on his watch. Two-twenty. He got up and put his tie on. While he was adjusting the knot he saw on the bureau a story he'd just finished writing. He picked it up, ran his eyes over the first page.

Then he dropped it and went out into the hall. He picked up the phone and dialed her number. He heard the buzzing, heard the receiver lifted.

"Hello," she said.

"Sally?"

"Yes." Rising interest, as if she were suddenly engrossed and anxious to know who it was.

"Erick."

"Hello." Then anxiously. "Something wrong?"

"No, no, I thought, well, I have a story I just finished and I thought you might, I mean..." He caught himself irritably. "I'd like your opinion of it."

"Well," she said, "Leo is sleeping."

"Oh. Who's that, your house mate?"

"Yes."

"*Leo*?"

She snickered. "Short for Leonora, dear," she said.

"Oh. Oh well, never mind about the story then. I don't..."

"No, you come out."

"Sure?" he asked.

"Come on out, Erick."

"Okay, I'll be right over."

"All right," she said, "*Bye*."

"So long."

He put down the receiver and went to his room. There he put on his suit coat and put the story in an envelope. He left the room and went down the corner for the bus. In a moment it turned a far corner and then, moments later, it jolted to a stop in front of him, he stepped on and the doors folded shut behind him.

LEAVE YESTERDAY ALONE

It was a long ride to her house. He wasn't sure where to get off. Three blocks past the top of the hill, she'd said. He counted three blocks on the left-hand side and then pulled the cord. It was the wrong street, he walked back a long block and saw the weeping willow tree she'd mentioned and turned in.

Her house was the first one on the right side of the street, a low slung, brick structure with a little stone porch. He looked around for the door bell when he reached the porch but there wasn't any. He tapped lightly on the glass-paned door. Through the white-ruffled curtains he saw a movement of skirt. The door opened.

She had a finger across her lips. She took his hand and led Erick across the living room. On the couch slept a short blonde girl.

In her room she took the envelope and told him to sit down on a chair. Then she stood smiling down at him as though he were something she'd been waiting to see for a long time and she was going to enjoy it now for all it was worth. She closed the door.

"I hope I didn't disturb her," Erick said.

"No," she said, "Leo sleeps like a log."

She stood before him again and smiled brightly. "Hi," she said.

"Hi."

She sat down on the bed.

"Did you have any trouble finding the house?" she asked.

"I got off a block too late."

"Did you count three blocks on the right?"

"On the left."

"Silly. No wonder."

Then she opened the envelope and took out the story. "Is it good?" she asked, without guile.

"I hope so," he answered.

She smiled back at him as if the remark were of prodigious moment. Then she started reading. At the first sentence her smile faded abruptly and a look of serious intent crossed her face. Erick smiled to see it. She was completely wrapped up in his story.

He looked at her as she crossed her legs.

She had on a light green print dress. Her brown hair was curled at the bottom and cut in a straight line across her forehead. Her full lips were red and moist. He watched them as she read, looked at them studiously and wondered how it would be to kiss her.

She sat very straight and silent on the bed, her breasts lifting sharply from the line where her shoulders started to her waist. They moved even as she read. Erick feasted his eyes on them as she read, feeling a brief tightening in his stomach. Then, with a slight shudder, he looked up again and ran his glance down across her face, her shoulders, the smooth arc of her breasts, her hips, stomach and long shapely legs. He closed his eyes and shivered.

When she finished the story she put it down on her lap slowly, and looked up at him, wide-eyed, lips slightly parted.

"Like it?" he asked.

She hesitated a moment, then said, "It's wonderful! So *good*."

"Really?"

"Yes! May I keep it and show it to Leo?"

"If you...if you think she'd like it."

"Oh, she *will*."

Then she smiled tenderly as if she felt that her enthusiasm hadn't been convincing enough.

"It *is* good, Erick," she said quietly.

"I'm glad you like it," he said.

It was past three and they decided to leave.

As they went into the living room Leo opened her eyes. She looked startled at first.

"Did we wake you?" Sally asked.

"Yes," Leo said, sleepily, then looked at Erick with groggy eyes.

"This is Erick," Sally said.

Leo looked at him and pressed down into the pillow with a sensual movement. "Hi," she said.

"Hello," he said, noticing the flesh of Leo's upper stomach where her body-tight sweater had slipped out of her skirt.

"We're going to the concert," Sally said.

"Mmm," Leo said, closing her eyes. "See you," she muttered indistinctly, turning on her side.

Sally closed the front door behind them and, as soon as she came up beside him, her warm hand took his.

"Isn't she pretty?" she asked.

He shrugged. "I guess."

"Oh, she *is*," Sally said. "I wish I had such perfect features."

"I think I said something about your features once," Erick said.

She smiled and squeezed his hand. "I think I'll remember that the rest of my life."

Then, after a moment's silence, she said, "What are they playing, do you know?" Her hand tightened in his and the feel of it in his hand brought her completely to him. It was as though with the one act of holding his hand firmly she had taken his life and their paths were forever bound together.

He told her he wasn't sure what the orchestra was playing but that Miss Spouse of the music department was going to play Tchaikovsky's First Piano Concerto.

"Really!" She gave his hand another excited squeeze. "I love that! Isn't that wonderful?"

He hadn't thought about it being wonderful but maybe it was. He smiled and the thought came distractingly to his mind that maybe this elation was just a pose on her part. Yet it seemed impossible to believe. She was too convincing, she wasn't the sort who could affect airs. Yet, whatever it was she was practicing on him, she made him feel as if this were the most wonderful date she'd ever had on the most wonderful day of the year and that he was the most interesting person she'd ever known.

"Isn't it a wonderful day?" she asked, she told.

"It's nice."

She took a deep breath of the warm, flowing air. "I love April," she said, and he thought—*she does*.

"Have you written any other stories lately, Erick?"

"No, I don't have the time. The show took it all up."

"Of course."

"And beside, it isn't easy."

"I bet it is for you."

And he thought that if anyone else had said that to him it would have sounded like blatant sycophancy. He believed her.

The bus came and she went in back. He sat down beside her and as soon as he did she took his hand firmly. *I like that!*—he thought with sudden delight. No girl ever did that to him before; making it seem as though he belonged. No girl ever talked to him like she did.

"How's school?" she asked, as if it were a question of most vital importance to her.

"Fine," he said. "I don't like most of my subjects but it's fine."

"Oh," she said, almost distressed. Then she brightened. "You're in Journalism School, aren't you?

"Mmm-hmmm"

"What do you take?"

"Oh, History of Journalism, ad prin, news…"

"Ad prin?"

"Principles of Advertising."

"That sounds good."

"Does it?"

"Yes, what do you do?"

"Oh, we sit in class and take notes until our arms fall off, then in lab we write in tall, graceful letters—'The quick red fox jumped over the lazy brown dog'—or something like that."

"I didn't know that," she said.

Did it matter? His other mind spoke the question and he had to stifle the words from finding his lips.

"It sounds interesting," she said and, again, his other mind looked squinting unpleasantly and speaking a puzzled—*Wha*? Then he smiled with a shrug. Maybe it *was* interesting to her.

"Are you going into advertising?" she asked.

"Good lord, no. They get ulcers, you know."

"Do they have to?"

"Of course. No self-respecting advertising man would be without his own private ulcer."

"Huh." She smiled in pleasant depreciation.

"No, no advertising for me," he said.

"What then?"

As if her words were magic, his mind spread out instantly, probing into the future he had dreamed of so often that the details were becoming almost stodgy. Writing success, shapeless visions of accolades and triumph on Broadway and in Hollywood. People speaking his name, a home in the country, pleasant, leisurely, creative life, a wife and lovely children fitting politely and quietly into the pattern.

Around there the pattern clouded and, sometimes, when he dreamed too much, he suddenly grew bored, as though he already had all these things and was surfeited with triumph and wanted something more. But there was nothing more and it made him feel ill at ease.

Then, every time, a second after, the house of dream cards would flop spattering to the floor and he'd be back in the present of unrealized potential.

"I want to write," was all he said to her.

"You will. You're good," she said confidently, squeezing his hand. *One story and she says that*, his mind told him. But, somehow, when she said it, it made him feel strong, and he felt inclined to say—*Yes, I will, after all, won't I?* But he didn't say it.

"What will you write? Sally asked. "Books?"

"Everything," he said, momentarily caught again in the great, shapeless desire. "Books, short stories, plays…everything. I'll even write singing commercials. No, I won't."

She smiled at him; like a loving woman, he thought.

"It's all bubbling in you, isn't it?" she said.

"Yes, it is," he said, and it occurred to him that Lynn was the only other person in the world he'd ever bared himself to, even this much.

"You'll do it," she said, and she tightened her grasp and her face shone as she looked into his eyes. The strength of her confidence seemed to pour into him. *She's excited*, he thought, *excited over a vague group of ambitions proclaimed in a creaking bus*. How much he liked her. She seemed to get so much out of life. Nothing was taken for granted. Life was an endless play to her, replete with new, ever exciting surprises, and she sat spellbound in the audience, clapping her hands in delight at each new development.

"Here's the stop," Sally said, and the bus ground to a halt. Erick got up and jumped down from the step. Automatically he held up his hand for her.

"*Thank* you," she said, as if his gesture had come as another completely wonderful surprise. He had the sense that a rare person walked by his side as they started down toward the campus. How different everything seemed being with her, as if she were a lens through which he saw a brighter world.

"That's where I go," Sally said as they passed the Methodist Church.

"Oh?"

"It's beautiful inside," she said. "You'll have to come some time. I sing in the choir."

"I didn't know you sang. I thought you danced."

"Oh, I'm talented," she laughed, then seemed to be embarrassed even at her little joke. "I'm not so good at singing," she added as if atoning, "but in all those voices no one can tell."

"I'll come to hear you drowned out."

She smiled. "Good. I hope you do."

They went up the cement path and under the archway into the campus. It was becoming bright green under the April sun. The carpet of grass was almost complete on the ground and the campus-lining trees were budding thickly.

"Isn't it pretty?" she said.

"Yes," he said, feeling completely at ease now although he was also aware of the fact that he didn't usually comment on the prettiness of anything.

"I like it here," he said. "I always wanted to go to a college like this."

"You're on the G.I. Bill, aren't you?" she asked.

"Yeah. Public Law 16."

"What's that?"

"For disabled veterans."

She looked alarmed suddenly. "What's wrong, Erick?" she said.

"Nothing much. I froze my tootsies in Germany, that's all. Long ago."

"Are they all right now?"

"They're all right."

Her hand tightened in his. "Oh, good," she said, relieved. She skipped once and changed her stride to match his. They walked in silence a little way, close together. Erick breathed in deeply of the fragrant air and it felt nice to be young and free and with Sally.

A girl in a long white dress handed them programs as they went in. The hum of soft voices touched their ears. The floor creaked beneath them.

"Where would you like to sit?" he asked her.

"Where do you usually sit?" she asked back.

"Anywhere," he said. "You lead."

She took his hand and started up the dress circle steps. "This all right?" she asked.

"Sure," he said as they sat down. "God, there aren't many people here."

"I think that's terrible," she said. "More people should come. Those poor kids go to all this trouble."

They looked at their programs and he wondered how old she was.

"I never heard this before, did you?" she asked, leaning over and pointing.

"No," he said. "Rameau." He sniffed. "Nice perfume."

"Mmmm. Do you like it?"

"Sure. *Night on Bald Mountain*"

"*White Shoulder*."

"I'm talking about the program," he said, smiling.

"Oh!" she laughed. "Yes."

The orchestra was starting to come out on the stage, girls in long dresses, boys in dark suits.

"We got here just in time," she said. "Oh, look, there's Felix."

"The cat?"

"Silly. You met him that night."

"Oh, the big one."

"Now be nice, Erick."

"Yes, dear."

She smiled at him, her eyes moving over his face.

"Do you play football?" she asked.

"Only in my dreams," he said.

And felt a slight separation for a moment. Sally was so wonderfully robust and athletic and, although Erick wasn't scrawny, he was no athlete. He felt vaguely that someone like Felix was more suited for her, more…more…
what was the word? He wondered. Bedable?

He was silent and the urge came to push her away from him because he doubted for a moment she could love him.

Then the audience started applauding.

On the stage the conductor was threading his way through the seated orchestra members. He stepped up on the podium and the audience grew silent. Sally reached over and closed her hand on Erick's, their fingers interlacing. He turned a little and she smiled sweetly at him. He looked away, his throat moving, and the orchestra started to play *Suite from Dardanus* by Rameau.

At first Erick didn't pay any attention to the music. The feeling of her hand in his was all there was. He felt blood pulsing into his fingers, felt them expanding between hers. The music was only an indifferent sound, her presence was everything.

Then, slowly, he began to relax and drift into the music.

He began to get the feeling which so often came to him; a desire to draw every impulse, every scrap of import from the passing seconds. He heard the music, smelled the ancient smell of the auditorium, powder, perfume, caught movements of color and light as people shifted in their seats. The slight movement of Sally's legs crossing caught his eye. He concentrated on the music, listening for harmonies, following one instrument through several phases, then switching to another, then relaxing and letting the overall sound swell untended in his mind. Then he was back to her again, held tightly, their hands grown into one comforting joint.

The piece ended and she applauded, then took his hand again as if it were essential to her. There was no doubt in the way she took it or the way she held it in her warm lap.

The conductor came onstage again, this time leading, amid applause, Miss Spouse.

She sat herself at the polished black grand. Breathless silence. Then a powerful blast of horns, the broad percussion of strong fingers playing the opening chord groups. Sally's fingers tightened in his, they both turned at the same moment.

For a second, something seemed to flicker between them, impelled by the music. An idea, a sensation, a sudden response. His hand tightened on hers, they drank in the sight of each other holding themselves fast with their eyes. Her lips moved slightly, as if she were about to speak, he saw her exhale through parted lips. Then she turned away quickly and he saw her strong breasts swell out and knew that her temples were coloring even though it was too dimly lit to see.

He turned back front.

Some moments he was deep in each pulsation of music. Others, he was deeply conscious of himself and of her. Once, he knew, she was looking at him, but he didn't turn. And, after a while, she returned her gaze to the orchestra.

During intermission they went down into the basement and Erick showed her the Dramatics Green Room. It was locked up and they peered in through the glass windows.

"Not very exciting," he said.

"That's because there are no people there," she said.

Their faces were close together as they looked. He could smell her perfume. His cheek brushed against hers and she took in a little shudder breath. He turned and kissed her warm cheek. She touched his hand.

"Erick," she said, softly.

♦ ♦ ♦ ♦ ♦

The concert ended and there was an encore and they all went out into the hall again. They passed Felix and two other football players. Felix looked at Erick with stolid venom.

"I hope he doesn't know where I live," Erick said.

"Why?" she asked.

"He'll come there and break my neck."

"Don't be silly," she said, "Felix is a nice boy."

"Brutus is an honorable man."

She gave him an off-glance. "I wonder what brought them here," he said to clear the air.

"I don't know," she said.

As they walked up the campus he asked her, "Do you have to go anywhere tonight?"

"No," she asked, "why?"

"Well," he said, "I th-thought you might like to see a movie."

"Why, I'd love to!" she said.

Sudden happiness welled up in him again, the entire series starting. *Just being with her*, he thought, *having her boundless happiness beside me, it does something to me*.

They decided to go to the Varsity Theatre. It was the least expensive show in town. Sally insisted she wanted to see the picture again.

"Hungry?" he asked her.

"Just a little," she said.

They went downtown to a café. A waitress handed them two menus.

"What'll you have, Sally?" he asked her.

"Oh, just a sandwich and a cup of coffee."

"Oh, have more than that."

"I never eat much Sunday night."

"But I'm going to have dinner."

"Well, of course, if you didn't have it yet. Really, Erick, all I want is a sandwich."

They ordered and while they were waiting he asked her how old she was.

"Twenty-three," she said.

"That old. I feel like a child."

"Why, how old are you?"

"Twenty-one next month."

"Oh! What day?"

"The twenty-second."

She seemed to concentrate a moment. "The twenty-second," she repeated, and suddenly he knew that he would receive a card from her that day. It would be just like Sally.

"You're two years older than I am," Erick said.

"That's nothing," she said. "My mother is fifteen years older than my father."

He felt himself start but she didn't notice. He wondered if her remark meant anything. *It couldn't, so soon*, he thought.

The food was brought and they started to eat.

"What do you want out of life?" he asked her after some idle conversation about food and music.

"Oh, I don't know," she said. "I'd like children."

"I trust you're planning on marriage first," he said.

She looked very serious.

"I'm glad you said that," she said. "Most of the fellows I know don't seem to think marriage is necessary."

"Really?"

"Yes. And it gets upsetting. Just last week a boy casually asked me to sleep with him."

He knew he winced. He didn't want to but he couldn't help it. It was as if, suddenly, she were revealed to him as a woman with a woman's body and desires and that he was not quite prepared to admit it to himself, thinking, perhaps unconsciously, that it would mar her attraction if he thought she could lust like anyone else.

"I hope you spat in his eye," he said, wanting to curse himself for the frailty of his voice.

"I let him know how far off base he was," she said.

"I guess that happens pretty often to you," he said, without thinking.

"Why *me*?" She looked concerned.

"Well, I mean...you have such a...a stunning figure," he faltered. "And...well, you're so warm and friendly. It gives a fellow ideas."

"You?" she asked.

"Here's dessert," he said, but he knew he couldn't get out of it that way. In a moment he said, "You can trust me, Sally. Does that sound ri..."

"Thank you," she broke in. "Oh, I'm sorry, what were you going to say?

"Nothing. I was just about to say—does that sound ridiculous, corny?"

She reached out her hand and closed it over his, tenderly.

"Oh, no, Erick," she said.

They walked up the block to the theatre.

"Popcorn?" he asked.

"No, thank you," she said. He got himself a box.

They slid in past a few people and sat down. "Good," she said, leaning over, "We'll see the picture from the start."

He smiled a little. It was a small thing, he thought, but he always hated coming in on a picture, too.

Her hand took his again. It was habit now, it would have seemed unnatural for her not to do it. He felt as though they belonged together.

A cartoon came on; a series of incredible sadisms in Technicolor, he recalled Lynn having called them.

Sally leaned over. "May I have some of your popcorn?"

"Sure," he said. "Don't you want me to get you a box?"

"No, no, I just want a little."

He took out his glasses and reached for his handkerchief. "Here," she said, and took them from him. She opened her handbag and took a tissue from it and breathed on the lens and polished them clean. Then she handed them back.

"Thank you," he said.

"You're welcome."

"Popcorn?"

"Mmm! Thank you."

They sat munching while a savage mouse degraded and tortured a cat, in order, smashing him flat, breaking his teeth like glass, pulling out his eyes and decapitating him. Every once in a while, Sally reached over and took some popcorn.

"Just a little, huh?" Erick whispered, kidding.

"Isn't it all right?" she said, almost wistfully.

He smiled. "Of course it is."

"I don't like to eat from a separate box."

He didn't know what it was. The words weren't romantic. It was what they seemed to say. They acted like a drug on him, filling him, choking off his breath. He turned to look at her but the light from the screen blurred his eyes and he couldn't see. But he felt her fingers tightening in his and she spoke his name. Very softly.

"Did you like that," he asked as they came out.

"I like the way Vera Ellen dances," she said.

"She *is* good. Do you dance like that?

"Not in a million years," she said determinedly. "Oh, hi!" she said to a young man who walked past.

"Gad, but you have acquaintances," Erick said, trying not to sound peeved.

"I dated him once," she said, matter-of-factly. Then she looked up at her watch. "The bus doesn't come for fifteen minutes. We have time for a cup of coffee if you'll buy me one," she said.

"Delighted, ma'am."

"Golly, I had a nice time today," she said as they sat waiting for their coffee at the drugstore counter.

"Good," he said. "So did I."

She smiled. "Did you? I'm so glad. We'll have to do it again soon."

"We will."

They had to run for the bus. They sat in the back puffing and his hand took hers for a change. It seemed natural but he knew he couldn't have done it with anyone but her.

"My coffee is gurgling," he said.

"So is mine," she said, and they laughed.

Then, as the bus started, he suddenly realized he couldn't say anything to her. A cloud of muteness fell over him, he felt tight and restless. They were almost to the end of the date and he knew how much he wanted to kiss her. But he didn't know how he would go about it and it made him ill at ease.

Every word seemed futile now. He heard himself saying various things but he couldn't remember from instant to instant what he'd said and he couldn't follow the thread of the conversation very well. She must have been equally as upset, he told himself, because she didn't seem to notice his confusion. After a few minutes she just smiled at him and tightened her fingers and leaned against him a little as if she understood everything and were consoling him. His stomach felt tight with unrealized desire for her.

When they got off the bus, his heart began to beat rapidly and he felt almost a desperate urge to put his arms around her and hold her tightly.

"Don't forget this corner," she said.

"I will," he said. "I mean I won't."

The words were spoken by someone else. He wondered why she was walking so slowly, as if she wanted to stop. And finally she did stop and he knew why. She took a deep breath and looked up at him.

"Leo is having some friends in," she said quietly.

It was everything; a statement, a sigh, an invitation. It happened so quickly and so easily it surprised him. How his arms slid around her and she moved in close. How there was nothing awkward about the way he kissed her warm cheeks, her ear lobes, her neck and how he buried his face in her warm silky hair and breathed in deeply of its perfumed fragrance.

"Erick," she whispered, her breathing faster. They rubbed their cheeks together. A sharp breeze flowed over them and she made a soft noise as he lifted her chin with a shaking hand.

Their eyes met. Her eyes were glistening as though the moment was too much and she had to cry. Her lips trembled. He moved his face closer and closer and their eyes were always on each other. Then he felt her warm breath on him and his lips touched hers. They pressed closer, she molded her mouth to his. He felt her convulsive shudder and the sudden sliding and tightening of her arms around his neck.

It was a long, passionate kiss. Her lips were full and soft, parted slightly. She moved her head gently as their mouths clung together. Finally, their lips separated and she pressed her cheek against his.

"Oh, Erick," she said, shaking.

"Sally."

"Why were you so angry with me that night?" she asked, almost unhappily.

"Angry? When?"

"When I met you. You didn't even look up at me when I said goodnight."

"I was…angry at myself."

"*Why*?"

"Because you were with Felix instead of me."

She drew back a little and looked into his eyes as if for vindication of his words. Then she said, "Oh!" and pressed her mouth passionately on his. She kept drawing her lips away a fraction of an inch and kissing his mouth again and again.

"Erick, Erick," she whispered, almost frantically, and clung to him with all her strength.

For a long moment they were silent, holding on to each other.

Then she said, "I guess…I better go in."

"All right."

They walked slowly toward the house, arms around each other.

"Say goodbye to me here," she said at the porch steps. Her arms slid around his neck and her mouth pressed softly and warmly against his. She kissed his cheek.

"Goodnight, darling," she said.

"Goodnight."

They moved apart and he went down the steps slowly, their hands being last to separate, as if reluctantly. He turned to go, then, impelled, he turned back.

She was standing motionless on the porch, watching him.

Everything seemed to vibrate beneath him and she came down the steps rushing and threw herself into his arms. She kissed him almost violently, her chest heaving, her mouth open and he felt as if he were lost in her, absorbed by her lips and clinging body.

"Oh darling, *darling*!" she whispered breathlessly when their lips had parted.

"This is incredible," he murmured, feeling dizzy.

"It is, it *is*," she said.

She held onto him a long moment, then she looked up with a smile of resignation.

"I have to go in," she said.

"All right," he said again and kissed her. "Good night, Sally."

"Good night, darling," she said and kissed him back, gently.

Then he turned away and walked dizzily down the path, the blood rushing through his body, her heat still clinging to him. He turned once and saw her blow a kiss from the door. He raised an arm, then, impulsively, he broke into a run up the street and stood panting under the lamp post, waiting for the bus.

"Oh my God," he said, trembling. "*Oh my God.*"

three.

She was always primping him, adjusting his tie with an adoring smile, brushing his blond hair back with a gentle hand. Doing all things for him with loving care.

Her general effect was one of all-pervading warmth. It shone out from her and touched him through her every word and motion. It seemed as if she could give herself entirely with a touch of her fingers, as if, in an instant, she were transferring herself wholly and filling him.

They went out a lot together, to movies, to concerts and plays, dancing. And, although the evenings always ended with her in his arms, they never mentioned love. Once she wrote him a poem entitled *Don't Speak of Love*. It entreated him not to speak of it until he was certain. He was never certain.

Because there were things he didn't like; little things, admittedly, but magnified by his never-resting mind.

The way she had of speaking so loudly in public. The way she spoke to everyone whether she knew them or not, either to speak a cheery "Hello!" to them on the street or to speak to them at length when she and Erick were waiting on movie lines or dancing in crowded places. It displeased him, he'd been taught it wasn't right to speak to strangers.

It appeared sometimes, however, that none of the men in town were strangers to Sally. He never suspected anything bad, yet it was incredible to him that she knew every man in the college. No matter where they went together, she'd pass a fellow she knew and then it was Hello Joe or Mike or Bill or Tom or Felix. It got to Erick, he was not the sort that took kindly to opposition. Competition made him shrivel. If he didn't win immediately, hands down, he gave up. And that feeling in regard to Sally produced many sullen moments in him.

Which she noticed. And when she did notice she would take his hand and look deeply into his eyes and smile, moving her lips just a trifle, as if she were kissing him. And the complete tenderness of the action would, always, melt him.

She could smile at him, too, with the healthy wickedness of a happy, young child. They talked about sex, kidded about it. Sally was frank and openly interested in the subject. After a while he began to caress her body and she didn't stop him, but seemed to enjoy it. That made him draw back for a while because he decided that she did it with all the men she dated and for while, he created in himself the belief that he was slumming. She was too open with her affections.

He was used to guarded smiles, chaste, unrevealing caresses. When he danced with Sally, she held on close, pressing her stomach against his, rubbing her cheek over his and singing to him. Softly she sang but everyone could hear it. *Like in the movies*, he thought the first time, a little disconcerted but pleased. Then it began to annoy him. He never liked being conspicuous so, during those times, he would stamp a look of parental resignation on his face and pretend to other people that he was treating her like an exuberant child.

She called him more than he called her. Once he tried to remember the last them he'd called her and asked if she was free on a certain night. But he couldn't remember. Somehow their dates were never single, detached affairs. They blended one into the other; the end of one including the plans for the beginning of another.

And, if there were no definite plans, any number of time she would call and he would hear her cherry voice saying, "Hi! Whatcha doin'?"

♦ ♦ ♦ ♦ ♦

He hadn't seen her for a week and a half. He was reworking the script and didn't get to rehearsals. Then one night he dropped over to the auditorium and sat through rehearsal. After it was over he went down to get Sally. Her face grew bright with a happy smile when she saw him.

"Erick!" she said excitedly and clutched at his hand.

They walked along the dark, silent campus, arms around each other's waist.

"I missed you," she said.

"Did you?"

"Yes. Were you angry with me?"

"No, I had to revise the script."

"Is it all right now?"

"It's okay."

"You didn't call me," she said.

"I'm sorry," he said. "I was so busy."

"You didn't feel like it."

He looked at her, then smiled a little sheepishly. "What can I say?"

She rubbed her cheek on his shoulder.

"Don't say anything," she said. "You're back, that's all that matters."

He leaned over and kissed her cheek. She turned and pushed against him, her arms sliding around him.

"I want to get inside of you," she murmured suddenly, almost desperately.

"Go ahead, get inside of me."

"Let's stop walking."

They stopped and faced each other in the dark. They held each other close and she breathed on his neck.

"Did you miss me at all?" she asked.

"Yes."

"Liar."

"*Sally*."

"I'm sorry, I hope you did," she said.

They stood in the doorway of a store waiting for the bus to come.

"Taking me home?" she asked.

"Sure," he said.

He had his arms around her. She sighed and held on tight, locking her strong hands behind Erick's back.

"Erick," she said. She looked up. "Please kiss me."

She raised her face and it shone in the dull green neon light from the store window. He bent over and brushed his lips against hers. She kissed him, her warm lips softening under his.

"Oh, I love you," she said simply.

His breath caught.

"You never...said that before," he said.

"I can't help it," she said quietly. "You know it. I know it. Why should I pretend?"

"I'm...glad," he decided uncertainly.

"I hope you are."

On the bus she rested her head on his shoulder. He put his arm around her and breathed in the perfume of her hair. He looked down at her breasts moving in and out as she breathed.

When they got off the bus, she said, "Are you sorry I told you?"

"No. Why should I be?

"I've spoiled the mystery," she said.

They sat on the porch steps.

"You haven't spoiled anything," he said. "I don't like mysteries."

She leaned against him.

"Well, my mystery didn't last very long," she said, and she pressed tightly against him.

"Your face is hot," he said.

"I'm feverish," she said, suddenly breathless. Her lips moved across his cheek and she pressed her parted mouth convulsively on his. She squirmed in his arms, a tiny groan starting in her throat. He felt himself growing restive.

"Take it easy," he said when their lips parted. He felt himself shiver at the way she clung to him, breathing in his ear.

"I can't," she said helplessly, "I *can't*! I love you, *I love you*! I want you so much!"

"Sally," he whispered, lost, confused. And felt cold.

He kissed her burning neck and was cold. She bent forward down on his arms and he pushed aside the hair on the back of her neck to press his lips against the hot flesh. She shook and gasped as though she couldn't breathe. And he was cold.

She straightened up suddenly and bit her lip. Tears came to her eyes. She sat looking at him, her body quivering. He almost winced under her intense stare.

Then, with a gasp, she threw herself against him and dug her fingers into his back.

"Oh, please love me! Please, Erick! *Please* love me!"

He held her tightly and said nothing as she cried in his arms, her body shaking helplessly. He disappeared from the spot. He was up in the black sky watching dark spots waver on the moon. He was in the trees, listening to them whisper dully among themselves. He was with the dog that barked up the street somewhere. He was in the bus that roared by on Main Street, sparks shooting from its exhaust, tiny figures sitting inside.

Then she shivered, back again to her, with her sobbing as if her heart would break. And, although he wanted to, he couldn't seem to care one way or the other.

"May I use your handkerchief?" she asked meekly.

"Huh? Oh, sure."

She dried her eyes and cheeks. "You mustn't mind me," she said. "Spring fever, I guess."

"I thought it was love."

"I mean me getting so upset."

"Sex, maybe."

Silence. "Maybe," she said quietly and gave him back his handkerchief. She rested against him and, after a while, she sighed.

"You're so nice and warm," she said.

And she lifted his hand and kissed it and pressed it against her cheek for a long time.

LEAVE YESTERDAY ALONE

♦ ♦ ♦ ♦ ♦

He was sitting in the darkened auditorium when she came in the side entrance. He pretended not to see her. She came over and stood in front of him. He looked up, annoyed.

"Hello, darling," she said cheerfully.

"Sit down," he said, and she sat next to him.

"How are you?" she asked.

"I'm trying to watch the play, Sally."

"I'm sorry."

They sat quietly until the scene ended. "Thirteen," Lynn said through the public address system. Some of the cast sitting in the auditorium rose slowly and went on stage. "You're wasting time," Lynn's voice crackled acidly through the darkness.

"Can you say hello now?" she asked.

"Hello," he said. Sullenly.

"Didn't they cut some lines in that last scene? I seem to recall…"

"Yes," he interrupted.

"Why did they?"

He twisted slightly in his seat.

"I don't know, they didn't ask me," he said irritably.

"But they can't do that without your permission," she said.

"They did it."

"Well," she said, "I don't think they…"

She stopped and was silent for a moment. Then she said, penitently, "Don't be angry."

He gritted his teeth and shook off her words with a twist of his shoulders. She said no more. When the next scene ended Lynn had the lights put on and went down front to discuss the first act with the cast. Erick noticed Sally looking at him and he turned down the corners of his mouth. Then, when she didn't turn away, he looked over. She didn't lower her eyes. Their eyes met. She looked so hurt that he smiled to ease the moment.

It melted her. She smiled at him and reached out her hand to touch his arm. Then she took his hand. Her palm was wet and that irritated him. It made his hand itch. He noticed suddenly how her skirt had slid over her stockingless crossed legs, making her right calf bulge out where it pressed against the left. And her dress was cut too low, he thought. He could see the edge of her brassiere, saw the fleshy line that ran between her breasts. He let his hand go limp and turned away from her.

"Don't be discouraged," she said. "It'll come out all right."

"Yeah."

When the next act started he noticed, with growing irritation, that she kept looking at him.

"The play is up front, Sally," he said, thinking his tone a patient one.

"Is it," she said.

He gave her a look of cold disgust and turned back front. After the scene ended the assistant director came back and dropped down next to Sally.

"How about ditching this jerk and coming with me after rehearsal," he said, jerking a thumb toward Erick.

Sally smiled a little. "Maybe," she said.

Erick drew back his hand and wiped perspiration from it with his handkerchief. He didn't turn to look at them.

The assistant director said, "Has he been mistreating you? By God, I'll kill him!"

Erich turned. "Why don't you go and *assist* the director?"

"Sally is going out with me tonight. Any objections?"

Erick glanced at Sally a moment and the look she gave him irritated him still further. "None whatever," he said.

"You see!" The assistant director was jubilant. "He has no appreciation of..." He leered at her, "The *better* things in life. Arf, arf!"

Sally said nothing and that made Erick angrier still. *Get the hell out of here!* his mind shouted. The feeling of triumph was draining quickly. He wanted to be alone, he wanted to push it away. It hurt him.

When the next scene started, Sally and the assistant director got up and left. Erick watched them leave as the side door opened, shooting a ray of light across the black aisle. Then he clenched his fists and stared fiercely at the stage, hissing in irritation, twisting uncomfortably, feeling sick. The play sounded ridiculous to him.

When the rehearsal ended he found Sally on the stage entrance porch. He walked up to her.

"Going home?" he asked her.

"I suppose so," she said.

"Want me to come?"

She looked away from him and he saw her throat moving.

"If you want," she said quietly.

He put an arm around her shoulders.

"Did I treat you terribly?" he said.

"Y-yes."

He took out his handkerchief and dabbed at the tears on her cheeks.

"Better?" he asked.

"As long as you're nice to me," she said.

"I'll try," he said, kissing her cheek.

They rode home and sat on the porch looking at the sky. "Look at all the stars," he said.

"Yes," she said, without enthusiasm.

"Let's sit on the lawn."

She hesitated, then said, "All right, I'll get the blanket."

They spread out the blanket, sat down on it. He put his head in her warm lap.

"I can see you," he said.

She said nothing. He closed his eyes and took a deep breath.

"I was burned up, Sally," he said. "The play's not going good, lousy test marks today. I took it out on you."

She stared straight ahead.

"It must be nice not to be a pushover," she said bitterly.

He sat up and put his arms around her, kissed her neck. "I'm sorry, Sal."

A moment later she was pressed against him, murmuring, "I couldn't *not* forgive you if I tried." And her lips molded themselves to his.

"Erick, Erick, if only I didn't love you so much."

He felt ill at ease again because every time she said it, he was more compelled to either say it back or leave. It made a vacuum on his side into which all her love was rushing, overbalancing everything.

"I wish you could love me," she said.

"So do I."

"You're afraid, aren't you?"

"Afraid?"

"Afraid that I'll interfere with your work. I wouldn't, darling. I'd help you."

"You'd want to help. I know that, but..."

He rested his head on her shoulder and she caressed his hair with her gentle fingers.

"It isn't just a matter of wanting and not wanting," he said. "Marriage brings responsibilities. How could I do all I want to do and still support a wife and children?"

"I could work too. I'd expect to."

He felt a slight, undefined resentment that she should keep arguing with him despite the fact that he seemed to have covered the objections adequately.

"You'd have time," she said.

"I'd have to work too much."

"You'll have to work after school anyway."

Was she goading him? He began to feel a desperate fear of being rushed, of being told what to do, of not being given a chance to do what he wanted to do. He almost pulled away forcibly and shouted in her face—No, I don't love you! I don't want to marry you! I *refuse* to marry you! I refuse to throw away all my work for a nightly bed and a squalling battlement called home!

He felt a fierce desire to escape what seemed to be methodically forging unbreakable links around him.

The topic passed. She didn't say anymore. And he found peace again as they lay on the blanket and pressed their bodies against each other. He felt the warm night wind on his face. He had her in his arms, but he was free, too.

"I wish it could be like this forever," he said.

♦ ♦ ♦ ♦ ♦

The curtain closed. He crossed his fingers, stretched forward and looked over the balcony railing. Applause flooded up from the darkness like a rushing of black wings. The curtain flew open, the cast stood lined up, smiling. Loud applause. The curtain zipped shut, in a second it rushed aside again and the principals stepped forward. The applause increased.

"Oh, boy!" Erick exulted.

The curtain closed and opened a third time, the cast all smiled broadly. They bowed gracefully, nodding their heads. Erick sank back with a satisfied sigh. There were two more curtain calls. He sat pleased while the light from the stage sprang into the auditorium, then was cut off by the rushing curtains.

The lights went on and Erick went downstairs, listening to the comments of the people as they went out of the auditorium.

Sally hugged him. "Wasn't it wonderful!" she exulted.

"Terrific!"

They embraced, then they stood in a big circle on stage and held hands with the rest of the cast. He grinned at Lynn and Lynn smiled a little, nodded to Sally. They all started to sing "Should auld acquaintance be forgot…" and their young voices swelled up to the high stage ceiling. They all rocked gently on their feet, their eyes smiling to one another as they sang. Erick looked at them all. It was a moment of utter nostalgia, he thought, closing of the show, all the separate components blended together now to become separated again. Sets to be scrapped, stage to be swept away of all the familiar magic. Then the show forgotten, the rush of studies for final exam.

And Sally was with him.

He looked at her. He was singing to her and she to him.

> "*We'll drink a cup of kindness yet*
> *for auld lang syne.*"

Everyone cheered. Hands were released, the spell was broken. Everyone lingered a moment, then the strands parted. The stage manager called for the stage to be struck and someone shouted, "Party at the Golden Campus!"

"It's all over," he said to Sally.

She pressed against him. "There'll be others," she said. Over her shoulder he noticed Lynn standing nearby, as if waiting to speak.

"You want to see me, Lynn?" he asked.

Lynn shook his head and turned away. "No," his voice came briefly in the swell of other voices. Lynn walked off stage, taking out a cigarette.

♦ ♦ ♦ ♦ ♦

They all clomped down the narrow, squeaky stairway into the Golden Campus. A pall of cigarette smoke hung just below the ceiling. The dance floor was filled with seated couples who were watching a small combination perform on the low platform. Shivery clarinet notes fluttered in the air like the sound of idiots laughing. The pianist beat out a tinny rhythm with claw-like hands while the bass man plucked wildly at his strings.

"What's going on?" Erick asked, squinting.

"A jam session," Sally said. "Didn't you ever see one here before?"

"No," he said, "did you?"

"Sure, lots of times."

He felt himself draw away from her a moment, then he went back.

"Oh," he said.

They went back to the big table that had been reserved and everybody sat down at it. The show's business manager brought armfuls of quart beer bottles from the counter. Hand shot out and plucked them from his grasp. The bottles skidded over the streaked table and glasses filled up with the dark, malty liquid. The thin music cut like a knife through the cloud of chatter, laughter and smoke.

"You want beer?" Erick said.

"What?"

"I said—do you want beer?"

"If you do."

"I don't like it."

"I'll have what you have."

"*What*?" he asked, bending over.

"I'll have what you have," she said.

He nodded and straightened up. He was jostled innumerable times as he moved for the counter. He had his feet stepped on, someone got the cuffs of his suit trousers dirty. A slight ire fanned into life. *Are they kicking hell out of the building code*, his mind commented.

He spilled half of one Coke on his jacket as he returned to the table. He cursed loudly and put the glasses on the table.

"What an ordeal," he said.

"What?"

He didn't repeat it. He took his handkerchief out and started to wipe the Coke from his jacket. She handed him a tissue from her handbag and he nodded his head and sat down.

"Thank you," she said.

"*What*?" he contorted his face into a grimace.

"Thank you for the Coke!"

"Oh."

The darkness seemed alive with arms and legs and a sea of faces. The air seemed to burst with an amalgam of cacophonous sounds. He drank in moody silence, listening to them all. He looked around, feeling the same sense of detachment he always felt when he was down there with a girl. It was different being with a couple of fellows. He could relax and talk and enjoy it. Unconsciously he felt that any girl who came to a place like this wasn't the kind he wanted to be with. It wasn't very logical but there it was.

A hand dropped on his shoulder and Lynn leaned over.

"The manager wants us to do a few routines from the show and a couple of the songs."

"Oh?" Erick said.

"Come on up," Lynn said, "I want to introduce you."

"No."

"Come on."

"Go on, Erick," Sally said, smiling.

They threaded their way through the sprawled audience. When they stepped on the platform, Lynn took the microphone from the band leader. Erick stood there awkwardly, watching Lynn, hoping that he wasn't blushing. One of the female vocalists from the show stood beside him.

Lynn blew self-consciously into the microphone.

"Testing, testing," he said, his voice blaring out over the audience.

"Ladies and gentlemen," he said, "latter term used advisedly." No reaction. "At the good musician has said we are members of this year's Campus show. We've been asked to present a few excerpts from the show which we shall proceed to do for, we hope, your entertainment."

Erick felt a sincere desire to kick Lynn in the pants for being so wordy and polite to these people. He felt himself coloring hopelessly with all of them staring up, seemingly at him alone. He saw several of them yawning. He saw one of the young men fall back into the lap of a girl behind and her pushing him up with a laugh.

"First, I'd like you to meet the author and the composer of the show," Lynn said, pointing. "Erick Linstrom and Bill Veezy."

Erick tried to smile but he knew it was a false grimace. He saw Bill Veezy beside him take a little choppy bow. "I thank you!" said Bill Veezy.

"*Boo*!" shouted the drunken young man in the audience. Erick felt himself tighten and his fingers twitched at his side.

"Now," Lynn said, "a brief comedy routine from the show by the two make leads, Al Spencer and Jack O'Brien. Take it away, men!"

Lynn stepped over next to Erick. Erick felt increasing warmth and tension in himself, as if someone were burning leaves in his stomach. He felt absolutely ridiculous standing there exposed. He knew he couldn't have felt worse if he were naked. He turned to Lynn and said, guardedly, "Whose bright idea was this?"

"Good publicity," Lynn said casually.

"Horse manure."

The two male voices slapped hollowly against the low ceiling. The comedy fell flat, it sounded pathetic. No one seemed to be listening. Erick wanted to pull the two actors away from the microphone and clout their heads together. He glanced at the audience. They were all talking, it seemed. Some of them were getting up and stumbling off toward the bar or the toilet. The drunken man stood up momentarily, accentuated a loud "*Ha*, *Ha*," and then he sank down again in a heap, waving his empty beer bottle.

Now Erick watched the audience intensely. He stared right at them, his muscles knotting. He felt as if he had been turned into icy stone. All except for the pit of his stomach. The fire still burned there.

The bubbling chatter of the audience continued under the thin, monotonous voices of the two men speaking his lines, which once had seemed funny. Erick turned and looked at Lynn. Lynn was staring blankly at the floor as if waiting for the end of his unfortunate incident. Erick opened and closed his hands in slow rhythm.

"Stupid Bastards," he murmured to himself, and looked at them all again. He felt a sudden overwhelming urge to have back his army rifle, to stand there with it at his hip and just pimp endless rounds of hot lead into their ranks.

The thought aroused him more. He shivered as he thought fiercely of them all screaming and falling dead with blood spurting out of great holes in their faces. He lost himself in that vision.

The routine ended and Lynn stepped up to the microphone.

"That's it," he said, "Don't fracture your hands, now."

Erick hated him suddenly, completely. A thin, dyspeptic applause moved around the floor. "Hooray!" cried the drunk, still waving his bottle, "Hooray, it's over!"

Erick tightened again. He could have chopped off the man's head with delight, he thought. He yearned to kill someone, wreak violence on someone. He shook with the crushing desire for revenge. He almost felt that if he let himself go at all, he would vault into the audience with an insane scream and bite and kick and tear at anyone who happened to be in his way. He never felt as close to insanity as then, with all of those white, raucous faces mocking his work. He felt his lips trembling and then he almost cried as he fought to stop the trembling. A sob filled his throat which one heard because of the noise.

"And now," Lynn said, still poised, still detached, "while you wipe the tears of laughter from your bloodshot eyes, Gloria Leeds will do the popular blues song from the play. Play, William," he finished, with an airy wave of his hand.

Bill started to play. Erick could hardly hear it. Bill played louder. The tinny resonance of the piano surrounded Erick and annoyed him. One of the notes didn't play and the dead thudding of it irritated him more.

Gloria stood in from of the microphone in a low-cut blue evening gown. The men howled. One of them whistled shrilly with two wet fingers shoved into his mouth.

"Sing to me, baby," yelled the young man with the bottle. "Sing me a lullaby!"

"Oh, you kid!"

Her thin singing voice was lost in the noise.

Suddenly Erick found himself lurching forward in a blind rage. He stepped off the stage not caring who saw him. He almost hoped desperately that someone would stop him. He yearned to commit violence. He pushed rudely through the seated ranks, stepping on someone's hand and feeling a bolt of pleasure at the "*Watch* it, for Christ's sake!" that exploded in his ear.

"Drop dead!" he snarled over his shoulder, and heard Gloria's voice barely coming over the microphone.

Sally looked up as he leaned over stiffly.

"I'm going," he said tensely. "You can come with me or stay."

She looked surprised, her eyes studied him curiously. He straightened up and turned away quickly and pushed through the crowd. He didn't look back at her, at anyone. He wanted to get away, to escape. He jumped up the steep stairway furiously, two steps at a time.

The cool evening air bathed over him as he stepped onto the sidewalk. He stood by the curb, staring at the street and breathing deeply, trying to get rid of the tight feeling of hate. His chest heaved and jerked with uncontrolled breaths.

He heard her come up beside him.

They started to walk. He didn't say anything. She didn't speak, didn't touch him.

"Lousy air in there!" he said, bitterly.

She made a tight, indefinable sound and he kept looking ahead, still breathing heavily.

"*You* didn't have to leave," he said angrily.

"I wouldn't stay without you," she said quietly.

It made him angry. *She's weak!* he thought, spineless. Then he realized that nothing she said would please him.

They walked a block without speaking, Erick moving in choppy, erratic strides, constantly looking around, up, down as if searching for some avenue of escape. Her walking smoothly and steadily beside him.

Finally, he felt her hand take his arm and he looked at her.

She was staring at him as if she couldn't understand him at all. It was the same look he'd seen on her face the first time he'd met her.

"Don't be angry with me," she said.

"Oh, for Christ's sake!" he said. "I'm not angry with *you*! You should know that. It's that stupid bunch of idiots down there. By Christ, it may be wrong to say I'm superior to anyone but *by Christ*, I *am* superior to them!"

His teeth clenched, he almost spat the words out.

"Their stupidity, their moronic shouts and grunts. I could have killed them all, by Christ, I could have killed every stupid son of a bitch in the pile!"

"I love you," she said.

He felt as if he'd been struck. He stopped suddenly and stared at her, dumbfounded. His face was a blank, everything vicious and twisted and bitter drained from it in an instant. He stared at her, unable to believe his ears, unable to appraise the sense of complete cleansing he felt at her simple words. Through his mind ran a phrase he'd heard in one of the churches, he forgot which—*And love is reflected in love*.

He sighed.

"Oh, Sally," he said, and his smile was a hopeless one. He put his arm around her shoulders, gently.

"I'm sorry I spoiled your party," he said. "I'm sorry I spoiled everything. Really I am."

He felt absolutely contrite for the first time he could remember in years.

"I understand," she said.

"I'm afraid you do," he said, "that's why I can't understand you loving me."

"I do," she said.

"But...how *can* you?"

"I understand you."

He shook his head and they walked in silence a while. They stopped at the drugstore for a hamburger and some coffee.

"I know how you feel, Erick," she said. "I felt it, too. I was so angry they paid no attention. But you can't blame them entirely. It wasn't the type of entertainment for a place like that. Especially for a crowd like that. All they want this late on a Saturday night is beer, sex and jazz."

"You're right," he said wearily, then he chuckled slightly. "Beer, sex and jazz," he said, "you hit it, Sal."

"You're too sensitive, Erick."

"I'm too something."

He reached over and patted her hand. "And I don't envy you for loving me," he said.

She smiled. "I'm happy as long as you are," she said. "As long as you don't hate *me*."

He gripped her hand tightly. "I could never hate you, Sally."

In the cab he held her tightly against himself.

"I think I love you," he said.

She started and her eyes were frightened and searching in the darkness. Then she leaned back against him, not pressing, just leaning.

"Don't say it, Erick," she said. "You don't have to just because you're grateful."

"Don't you believe me?"

"Do you believe yourself?" she asked.

He thought, then after a moment he said, "I don't know."

They were silent the rest of the way to her house.

four.

One Sunday near the end of the term, she invited him to dinner at her house.

The lawns of the houses were covered with a closely-cropped layer of grass. The deep blue sky was spotted with puffy white clouds. A warm breeze spurted through the fingers of the day, flooding through the open bus windows as he rode out, bathing him with its rushing fragrance.

Sally was sitting on the porch in a canvas chair. Erick walked up the path and flipped open an imaginary suitcase.

"I have here," he said, "a tasty little line of brushes for any and all occasions. You say you have teeth? I have a brush for them. Your back? I have a long brush with a crooked handle. Brush your chestnut locks? Madame, I have the brush!"

She smiled as he bent over and kissed her warm mouth.

"Mmmm," he said.

"Mmmm?"

"Mmmm."

"Taste good?"

"Tastes like more."

She put her hands on his shoulders and he kissed her again. As they parted she asked, "Love me?"

"Yup."

"Liar," she said.

"Madame."

"Put away your suitcase and sit down," she said, getting up.

"Where will you sit?"

"At your feet."

He eased himself down into the chair, sighed and stretched out his long legs. She sat down and rested her elbows on his knees. He yawned and sniffed the air. Then he looked down at her.

"Well," he said, "what mischief have you been into since last we met? Last night, I believe it was."

"That's right."

"What mischief?"

"None."

"Oh, come now."

"You know there's no mischief in me."

"As there is no water in the ocean."

"None."

"There must be."

"Not a drop."

"Bless you."

"What have you been doing, darling?" she asked.

"Studying for finals. Dying. Five of them, count them, five."

"You have circles under your eyes."

"I'll have squares before long."

"Don't study too hard," she said, and put her chin on his knee and looked up at him with an adoring smile as though, loving him, she were climbing a sun-drenched hill, breathless and blind, but happy.

"Isn't it beautiful today?" she said.

"It is," he said. "It's living weather. Trees bursting with color and life. Grass. Warm air. Makes you feel more alive than you even are."

She shivered. "Yes! Just like that."

"Speaking of the weather," he said, "why don't you sit in my lap?"

She smiled. "Won't I be too heavy?" she asked.

"Nonsense, my dear, I have a king-size lap."

She sat on his lap, sliding her arms around his neck. The chair groaned. "Steady, Bessie," he said.

"Am I too heavy?"

"Nope, if the chair can stand it."

"I hope so."

"You mean you haven't tried it out before?"

"What do you mean?"

"You never sat in another man's lap in this chair?"

"No."

"Not even the football team?"

She pressed her face against his. "Please don't tease me," she asked quietly. He tightened his arms around her.

"Sal," he said, "you know what a mistake you're making."

She sighed. "I know."

"Trouble with you is you don't know a bad thing when you see it."

"I know."

"All right." He felt relief to see the exit sign polished off again.

"Don't you want to know what I'm making you for dinner?" she asked.

"Yeah!"

"That reminds me, I'd better go in and look at the chops."

"Chops, chops?"

"I'm broiling some lamb chops."

"Darling, I love you," he said.

"The way to a man's heart."

"You think me callous?"

"Honey," she said seriously, "If I thought lamb chops would win you, I'd broil you a mountain of lamb chops."

"That is the sweetest thing anyone ever said to me."

They smiled at each other, then she put her lips against his and pressed close. A car drove by in the street and Erick wondered if the people in it were watching them kiss. Their lips parted.

"Let's eat each other for supper," he said.

"Cannibal."

"Just imaginative."

She smiled and tried to get up. He wouldn't let her go. He kissed her neck fiercely. "Now stop, *stop*," she laughed, squirming in his tight embrace. "Do you want those lamb chops to burn?"

"I fiddle while the lamb chops burn."

"Oh! After that, I refuse to admit I know you."

They got up and he followed her into the kitchen. He watched her open the broiler door. "See?" she said.

He peeked in and a blast of hot air jumped out on him. He stepped back with a stage shriek. Then he licked his lips at the sight of the two large brown chops oozing fat on the grill.

"Mmmm, those are magnificent, beautiful, superb, grandiose."

"And I have french fries, peas and biscuits and pie and coffee."

"I love you," he said.

"You have no soul," she said.

"I sold it for a broiled lamb chop."

"I thought so."

She took some peeled potatoes out of a pan in the sink and started cutting them up. He went behind her. She had on a light cotton dress with a low-cut neck. He pulled aside her hair.

"Now stop tha..." she started, then she writhed in breathless silence as he kissed the back of her neck.

"St...*op*."

He put his arms around her and squeezed. Her knife dropped to the floor.

"Don't you want to eat?"

"Want to eat you."

"No, I have lamb chops."

"Want to eat you." He nuzzled her throat.

"Don't hon. Not in fun."

"Who's doing it in fun?"

"No." She reached up and took his hands off her breasts. He put them back and she took them away again. Then she twisted around in his arms and pressed forcibly against his body and molded her lips on his. She moved her head from side to side, she opened her mouth and he felt her hot breath in him.

Then she pulled away and rested her cheek against his.

"Now for God's sake go read the funny papers," she said.

"Yes, dear," he said, and kissed her cheek. Then he picked up her knife and handed it to her. He went into the front room and sat on the couch.

"Would you rather have milk?" she asked.

"Yes," he said, "It's so warm."

"Okay."

She came out with an apron over her dress.

"Honey, will you tie this?" she asked. "My hands are greasy."

"Okay."

He tied the strings as she stood in front of him, then he stood up and kissed her neck.

"Not again?"

"You resent mah attentions, ma'am?"

"I don't resent them, suh, I just have to make dinner, that's all. You make me forget about making dinner."

"What do I make you think about?"

She looked into his eyes and smiled, tongue in cheek. For some reason, she looked sly to him, and he felt the suggestion of a shudder.

"You expect me to answer that?" she said.

"As you would answer the Lord."

She pressed against him and he shuddered again. Then her warmth flowed into him and his breathing grew faster. He hugged her.

"I'll get fat on you," she said.

"No you won't."

"Stop it."

"What do I make you think about?"

"I'm not talking."

"You must tell the truth or you must pay the consequence."

"Either way, you got me," she said. "Let go now."

"For a ransom. A kiss, that's my ransom."

She kissed him gently.

"Another," he said.

"You're cheating," she said. "You said one."

"That's what you get for being involved with a blackmailer. We bleed our victims dry."

"Darling, don't you want me to get those potatoes nice and brown and crisp?"

He kissed her throat.

"Don't you want the peas nice and warm and don't you, oh, want the, uh...biscuits...nice and...oh, stop!"

"One kiss."

She raised her lips. He kissed them. Again.

"Now that's three," she said. "What is this, bank night?"

"More."

"No more."

"Later?"

She pursed her lips thoughtfully.

"You got an outside chance, kid," she said. She turned away and he patted her on the rear as she went out.

"Watch that," she said.

"I am," he replied.

He sat down and glanced at the paper, then he lay down on the couch and closed his eyes. He felt the sounds of the house dying away. It was quiet and warm and Sally was in the kitchen, moving about, making dinner for him.

♦ ♦ ♦ ♦ ♦

He started as she sat down next to him.

She had fresh lipstick on. There was a bright red ribbon in her hair.

"Dinner is ready, honey," she said softly.

"Have I been asleep long?"

"About twenty minutes."

"Oh."

"Hungry?" she asked.

"Always. You look pretty."

"*Thank* you."

"That's a new dress. I never saw it."

"I bought it last week. I'm glad you like it."

"Pretty," he said drowsily.

"Come on now, wash up and we'll eat."

"Okay."

He sat at the table, then got up again and helped her into her chair as she came in with the food.

"This looks good," he said.

He didn't know whether it was the sleepiness or the quiet or what, but he felt different. As if he could say what he meant, what he felt, that all restriction of mind were gone. That Sally was his love and everything was settled.

"You sound sleepy," Sally said.

"I guess I am a little."

"Go ahead and eat."

He took a drink of water, then sipped down the tomato juice and made a satisfied noise. "Good," he said. "Good," she echoed. He ate. Everything was delicious. The potatoes were brown and crisp and piping hot, the meat tender and pungently tasty. The peas were bright green and like hot bubbles in his mouth and, when he opened the biscuits, the white insides smoked hotly and the butter melted right into them.

"Delicious!"

"I'm so glad."

"You're a good cook, Sal."

"I had a good teacher."

After a moment he noticed her looking across at him and he looked up. She said, "See what you're missing?"

He smiled.

"I'm plugging," she said.

"I think you're sweet," he said, wondering how such words ever came from him.

When she took away the plates the dining room was getting dark. Looking out through the front screen door, Erick saw the sky bright with red and yellow. It gave him a feeling of satisfied peace to sit there in the house, quiet and still except for the pleasant sound of dishes and soft footsteps in the kitchen. He closed his eyes and tried to pretend it was his house and found it not too hard.

She brought in pie and milk.

"Did you make that, too?" he asked.

"I could lie but I won't. I bought it."

"You bought it with your very own hands."

She laughed quietly. "Stinker," she said, and went into the kitchen and came back with her own pie and milk. She sat down.

"I like this," he said.

"It *is* good pie," she agreed.

"I don't mean that," he said. "I mean, oh…just sitting here with you in this nice house on a lovely spring evening. It's like…like we were married and living here. It's a nice feeling—like I belong here."

She reached across the table and touched his hand.

"Honey," she said softly and, in the dimness, they smiled at each other. And he loved her then. But didn't tell her.

They went back to their pie and, after he'd finished eating, he stretched lazily. "I could sleep ten years," he said.

"Why don't you take a nap?"

"I'll help you with the dishes."

"Don't be silly. There are only a few. Go take a nap."

"You aren't making a very good argument for me to help you with the dishes."

"I don't want you to, honey."

"Sold."

He stood up and went behind her chair. He put his hands on her shoulders and, bending over, kissed her warm neck.

"It was wonderful, Sal," he said. "Really."

She crossed her arms and put her hands on top of his and patted them.

"I'm glad you liked it," she said happily. Then she said, "It *is* like it's our house and we were having Sunday dinner all by ourselves."

"Yes."

"Oh, if only it were so."

"Maybe it will be," he heard himself say instinctively, but immediately felt a drawing back in himself.

"Don't say it, darling," she said. "I love you so much but I don't ever want you to feel to owe it to me. Unless you feel it in your heart, just let it go."

Then she said, "Remind me to show you something later."

"All right."

She got up to do the dishes and he went into the living room and lay on the couch.

"Why don't you turn on the radio?" she called.

"I don't want to let anything in the house but you and me."

She didn't answer. He wondered what she was thinking, what sort of expression was on her face. Then the dishes started to rattle again.

When she came in and sat down he said, "Boy, I'm half gone."

She stroked his hair and bent over to kiss him.

"You read about the homosexual ring they broke up at the college?" he asked as she straightened up.

"What made you think of that?"

"Just looking through the paper before."

"Wasn't that awful?"

"It was."

"I…was a little worried."

"What for?"

"Oh…"

He laughed. "You mean you knew some of them?"

"I wasn't sure."

"Who, Felix?" he said.

She didn't smile and he suddenly felt himself shudder. His laugh was strained.

"*What*?" he said.

"Well..." The look in her eyes frightened him.

"Well," she said, flustered now, "You're so...pretty."

"Pretty!"

"You are," she insisted. "By...*their* standards. You have a good build and you're...well, good looking."

"Oh Christ, Sally."

"You're angry with me?"

"No," he said. "Amused, mostly. That you should have thought that of me."

"Well," she said, "your...your friend."

"Who's that?"

"Lynn."

"Lynn!"

He felt as if something were wrapped around his chest and starting to crush him and he wanted to tear loose and run from the place.

"I'm sorry," she said. "I...just pretend I didn't say anything."

"But...oh, all right," he said moodily. He felt almost like a child in the darkness who hears a noise—afraid to investigate and see what it is.

"And you'd still love me?" he said.

"I'd be unhappy," she said, resting her cheek on his chest so as to avoid meeting his eyes. "But I couldn't stop loving you. I'd...want to help you."

He sighed.

"Sally," he said, "that I should have given you that concern to add to all the rest."

"You're a concern, all right."

She raised up and looked at him with a smile.

"So you thought you were in love with a fairy," he said.

She tried to keep smiling.

"Are you blushing?" he asked.

"Yes," she said. "I am."

After a few moments she lay down next to him and they fell asleep for a while.

♦ ♦ ♦ ♦ ♦

"Would you like to go out in back?" she asked.

"Back yard?"

"Mmmm. It'd be cooler."

"Sure."

"I'll get a blanket and you can take the radio out from my bedroom window. I have an extension cord."

She handed him the radio after opening the screen. He put it down on the spread-out blanket. He turned it on as the house lights went out and Sally came out on the back porch. He heard the tread of her bare feet on the wooden steps. She sat down beside him. He took her in his arms and they kissed. But he kept thinking of what she'd said. Even while her mouth was crushed on his and her body rubbing against him he kept thinking of it. And wondering.

"It's nice out here," she said at last.

"Yes."

They lay in each other's arms, listening to the music. He felt the flow and ebb of her warm breath on his cheek, her soft stomach resting against his. And a little of the feeling of before came back.

He began to caress her breasts. First she tried to take his hands away, but then she slid her hands behind his back and pressed close. He opened a button of her dress, not because he desired it, he suddenly realized. It was more in the nature of a challenge. He just had to open her dress, beyond that there was no plan.

Dead silence, then, "Erick?"

"Yes."

"What are you doing?"

"Opening buttons."

"Why?"

"Good question."

His voice trembled a little. He opened another button and drew the dress over her shoulder. He pressed his lips into the warm flesh. She sighed and held on tightly. He opened another button, a fourth, then feverishly, a second or two, he went down the front of her dress and opened them all. He forgot why he wanted to do it or if there had to be a reason at all. He just couldn't stop.

She didn't say anything. Not when he pulled the dress over her shoulders. Not when he caressed her breasts through her brassiere. Not when he held her arms at her sides and slid the dress to her waist. She was docile. He pressed his fingers on her warm back. He held her tightly and kissed her. She was starting to breathe heavily. She rubbed her breasts against him and his breath caught.

Then his mind started in.

He kissed her neck and ear lobes passionately, almost desperately, trying to outdistance analysis. He felt for the catch of her brassiere. It slid to the sides and he felt her uncovered breasts swell up against him, large and firm.

"Oh, Erick," she murmured, "no."

Don't be ridiculous—the words started in his mind—*why the hell do you say no when you mean yes, yes, yes. Why do you…*

He cut it short, feeling unbounded rage at himself. *Stop thinking, for Christ's sake*, he demanded of himself. Anxiously he tried to recapture excitement. He jerked off her brassiere and pressed his lips on her breasts. They were burning hot, yielding softly to his kisses. She caught her breath and moaned softly as he kissed her nipples. She dug her suddenly hard fingers into his hair and almost scratched him.

"Oh, Erick. Darling!"

Breathing heavily, she pressed her cheek against his.

"You're not very nice," she said.

"Yes, I am."

"I wish I could stop you."

"You have a lovely body."

I'm glad you like it! mimicked his mind.

"I'm glad you like it," Sally said.

"I do." He almost laughed out loud.

He kissed her throat, tightening his fingers on her soft shoulders. He ran his lips over her shoulders and down to her breasts. He rested his cheek against their large white softness.

"Why can't you love me?" she asked.

"I could tell you I love you," he said, feeling almost sick. "I could tell you to make you happy. But I respect you. I think too much of you to lie just to take advantage."

Noble soul—sneered his mind—*cut the crap, buddy.*

He pressed in close to her.

"You couldn't get much more of an advantage," he heard her say as she stirred against him restively.

Then she said softly, "Make me happy."

"What?"

"Tell me you love me. For now. Tell me over and over. I don't care if it's a lie, just tell me."

She gasped and pulled his lips against her breasts. "Tell me you love me!"

He lifted his head, feeling like someone powerful in a great position of eminence. He waited dramatically, knowing the moment in every sense, experiencing her feeling.

She had her eyes closed and he looked hungrily at her breasts in the dim light from the radio dial. They were very white and large, standing out firmly from her body. He bent over her mouth suddenly.

"I love you," he said.

He tightened his arms on her, feeling free and powerful. He could say it and she would not hold him responsible. It was, he knew, a feeling he yearned for always. To have and have not.

"I love you Sally!" He said it again, again.

She began to sob and her arms tightened around him. Their mouths clung together and he ran his hand over her upright breasts and rubbed the erect flesh. She twisted and moaned, saliva ran across the cheek. *Messy love affair*, said his mind, *quite messy*. He fought it off. His hand moved down impulsively to her thigh and he felt her bare flesh and knew, with a start, that her dress had worked its way up to her waist. *Or she's pulled it up, idiot*! his mind howled with raucous laughter, watching him fail.

He gasped for breath and ran his palm over her leg, feeling his heart beat rapidly, thudding like maniacal fists against the wall of his chest. But his mind ticked on calmly and dispassionately—*now I'm caressing her thigh, yes sir, oh yes. Now just a little bit higher and my hand will touch…*

She wrenched her lips away with a sob.

"Oh, Erick, please don't!"

"Sally, please!"

He was utterly appalled by the husky, grinding sound of his own voice. He almost jumped up.

She sobbed, then she made a helpless sound and her head fell back and her body went limp.

"Oh, I don't care," she said, shaking uncontrollably. "I don't *care*."

His stomach was drawn and tight. *Now!* cried his mind. He felt a wild uncontrollable heat bubbling up in his limbs which his mind could do nothing to stop. He pressed his hand down on her warm, heaving stomach. She lurched a little and his mind clicked on. He wanted to scream in rage. *Well, well, what are we up to?* said his mind. *Let me alone! Let me alone, for God's sake!*

He touched the edge of her pants. He ran his fingers under the edge and felt the soft flesh of her stomach under his palm. He bit his lip. *She's too healthy*, he thought, *baby,*

baby, watch that stuff. His mind droned on—*Too dangerous, watch that, baby, baby, baby!*

He clenched his teeth and sobbed out loud as his hand jerked back.

"No," he said. "*No*!"

Abruptly she began to cry helplessly, clinging to him. Cooly, calmly, he pulled part of the blanket over her. He felt the cool breeze on his body. His breath was suddenly even. She had no attraction for him, she was just a sobbing girl. He was apart, aloof. He sympathized with her mildly. The heat in his body seemed to drain out into the ground like water from an emptied pitcher. He felt cold in mind and body. The radio music played on and on and it became a mass of empty sounds. He felt lifeless.

He looked up at the stars. I've lost it, he told himself, without knowing what he meant—I've lost it.

And didn't care.

After a while, she pulled away a little and drew up her dress without buttoning it.

"I'm sorry," he said as he might say if he had spilled something on her or stubbed her toe while dancing.

"It's nothing," she said.

"I wanted to do it. You know that." *If you do, you're out of your mind*!

"I'm glad you didn't," she said.

"I knew I shouldn't," he said.

"It's all right."

"Is it? Really? You wouldn't have stopped."

"I would have let you do anything," she said. Almost grimly.

His muscles tightened involuntarily and something cried out in anguish in his mind.

"I'm glad you had the sense I didn't," she said.

"Sense," he said, dully.

She was silent, breathing evenly. She arranged her dress.

"What time is it?" she asked.

He squinted at his watch by the radio light.

"Ten thirty."

"Oh," she said, "we'd better get up. Leo will be coming home soon."

She sat up and Erick saw the whiteness of her breasts as her dress fell open. He put his hands inside and she didn't stop him, but she didn't shiver of seem to be affected.

"Are you angry, Sal?"

"No."

They pulled out the radio plug and carried the blanket and radio inside. When she came into the living room her dress was buttoned up.

"I'm not really angry," she said, sliding her arms around him. "I can see that you did the right thing."

"I hope I did the right thing."

"You did."

"I hope so." He was conscious of the two of them standing there and talking, to his mind, errant nonsense.

He kissed her forehead. "I wish I'd done it," he said.

"It's all right," she said, and every time she said it, it made him sicker.

They stood silently. He looked over the walls and the ceiling. Then he said, "I'd better go."

"All right."

"I bet you're glad to get rid of me."

He looked at her and wasn't sure what he saw—love or sympathy or amusement or all of them together. She just shook her head. "No," she said.

"Maybe you think it's a sign I do like…men."

"I don't think so."

"I don't think so either," he said, a little irritated at his own tone of self-defense.

"Good night, darling," she said, kissing him on the cheek.

"Thanks for the dinner," he said.

"Oh. You're welcome."

He pressed her breasts as he kissed her. "I'm always yours," she said, but he didn't believe her.

He stood on the cool corner and leaned against the lamp post. He felt an urge to run back and take her by violence. He didn't move. He saw a car pull up to the house and Leo jumped out and kissed some boy goodnight through the window. Erick saw the boy's hands reach out to grab Leo's breasts and she pulled back with a loud giggle and went in the house.

He sat in disgruntled silence on the bus. The night was ugly.

It wasn't until two days later that he found the poem in his jacket. She'd probably put it there when he was asleep, he decided. It was what she had mentioned showing him. He also guessed she was sorry he had it now. He read it so many times it filled his memory.

Deep in the dark center of life
You came and drew breath and lived.
Time took you and held you awhile
Then set you free.
Out of the dark center of life
Somehow you came to me
And the breath life had given me
Stopped for a moment, then caught again
In time with yours.

five.

The term was over. The streets were empty and barren. Erick walked around distractedly with nothing to do. The summer semester didn't start for five days.

He went into a drug store and had a Coke. Then he went in back and called Sally. He hadn't seen her since that night, except once briefly on the campus.

"Hello, Erick," she said. "What's the matter?""The matter?" he said. "Something have to be the matter?"

"No. I thought we said goodbye, though."

"Well..."

"What is it?"

"I...just wondered what you were doing," he said.

"Cleaning up. Packing."

"When are you leaving?"

"I told you. Tomorrow morning."

"Oh."

"You're staying till August?" she asked.

"Yes."

"That's too bad."

"I suppose so."

Silence a moment. "Look, Erick, I'm awfully busy."

"I just thought I'd come out and see you." He almost bit his tongue in saying it.

"Oh," she said, sounding pained. "Well, if you think you'd enjoy watching me run around like a chicken without a head..."

"I'll stay out of your way," he said, unable to stop himself. He didn't care what she said, he didn't want to be alone. Being alone was the most awful thing. There were long periods of time when he craved solitude but then, at times when mental activity slowed down, the loneliness would come and he would be thrown into a panic at the thought of being alone with nothing to lose himself in, no activity to swallow up introspection.

LEAVE YESTERDAY ALONE

The front screen door was open when he got there. He let it slap into its frame as he went in. She looked out from the kitchen.

"Hi," she called.

"Hello."

She was at the sink scrubbing some white tennis shoes with a small brush.

"Washing out a few pairs of shoes?" he said.

"Getting the dirt off."

He stood by the sink and watched her strong brown fingers hold the white rubber taut while she scrubbed suds into it. Water ran slowly from the faucet, dribbling onto the white enamel.

Sally was wearing a wrinkled cotton dress. Her hair hung in damp wisps over her forehead. There was a line of sweat on her upper lip. Erick took out his handkerchief and dabbed at it.

"What are you doing?" she asked.

"Blotting your perspiration," he said.

He sat down at the table and watched her, feeling a rising lack of ease. She said nothing. With his gaze he followed the line that ran from her right armpit to her waist, swelled out at her hip, and then angled down to her calf. He looked at her well-muscled legs, her arched feet stuck into floppy white sandals. He looked up again. Her shoulders were very broad for a girl's. She stood erect and firm.

"You're a healthy looking creature," he said.

"What?"

"Didn't you hear me?"

"You don't speak clearly."

"I said you're a healthy animal."

"Thanks."

"Nothing."

He leaned against the wall disgustedly and watched her for awhile. He drifted away for a moment, held by the heat and the near silence and the sound of running water.

"Going to write me?" he asked.

"What?"

He hesitated. "Going to write me?" he said loudly.

"Why?"

"I have a crack in the wall of my room and I need some paper to stuff it with."

"I wouldn't be surprised."

She finished washing the shoes and walked out of the kitchen without a word. He wanted to leave but he kept seeing his empty room and all the theatres closed and his friends gone. With a sigh he got up and went into her room, following like a mute.

A big steamer trunk stood open on the floor, drawers sagging out like cardboard tongue, dresses, suits and coats hanging inside. On the bed a large suitcase was flopped open, half filled. She was putting the tennis shoes in a bottom draw of the steamer trunk.

"You taking everything?" he asked.

"No."

He moved toward her bed, accidentally kicking over a waste basket filled with papers. He picked it up and set it down beside the bed.

"Be careful," she said.

"Yeah," he said, taking off his shoes and putting his feet up on the bed. He sank back into the soft mattress.

"Boy, what a nice bed."

Silence. He stared at the ceiling.

"Aren't you going to write me, Sal?" he asked.

"You don't want me to," she said, folding skirts.

"Sure I do," he said, after a brief pause. "Why should I ask you if I didn't want you to?"

She shrugged her shoulders. And he failed to sound amused as he said, "You don't love me anymore."

"Why should I?" she said.

"You got me," he said. "I've been trying to talk you out of it for the last two months."

"Maybe you did."

"Oh, I see." He fell back on the pillow and closed his eyes. He blew out a breath of air. "Here I come to see you and you insult me," he said.

"You invited yourself."

"Oh."

"You're lonely and you don't know anybody," she said.

"Oh, I see."

He opened his eyes and watched her putting blouses in the trunk grimly.

"What are you mad at, Sally?"

"I'm not."

"Sure you are."

She tightened her mouth and took some stockings out of a dresser drawer and started rolling them up.

"What have *I* done?" he asked.

He waited for her answer but it didn't come. He fell back on the pillow and sighed. "All right," he said.

She moved around the room quickly, pulling out drawers, irritably tossing clothes into the trunk and suitcase.

"When are you leaving?"

"I told you twice."

"I *forgot*."

She said nothing. He closed his eyes again, his ears following her quick, jerky motions around the room. He smelled the overall perfume of the room and thought of the first time he'd been in there, that Sunday in April. He thought of the time he'd stood in the doorway watching her put lipstick on. She'd been wearing a blouse and slacks. When she'd turned out the light he'd blocked the way and she pressed into him willingly and they kissed in the darkness, her hot, wet lips teasing him, her stomach pressed tightly against him.

He sat up, threw his legs over the edge of the bed, and stood up. He kissed her lightly on her flushed cheek.

"Goodbye," he said coldly, and left.

The landlady called him to the phone in the morning.

"Hello, honey," Sally said. "I'm about to leave."

"Oh. That's nice."

"Did you just get up?"

"Yes."

"Erick, I'm sorry about last night. I was tired."

"I know."

"Don't say it like that, darling. I'll write to you, you know I will. You answer me, too, hear?"

"All right."

"Don't work too hard this summer, honey."

"No."

"I'll see you in September," she said.

"All right."

"G'bye, honey."

Afterwards he sat on the bed and stared at the dust blobs on the floor and pushed his toes into them. He sat there half the morning, just staring.

♦ ♦ ♦ ♦ ♦

Two weeks after, she sent him a letter.

Dear Erick, it read, *Golly how time slips by. And how it must be dragging for you. I'll bet you'll be glad when you get home.*

Home, he thought. A couch at my sister's house, a cantankerous brother-in-law.

Let me pause right here and say I know I'm a fool but I'd give anything to be with you today. I miss you so!

News of her family.

I got that job in a day camp near home. I'm getting nice and brown. Swimming a lot.

The kids at the camp.

I've been thinking of the swell times we had last year. Going dancing, walking together on the campus, the show. The sound of the bus stopping at the corner when you came to get me. The time at church when we went square dancing.

All the wonderful talks we had. Yeah (as you'd say) I miss you Erick. Darn it!

Are you still writing? I want to read everything you do this summer!

I'm even writing poetry again. See, you inspire me! You never did tell me what you thought of that poem I put in your jacket.

More about the past year.

Have to close now Erick. Missing you. And loving you.

Sally.

In August when he got back to New York he got two more letters from her. One was just a recital of sunny information. *Summer going too fast, darn it. Mother and Dad fine, ask about you. Brother and wife well, niece a darling—walking! Guess who I heard from? Do you ever see Leo in New York, she lives there you know. Got a new dress, I hope you like it, I think it's slick.*

The other letter was different. He read it seven times. She must have written it at night, he imagined, when everybody was asleep. When the moon hung moodily in the black sky, while the lazy rasp of crickets filled the night air, while frenzied bugs beat insane wings against the burning bulb until they perished. And there she sat, writing.

I've been trying to convince myself, Erick, that I don't want to see you anymore. But after I say it myself I have no way of making myself believe it.

I'm trying—so hard. Harder than I ever tried. I never had this happen before, just like this. I've had small loves in the past but they never ever came close to this.

It's been wonderful to know you...and terrible. I've loved you, hated you, and sometimes...I was even afraid of you. Does that sound funny? You can be pretty awesome at times.

But you can be so wonderful. Understanding, kind, a perfect companion.

I don't know where to turn. I want to stop loving you. It isn't any use though. I know it. But, even knowing it, I find myself hoping.

It's such a terrible problem.

Forgive me. I shouldn't pour my troubles over your head.

Sally

♦ ♦ ♦ ♦ ♦

Days passing uneventfully. Idle couching on beach sands. Dreamless sleep at night. A sluggish plodding through the hot days of August. Days and nights of reading. Days dying. Retreats to Lynn's house, seclusion in Lynn's large, quiet room. Talks. Hopeless lethargy of brain and body. Waiting for something. Return to her?

Thinking of her largess of affection.

six.

"Oh, honey, hello!"

Her voice shook with excitement. The warmth seemed to reach him all the way from her house.

"Are you coming out?" she asked.

"I'll be right out."

"I don't want to keep you a second. Come out now."

"Okay."

Her voice was filled with affectionate urgency. "*Please* hurry," she said.

He went back to his room and Lynn looked up as he entered.

"I must be out of my mind," Lynn said, "to move into this squalid cell just for the sake of your dubious company."

"You know you're delighted."

"Benighted is the word."

Lynn watched Erick pull on his jacket. "Where are you going?" he asked.

"Sally."

"What, already?"

"Already."

Lynn shook his head. "You're gone," he said. "There goes your soul right down the drain."

"Horse manure, dear friend," Erick answered. "See you later."

It was a warm, sunny September day. Erick waited at the corner for the bus. He began to get a little excited as the bus left the downtown section and started chugging up the long hill to her house. He began to feel like a little boy returning from a summer in camp, looking at everything with new eyes and thinking—there's the good ol' campus, there's the good ol' bus, there's the good ol' Main Street. Although he'd only been away for little over a month, everything seemed fresh. The people, the cars, the houses standing back on their green lawns. He decided the excitement was due to the fact that he was back at school.

But when he got off the bus, he knew it was more. He stopped and stood on the corner, the warm breeze on his face. There it was. For a moment, the sense of being home surged over him.

The screen door opened and she came out.

They started walking toward each other. Her face was radiant, it seemed to draw him in. They were like attracting poles. He hardly felt his feet on the ground, he seemed to float. He'd never felt her love more powerfully than he did in those few seconds when she started to run and threw herself into his arms. Her words flashed through his mind—*I want to stop loving you.*

She was quiet a long time as though she couldn't catch her breath enough to speak. She clung to him tightly and held her warm cheek against his.

Finally, she whispered, "You're back."

"I'm back."

They kissed. Her lips were hungry for his. Then she smiled happily and sighed, rubbing a little lipstick off his mouth with the edge of her right forefinger. A tear started in the corner of her right eye. She brushed it away.

"My goodness," she said, shakily. "I'm all upset."

"Sally," he said.

They started for the house and she took his arm tightly. She kept looking at him, her eyes drinking in the sight of him. She seemed to be looking enough to make up for the two-odd months they'd been apart. Her eyes seemed to speak—I can't believe it, you're back but I can't believe it.

She stroked his arm.

"Oh, see how tan he is," she murmured, her voice vibrant with love. "You must have gone to the beach a lot."

"I did," he said.

She smiled at him as if his words were the most fascinating she'd ever heard. And he smiled back affectionately, feeling a rush of love for her.

At his smile, she made a sound of unrepressed delight and pushed her cheek against his shoulder. It reminded him of his sister's two-year-old daughter pressing her face into a pillow when her birthday party was just too exciting for her. That was how Sally acted, unable to contain her joy. It flowed over the edges of her smile, her touch, her words. She was like a joyous child and he was her Christmas morning.

"Leo told me I shouldn't come out and meet you," she said. "She said I shouldn't show you how much you mean to me. But I don't care, I did it anyway. I tried to walk, I tried so hard just to walk. But I couldn't, I couldn't walk slowly, like a lady should. Not when I saw your face. And when you smiled at me—Oh Erick!—I had to run to you!"

He put his arm around her and squeezed. "I'm glad you did," he said. "I want it that way. You look pretty. I like that ribbon in your hair."

Now he was starting to talk like her.

"Thank you, darling," she said. "How have you been? I want to know everything you've done this summer."

"That would take some telling," he said, with a smile.

"I don't care how long it takes," she said, "if you don't."

Leo looked up as they came in.

"He's back," Sally said.

Leo looked amused. "So I see," she said.

"Hello, Leo," Erick said. "Have a nice summer?"

"Pretty nice," she said. "Why didn't you give me a buzz?"

"Got me," he said, "didn't know your number, I guess."

"Fine excuse," she said.

Sally took his arm. "I want to show you something, Erick," she said.

Leo watched them leave. "See you," she said to Erick.

"Sure," he said.

Sally stopped in her bedroom doorway. She looked up at him and he felt enveloped by the surging of her love. There was no seeming transition, suddenly they were embracing and her warm mouth was clinging to his. They trembled under his kiss. Her fingers opened and closed on his back. Erick wondered if Leo were listening to them.

"Oh, *darling*," Sally gasped, "I'm so happy you're back. I've missed you. So terribly."

"I've missed you too, Sally."

"I hope so. Oh, I hope so."

They say on her bed and she snuggled against him as he put his arms around her. She raised her lovely soft face and kissed his cheek. "Sweetheart," she said.

He looked down at her. She was bronzed, even the red of her lips seemed to pale against her skin. She wore a low-cut pink dress which revealed her figure, as beautiful as ever.

She kept on glancing at him every few seconds as if she were afraid he might disappear if she didn't keep looking.

"Thank you, darling," she said.

"What for?"

"For coming back to me."

"Oh, Sal."

She leaned forward and her soft lips brushed over his. He pulled her against himself and held tight.

"It seems so long since I was in your arms," she said.

They didn't say anything then. He kissed her temple and looked down at the swelling of copper-colored flesh where the bodice of her dress fell away. He didn't want to do anything but sit there with her in his arms. He was perfectly content for the first time in months.

"I love you, Erick," she said. "I always will."

Then, as if relieved to have unburdened herself, she sighed deeply and rested against him. Then, after a moment, she lifted her face again and looked into his eyes. Her hands moved up and she stroked his cheeks very slowly and gently. She leaned over and kissed his mouth over and over, barely touching her mouth to his. She whispered of love in his ear. She kissed his eyes and cheeks and, suddenly, he grabbed her wrists and pulled her close to him as he kissed her.

"I have missed you, Sal, I *have*," he muttered.

Her warm arms slid around his back. He could feel the heat of them through his shirt.

"Oh, thank you, thank you," she whispered, almost fiercely.

They sat in silence, every once in a while shifting a little to get closer to each other, their arms tightening, their bodies pressing harder. Tiny sounds of love filled her throat. He felt a severe desire to tell her he loved her. But he didn't.

"I'm too obvious," she said. "Leo says I am. Is that all right?"

"Yes, that's all right."

"I can't help it. I want you to know just how I feel. I can't hide it."

He kissed her cheek.

"When you didn't call last night, Leo said you were probably out with another girl."

"Good old Leo."

"Oh, I don't care. You can go out with a hundred girls as long as you keep some time for me."

"Sally."

"No, really," she said, pouring her love at his feet. "I don't mind if you go out with anyone else. Just keep seeing me, too, once in a while. You don't have to call me all the time. When you get tired of me, don't call. Only call me when you want to. We'll do what you want to do. I'll be anything you say."

The words tumbled from her lips, warm and eager.

"Sally."

It was all he could say as he held her tighter and tighter. She was throwing herself at him. *If she really meant it*, his mind suggested, *you could*...he shunted aside the thought.

"You shouldn't talk like that," he said. "You know how spoiled I am. You'll make it worse."

"I can't do anything else," she said. "I can't be strong with you. Maybe another could but I love you so much I just have to tell you and I just want to do anything you say."

She seemed to know his thoughts suddenly, for she said then, "I trust you."

They started to plan out the coming term.

"Shall I get season tickets for the Drama Workshop plays?" he asked.

"Oh yes!"

"And we'll go to the concerts together."

"Yes! And dances too, Erick?"

He smiled. "And dances too."

He began to feel the rare sensation of genuine happiness. It made him want to open wide his arms and embrace the world. He was happy being with her, making plans, settling the future. Once more he began to feel the bubbling excitement in her that has more or less amused him the first times they'd gone out together. It filled her to the brim, this intense love and enjoyment of life. It transferred itself to him, he could almost feel it like a flow into his body, a transfusion of spirit. Her vitality spread upon him, she was life for him. He felt it strongly. She was what he needed more than anything else—a clear and shiny lens through which to see the world anew.

Happiness such as he had rarely experienced came to him that afternoon. Sometimes, alone, he had experienced an ecstasy of ambition, a delight of mental effort. But these feelings always drained him in the end, he had to rest between them. The happiness she gave him was its own source, its own renewal.

The moments flew by that afternoon. The details obscured, there were so many, and his head whirled with excitement and happiness. What stood out clearly was the glow in her eyes and the steady rush of warm delight he felt in being with her. Happiness welled in him until he felt he would burst if he didn't shout it out to everyone. He felt secure with her, at ease with her, without need of anything else than her touch, her smile, the gentle impelling of her love.

♦ ♦ ♦ ♦ ♦

One evening Sally and Erick went over to the house of Sally's singing teacher. As they were going up the path to the porch a car ground to a stop at the curb.

"Is this Professor Walton's house?" asked a voice from the back of the cab. Sally said it was.

A young girl came up behind them as they stood waiting for Professor Walton to answer the door bell.

"Hello," said Sally.

"Hello," answered the girl, a little timidly.

Professor Walton came to the door and they went in. The girl was several inches shorter than Sally, Erick noticed. Professor Walton introduced her as Melissa Crane.

They all took chairs. Two other male students were there and Sally introduced them to Erick. Then they listened to recorded singing.

Melissa sat in a chair near the record player. She was wearing a light green dress. Her figure was exquisite, Erick saw. He noticed her legs as she crossed them. Sally and he were sitting across from her on the couch, next to Professor Walton.

They sat in silence through the lieder cycle, then most of them talked about vocal technique and Erick sat in silence, listening. Melissa and he were the only ones who didn't have anything to say and it made him feel on common ground with her.

He seemed interested, though. Her green eyes moved around from speaker to speaker. *She's lovely*, he thought. Dark, dark hair. Something about her face. Gentle, yet vitally strong.

"Erick?" Professor Walton was asking.

"What?"

"Anything you'd like to hear?"

"Oh...how about, have you got Scriabin's *Poem of Ecstasy*?"

"Yes." Professor Walton stood up and Erick's eyes touched Melissa's for a second and held them. He felt his breath catch. *Then caught again in time with yours*. The words moved through his mind.

"What's *The Poem of Ecstasy*, honey?" Sally asked, too loudly, he thought. *Don't call me honey!*—his mind exploded. *I wish I were alone*.

"Scriabin."

"Is it good?" So anxious, so interested in what he had to say.

"I don't know," he said hastily, "I never heard it, that's why I want to hear it."

She was silent then and the fingers on his arm seemed to go limp. He felt uncomfortable. *I'm sorry*—his mind apologized—*but for Christ's sake, don't hang on to me. Eat your cake and have it too, eat your cake and have*...his mind chanted.

The music began. "Tell me if you think it's religious music," said Professor Walton.

Erick fell away with it and knew right away Professor Walton was joking. The music wasn't religious in any sense, it was a sensuous mass of sound. He felt it in his blood.

This isn't music, his mind declared, *it's part of thought, an opiate that dulls and expands yet leaves no remorse*. He felt himself shiver and recalled what Lynn had said once about music listeners being like smokers. The true smoker, Lynn had said, doesn't show his reactions in an overt manner. The smoke is inhaled deeply and not much comes back out. It is not like the sniff-snort puffings of the neophyte smoker. The nicotine fumes are drunk in and savored deeply in the far passages of the lungs. There is no wild exhalation and the enjoyment is expressed only with the eyes, the face is generally a blank. The enjoyment is within.

Thus it is with the music listener, Lynn had said. The music is inhaled deeply. There is no combination of listening and overt action, no whistling or humming or movements of extremities. The body and face are placid. The music is taken down deep and there it stirs. Only in the eye can the tale be read.

His eyes fell on Melissa again. They could not help but gravitate toward her, his glance was weighted in her direction. He ran his eyes over her body. It was as lovely as Sally's, a little less robust. *Look at those eyes*, said his mind, *those eyes*. And features carved delicately with a loving and expert hand.

He felt Sally's eyes on him as the music surrounded. He could tell she was looking at him now without even glancing aside. He didn't know when the ability had become full-blown but it was there.

She gazes for the thousandth time at me, he thought. What was she thinking? *There he sits, damn him, my only rival his career. I could help him if he only knew. But he has to be as free as the air. I know that and still I love him. It is tragic.*

Did she think that? He kept looking at Melissa while he wondered.

The music ended. "Religious?" Professor Walton asked.

"Carnal," Erick said, and they all laughed.

There was conversation a while which Erick didn't pay much attention to. All he kept thinking was that it would be better if Sally weren't there. It didn't occur to him that he would never have been invited there at all if it hadn't been for Sally. Desire overshadowed reason. He didn't want Melissa to think he was engaged to Sally. They had such an easy air of familiarity between them. They might even be married. The thought made him shiver. He found himself displaying his left hand prominently so she could see there was no ring. *But lots of married men wear nothing*, the thought came, *what if...*oh, shut up!

He listened carefully when she spoke. She was a freshman student. She must be no more than eighteen, he decided, quite a drop from Sally's twenty-three.

After a while they all had cocoa and crackers. Melissa brought cups to Sally and him and he felt a chill as she smiled at him.

"Thank you," he said, and she said, "You're welcome," and her voice sounded mysterious to him.

The cocoa burned in his throat. He tried to talk to Sally but he couldn't get interested in anything she said. He was beginning to feel the same eating hunger he'd felt the first time he met Sally. It was an emotion he distrusted, a de-enervating loss of mind, something he could intellectually curse but something that made the different in spite of everything.

Going home on the bus they were silent.

When they got off, Sally said, "What are you thinking about, darling?"

"Nothing."

"You've been away from me all night."

"Sorry." He took her arm from habit, not desire.

"Why do you stand for me?" he said, conscious of the fact that there was more belligerence than amusement in his voice.

"Because I love you so."

He closed his eyes for a moment. She was a she-devil in the way she knew how to get to him. He put his arm around her and looked into her eyes and forgot about Melissa for a moment.

"I kick you around and you still say that," he said.

"Just a faithful old shoe," she said.

On the porch she asked him if he was coming in.

"I can't, Sally," he said. "I have to get up early tomorrow."

"Oh," she said quietly, "all right."

He put his arms around her.

"Sweetheart," he said, "do you want me to fall asleep in class and tumble out of the chair?"

She laughed sadly and pushed her face into his shoulder. "Oh me," she murmured and he lifted her chin and kissed her.

"Oh. I love you," she said, as if she would rather it were otherwise.

"Sally."

"Go home," she said. "Go to bed and dream of me cold and alone."

"I'll stay if it's that bad."

She smiled. "No. Thank you for taking me home."

"Good night, Sal."

He couldn't sleep for several hours. Lynn was snoring delicately in his bed but even when Lynn turned over and the noise stopped, Erick lay awake, eyes shut, trying to see Melissa's face in his mind again.

At least, he told himself, it shows me I'm capable of emotion toward a girl. I'm still human to that extent. And it must be more than physical attraction. Sally has as much of that but I don't even pretend to love Sally.

And now this girl, with her angel's face, reduced him to thoughts of love. It was pathetic, that's what it was, spoke up the Ned Sparks of his intellect. He drank down mental draughts for months on end, then, in one swoop, he was gone. One unknowing flap of eyelashes and he was a dead duck. From one extreme to the other.

Perhaps that was the cachet.

He stretched his body taut and then relaxed. He listened to the silence and made believe he was back in his army tent after a grueling day on the obstacle course. The branches rustling outside were the swaying Georgia pine tree branches high above. The mattress was softer than the ground but he could still pretend. He fell asleep and dreamed that he was trying to get over to that chair by the record player but people kept putting obstacles in the way and he couldn't get close enough to see her face.

LEAVE YESTERDAY ALONE

♦ ♦ ♦ ♦ ♦

He walked right by her in Sociology class.

He didn't realize it for a second. It was only at the last moment that he recognized her and returned her smile hastily. Then, instead of taking the empty seat beside her, he walked back about five rows, his heart beating rapidly. He cursed himself.

He looked at her after he sat down. Once she turned around and looked over the classroom without looking at him. Maybe she disliked him, he thought. He consulted memory. He hadn't done anything particularly odious at Professor Walton's house that night, had he?

All through class he had the fear that when he got to speak to her he wouldn't have the courage to ask her to attend the first Drama Workshop play with him. His heart kept beating violently, his hand shook so that he couldn't write his notes. When the bell rang at the end of the class, he almost jumped up out of the seat.

He got up shaking and went out of the room, heart thudding furiously. He stood in the hallway, waiting. *If she comes out with a man*, he thought, *I'll go mad and hurl myself out a window*. Then, as he was reluctantly smiling at his own hopeless urges, she came out with two girls.

As she passed he swallowed a lump in his throat and said, "May I see you a moment, Melissa?"

"Yes," she said, and stood before him. He felt as though his legs were turning to water. Her lips were so red, her yellow sweater double-pointed, her green eyes directly on him.

"A friend of mine gave me a couple of tickets to the Workshop play tomorrow night. I wondered if you'd care to go with me."

"Why, I'd love to," she said.

A warm wave of joy and relief flooded through him. He felt like tearing down the building, grabbing her in his arms and kissing her, shouting something noble.

"Fine," he said.

"I don't know whether they'll let us stay out that late, though," she said. "We have freshman hours, you know."

"Oh yes, of course," he said. The shaking was back, he felt like squirming.

"But I think they should let us out for that."

"I should think they would."

Damn!—howled his mind. Rational conversation when he wanted to crush her in his arms and kiss her lips and neck and eyes and shout—I love you, Melissa! I don't know why or how but suddenly I love you completely. I want you, I need you. Everything is meaningless but you. *I love you, Melissa*!

He went to his next class, imagining himself pouring out those tempestuous words in that moth-eaten hallway. It made him chuckle in spite of himself. He imagined Lynn standing by, listening. That amused him even more.

When he called her that night, she told him she couldn't go to the play. Quickly he suggested the next Saturday and she said yes. The next night he went to the play with Lynn and didn't go over to speak to Sally when he saw her.

Wednesday he sat in class with Melissa and they talked about trivial matters. All he found out about her was that she was seventeen and came from a small Illinois town whose name he immediately forgot. He told her they would go on a hayride Saturday night. She smiled.

♦ ♦ ♦ ♦ ♦

He called for her at seven. When she came down she had on blue jeans with a white silk blouse and a red corduroy jacket.

"Hello," she said, smiling.

"Hi. How are you?"

"Fine. How are you?"

They walked to the church and she told him about her family and her school. At the church they waited in the basement for the trucks to come. The basement was crowded with young couples from the college.

Melissa took off her jacket while they waited. Erick noticed the contour of her breasts through the blouse. They were more graceful, more Grecian in outline than Sally's upright, swelling bust. But he tried not to think of Melissa that way. It was different, he told himself. The thought of holding her hand was a mountain of expectation. The expectancy of their first kiss was endlessly burning in him.

They went outside holding hands when the trucks came.

"Gawd," he said, "here I visualized mountains of hay on a wagon and all we have is a few moldy straws on a truck floor."

They sat down inside the truck, their backs leaning against the side boards. Dust rose from the thin layer of straw as people stumbled and trampled in and arranged themselves. Melissa didn't like the dust. She sneezed once, prettily, and made a displeased face. Erick felt angry with everyone for making the dust.

The truck filled up fast. The couples were laughing and some of them started singing. His leg pressed against Melissa's. There was a chain stretched across the top of the truck for the standees to hang onto.

"Walk it," Melissa said to him.

"Wite a minit," he said. "Wite till the veehickle is in motion."

She laughed and her green eyes glittered in the light of the street lamp and he loved her with all his heart.

They were all pressed and massed together. The motors started up and the trucks moved away from the church. The wind whistled overhead and swooped down to rub its cold fingers over them. Everyone huddled down together in the lurching truck. Street lights winked down on them and were gone in a flash. The trucks roared through the cold night into the country.

After a while, Erick took one of her hands and intertwined his fingers with hers. She said nothing. It felt good to have her warm hand against his. It was getting cold now. Everyone slid around the floor, changing positions and saying brrrr. There wasn't much chance to talk. The rushing wind and the roar of the motor was too loud. All Erick could do was caress her hand and hope that she understood what he felt.

She leaned back, and when he looked at her, she was looking at the stars. He took her other hand and moved close to her. Sometimes their heads rested against each other's, and her hair blew down over her face and some of the long dark strands whipped in fragile tautness against his cheek. Oh God, to kiss that black gossamer hair, he exulted, to feel that perfumed breath on my cheek!

He rested his head on her shoulder. She took back one of her hands, both, and brushed back her hair. Then she plunged them back into Erick's hands and they held each other tightly.

The ride seemed endless. He had on only a thin sweater and he was chilled before the trucks stopped and his feet were numb. At last, though, the trucks rolled into a dark glade and everyone got up and stretched. Erick felt the warmth suddenly as the wind stopped blowing on them. He jumped down from the truck and held up his arms for her. His hands tightened under her armpits as she swung down.

They all went into an open field. No one seemed to know where to go. People stopped and waited for instructions. Melissa hesitated in front of him. He put his arms around her and crossed them over her stomach. She leaned back against his chest and he felt how soft her stomach was under his hands. He looked down and saw the swell of her young breasts through the silk blouse. He saw her face, the shining eyes, the cryptic half-smile, the white, flawless skin. She put her hands over his.

Then, out in the field, three bonfires flared up, and the moved out there with the rest of the couples.

They stood in front of one yellow crackling blaze and thawed out. When it got too warm they moved away a little. He put his arms around her and she rested her cheek against his chest and looked into the fire. He hoped someone saw them there. He felt proud to stand there with her. For some reason he wished, more than anything else, that Lynn could be there, watching them. He had tried to talk Lynn into getting a date for the hay ride, too, but Lynn only looked vaguely disgusted and went back to his Gide.

Her warmth flowed into Erick. He looked up at the stygian sky, saw the stars clustered in the night, felt the heat toss back against his face and the cold wind at his back. He saw the fireflies of sparks born in the flames and dying in a second in the cold blackness. And, for a split second, he thought he had the complete meaning, the complete sensation of love and beauty.

It was a delight to forget the intellect and the philosophies and absolutes. It was wonderful to think only of love for a girl in his arms. He felt an awe at simple things; a sky above, a fire with young people around it singing their well-known songs, their faint voices rising up into the huge night. A girl and night and love—it was an end in itself. There need be nothing more. And if, as the last efforts of his deeper mind would insist, it was all a trick of nature, then it was a pleasant jest. One that defied deep-sought analysis, one that he was, happily, not immune to.

Only briefly he wondered why he had never felt like this with Sally.

Someone called out for everyone to come and eat. Erick and Melissa went over and stood in line. His hands rested on her stomach again, her hands over his. The line moved slowly. There was only the sound of feet shuffling on the ground, the wild crackle of the fires. He felt drawn into it all. And, suddenly, as her hands caressed his in mute tenderness, a surge of emotion went through him. He tightened his clasp and felt her fingers tighten in turn. She moved her head a little as he kissed her temple, then her cheek. Then he pulled her around tautly and pushed his mouth over hers, breaths hammering at his chest.

He straightened up dizzily. She was breathing heavily, too, but they didn't speak. All they did was hold hands tightly.

It seemed as if words were out of place in the darkness and the coldness, as if their's was some sort of primitive attraction predating words.

They stood before the fire again with frankfurter and coffee and doughnuts. And once she smiled at him, but that was all.

It seemed only moments before they were going back. He put his arms around her and her arms moved around his waist. They walked back through tall grass to the truck. They sat on the hard floor again and he put his arm around her and she moved closer. Someone offered them part of a blanket and they huddled together under the heavy folds.

His hand went under her jacket and he felt the warm flesh through the silk blouse. He pressed against her, bent over and kissed her throat. It was so completely different from being with Sally. Maybe, he half-guessed, the magic came from the silence, from the utter needlessness of words. It was almost as if they communicated by touch and looks and he, with his eyes, told her over and over that he loved her.

They walked from the church to her sorority house in dead silence except for a word here and there. At the door to her house there was too much light and too many couples lined up making love. He could only touch her hand before leaving. He asked her to go to the movies with him the next night. She said she had to study for a test Monday morning. He walked home muttering to himself. He loved her.

When he got home Lynn was still reading. He looked up.

"Hello, Lover," he said.

♦ ♦ ♦ ♦ ♦

Dear Sally, he wrote, *I guess you've been wondering why I haven't called you. I may as well tell you right away. It's that girl we met at your singing teacher's house. Melissa. I'm in love with her. I think it's kinder to tell you right away. I can't help it. But I have to see her as much as I can. I know you'll understand. You always have.*

When he dropped it in the mailbox he felt a jolt of prescience. He had an inclination to stand there until the mailman came and take it back. Why did he have to do it? He could have still seen Sally without telling her. Why didn't he always have a need to feel clarity in situation, a sense of one thing at a time? Why could he never combine, wait and see?

He wondered what Leo would say if she read the letter.

The afternoon of that day he accidentally mentioned it to Lynn. Lynn looked at him strangely, then shook his head and blew out a disgusted cloud of cigarette smoke.

"One down," he said, "one to go."

"What the hell does that mean?" Erick asked coldly.

"It means you're a fool," Lynn said.

seven.

Monday morning he sat next to Melissa. A girl friend wanted to sit by her to tell her something. When Melissa asked him to let her friend sit with her he said no, smiling. This made her surly instead of pleasing her. Then one of his jokes about small towns offended her. She wanted to know what was wrong with small towns; just because she didn't live in a big city didn't mean that...

He passed the day in a fog of agony. He couldn't study. He called her five times at her house before he got her. He tried to sound casual. He asked her to save him Saturday night. She told him that a friend's brother was visiting the college for the weekend and she had to go out with him.

He stuttered a few words and then hung up, and felt as if the walls were going to fall in on him. Rage built itself up. Oh God, you stupid bastard, he stormed at himself, what's the matter with you, anyway!

"Where are you going?" Lynn asked as Erick threw on a coat.

"I don't know!"

Erick heard him laughing as he slammed the door. Then he heard the door open quickly and Lynn called, "Wait, I'll go with you!" But Erick went out the front door quickly and had turned the corner before Lynn got out of the house.

He paced the streets, muttering to himself. "Damn, *damn*!" He couldn't think straight for dreaming of her. What kind of idiot was he? He had renounced romantic love, eschewed the ways of the mind, and then fell over dead with love at the first provocation. Ended up deep in the pit of it.

"Oh, Christ!"

He could see it all coming. Heartbreaks. Her busy when he wanted to see her, when he *had* to see her. Her with other men. God!—in love with someone else! Or the other way. His love returned. Arguments and sleepless nights. Reconciliation. Him getting distant as her love became a thing of assurance and became taken for granted. More arguments, her crying. More sleepless nights.

Oh, Jesus, what a stupid world it was!

♦ ♦ ♦ ♦ ♦

A week passed. He stayed in Saturday night reading while Lynn slept. Later they went to a midnight show which he didn't enjoy at all because he kept looking around for her all through it, dreading the possibility that he might see her laughing with another man. He saw Leo in the back row with a man and turned away quickly.

Melissa's friend was sitting next to her on Monday morning. He had to sit three rows behind her. He left the class without talking to her although it almost tore out his heart. He made up his mind never to see her again. That night he called her seven times.

He finally got her to accept an invitation to see a concert at the field house two weeks later. She told him she should really study that night and he wanted to scream—For Christ's sake, that's two weeks from now, what the hell are you, a clairvoyant?!

"I see," he said. "I know you'll enjoy the concert, though."

♦ ♦ ♦ ♦ ♦

Somehow the two weeks passed. By the night of the concert he was weak with tortured thoughts. He felt stolid, beaten.

He called for her at seven-thirty. She wore the same dress she wore the night he met her at Professor Walton's house. He told her he liked it. She said it was the only good dress she had in a tone that seemed to blame him for the situation.

He tried to think of something to say as they walked toward the field house. But everything he thought of he's said a dozen, a hundred times in his imagination. He had visualized so many conversations with her that there was nothing left. It was as if he had lived this moment already, and when it finally came, he was bored and surfeited with it. Only the throbbing of his heart showed him that he was still excited by her.

They got to the field house and took two seats in the stands. With trepidation he asked her if she'd mind moving two seats over so they could save two places for Lynn and his date. Melissa looked annoyed. She clutched her coat and edged along the row. He thought he was going to scream.

They put their coats on the two extra seats. They looked around. He dreaded the thought of seeing Sally. He hoped she wasn't there. He felt tight and ill at ease, afraid to speak. He went over every thought that occurred to him, turning it over reflectively in his mind to see if it could possibly offend Melissa if he spoke it.

Melissa took a small book from her handbag. It was a catalog from the University of Michigan.

"What's that for?" he asked.

"I'm going to transfer next semester," she said.

His heart jolted.

"W-why?" he asked, wondering if his voice could possibly be as thin as it sounded.

"They have more to offer," she said.

"Shucks," he said.

He looked over her shoulders and noticed her breasts moving as she breathed. He felt a weighted, sickening sensation of loss, as if in the next second she were going to disappear completely and he would never see her again. He felt almost an uncontrollable urge to stroke her arm, put his hands on her body, kiss her and tell her he loved her.

"No grass on the campus," he said, commenting on a picture in the catalog. "How can you to go to a place with no grass on the campus?"

"As if *that* was so important," she said disdainfully.

Melissa!

"Has it a good music school?" he said, trying to please her.

"A lot better than *this* one," she said.

"Oh."

From then on, no matter what he said, she took it the wrong way. He finally began to accept the fact that he just wasn't going to please her. He began to feel almost a masochistic pleasure in saying one thing after the other that made her grow sharper and sharper toward him, made her face more and more unpleasant.

He felt as if he had himself in a vise and she were slowly tightening it, crushing his organs. He felt as if someone poured him full with concrete and it was hardening, pushing him out of shape, pressing his intestines to pulp. He was physically ill. His mind, in futile machinations, kept trying to convince him that he didn't even like the girl, much less love her. That she was a stupid, spoiled child. But he couldn't do it. He loved her. Like a blindly adoring fool, he kept turning one helpless cheek to her after the other, withering under her words, jolting in agony as she struck. It was a flagellation of the mind.

By the time Lynn and his date, a girl named Virginia Greene, came, Erick was weak with misery. Lynn saw the agony on his face immediately and his mouth tightened. Erick saw his discriminating blue-grey eyes running over Melissa's face as he spoke to her, appraising her petulant expression, tearing down. Once Erick almost shoved his palm into Lynn's face and shoved him off the seat. His hand twitched in neural beginning of the act.

The concert started.

Erick tried to say something to her once in a while but she wanted to hear the music. During intermission, she said she wanted to read, then she poured over her catalog while he sat dumbly at her side, shivering every once in a while. He talked disjointedly to Virginia and Lynn, then saw, with added shock, that Melissa resented him talking to anyone else when he was with her. He almost felt like handing her a knife and yelling—Go ahead! Cut out my Goddamn heart and get it over with!

He kept noticing Lynn looking at Melissa. He remembered then telling Lynn that Melissa was beautiful. She didn't look beautiful that night. He was getting the first hint that of his life that beauty was a thing of more than features. Melissa looked old and sour and mean.

Throughout the rest of the concert he maintained a strict silence and tried to figure it out. He didn't even hear what the orchestra was playing. He banged his hands together when the thunder of applause started. He answered questions and heard nothing. The suffering had all chilled in him, tightening and contracting him.

He had loved her. Now, suddenly, he realized that he had hypnotized himself. It proved his old thesis: there was no such thing as romantic love. He would return to his books, Sally was lost. The pattern grew clear. He would throw aside everything but the mind.

When the concert ended Melissa hurried him out of the field house. He walked quickly beside her, feeling now an almost uncontrollable urge to slow down and let her steam on ahead, and see if she'd turn to see why he wasn't tagging along. She kept saying she had to get back and study. She said, "I hope you don't think I'm rushing you."

"Oh, *no*," he said.

At the door to her sorority house a moment of fear caught him. Then he realized he didn't care and the memory of the night's blows came to deaden his feeling about leaving her.

"Thanks a lot," she said, smiling nervously. "Better not stand here. The girls will talk."

"Goodnight," he said coldly, and walked away.

As he went back to the room, the fury mounted, finally exploding in his mind.

The great judge!—snarled his mind—*The superlative picker of womankind! See him in action!*

"I'm priceless," he muttered to himself. "Oh, I'm an invaluable gem!"

He shook as he walked. He felt like striking something. Back in the room he undressed and went to bed. When Lynn came in he turned his back on him.

"Is that you?" Lynn said lightly.

Erick said nothing.

"Lovely girl you have."

"I had."

"Oh," Lynn inquired, "hic jacet? Demise?"

Erick took a heavy breath and tossed on his stomach.

"How so?" Lynn asked. "Just today you were hurling hosannas at the sky."

"Oh, shut up."

He heard Lynn's irritating chuckle.

"You're a stupid bastard," he said.

"Goodnight, baby," Lynn said cheerfully.

♦ ♦ ♦ ♦ ♦

Another week. He studied five hours a day. He tried not to think of Sally. He spent some time trying to analyze his feeling for Melissa.

He decided that the girl had never really existed, everything was in his mind. The total design of her in his imagination. And, under honest appraisal, he realized that Sally represented to him all those things of possible and substantial comfort in life, while Melissa, only a token of the larger dream, stood for every mountainous delusion, every hunger for elusive beauty—the sort of beauty which was never found, because it existed only in the imagination of the searcher. And this was his malignant obsession, always—to embrace the hopeless.

At least this phase was over quickly. That was a satisfaction. Once he might have been mooning and cowsick, now he was filled with a fierce pleasure that it was over. It was progress of a sort. Now he could go back to his life work with a sigh of relief.

Except that he started to miss Sally.

One night he saw her in a café as he was having a hamburger. He got only a glimpse of her face but, to him, she looked unhappy. The next morning he sat down and wrote her another note.

Sally, it read, *I was wrong and I'm sorry.*

That night he waited for her to call. It never occurred to him to call her. He sat waiting until almost nine, then he went to a movie.

The next evening, when he came from the library, there was a scrawled note from the landlady. *Sally called*, it began.

He closed his eyes and could not stop the tear that ran from his eye. His throat closed tightly.

"Sally," he whispered.

♦ ♦ ♦ ♦ ♦

He called her later that evening. She was at the woman's gym, Leo told him. He was to meet her there at nine if he wanted to. He went over to the gym about a quarter to nine and waited down in the hall. After a while she came down in shorts and a tee shirt, her healthy figure bulging through.

"Well!" she said, with a roguish smile.

She told him to wait while she took a shower and got dressed. He sat in the hall, waiting. Finally she came and they left the gym and started walking toward Main Street. They were silent a while. He knew she was waiting for him to speak.

"Well, tell me all about it," she finally said.

He smiled awkwardly. "Nothing to tell."

"Now just *who* was it?"

"Girl we met at Walton's house."

"There were two of them there."

"You know darn well which one."

"Mmm-*hmmm*." Briskly. He almost drew back in anger. Then he let it slide, feeling in no position to take offense.

"So it's all over, haah?" she asked.

"All over."

"What happened?"

He wasn't sure whether she was actually curious or just needling him.

"Are you sure you want to know?" he asked.

"What happened?"

"I found out she was pregnant by the dean."

"I see."

They stopped off for coffee. As they sat there he felt an ineffable sense of comfort in being with her again, doing the old familiar things.

"I saw you that night in here," she said. "I was going to say hello but you left right away."

"I know."

"How's Lynn?"

"He's all right."

He saw the half-impish smile she was trying to hide. He didn't smile. He turned away suddenly, sorry that he had written to her a second time.

At the bus stop she asked him if he were taking her home.

"Of course," he said.

"Will wonders never cease?" she said.

"Have your revenge," he said quietly. "I'll take it."

"No revenge," she said.

They rode out in silence and half way there she hooked her arm in his. They walked to the house together.

Leo looked up from the couch as they came in. Her wrappered body was draped over the cushions, her head propped up by one hand as she studied.

"Look who's here," Sally said and, for the first time Erick could remember, her voice sounded strained.

"Well, well," Leo said, "the Prodigal Son."

Erick smile self-consciously. "Hi," he said.

"Take off your jacket, Erick," Sally said, moving toward the hall and her room. Erick took off his jacket and tossed it on a chair.

"How you feeling?" he asked, restive under Leo's frank stare.

"Oh, tumescent," she said.

She crossed her legs and the wrapper slid off her knee, revealing her legs. Erick swallowed, pretending not to notice. Leo didn't cover her legs.

"What're you reading?" he asked her.

"Sex book," she said. "It stinks."

"Oh? Well, that's a dull subject anyway, don't you think?"

She looked at him. "You really think so?" she said in a low, amused voice. Sally came in before he could get his mind to work defensively.

"Erick thinks sex is a dull subject," Leo said. "I told you you picked the wrong guy."

Sally's mouth drew into an irritated line and she didn't answer Leo. She smiled slightly at Erick.

"Come on down the cellar, Erick," she said. "I want to show you some kitchen furniture the people next door gave us. We're going to paint it."

"Okay." He followed her out of the room.

"Have a good time, kids," Leo said suggestively.

Sally flicked on the cellar light angrily. "Sometimes she makes me mad," she said.

The furniture was chipped and ugly.

"Isn't it nice?" Sally said.

"Uh…yeah."

They stood silently, the excuse given its proper allowance of time. Then Sally looked at him. Her lips started to tremble and she bit them to stop the trembling. Then, suddenly, she moved against him and slid her arms around his back. Her lips pushed against his.

After the kiss, she pulled back and he saw the color in her face. She forced a smile.

"It's nice to have you back," she said.

"I'm listening."

She pressed her cheek against his convulsively.

"It *is* nice," she said, almost frightened.

"I missed you," he said.

"You don't have to say anything pretty," she said.

"I did though. Why do you think I wrote to you?"

"I don't know."

"I'm sorry it happened," he said.

"It's all right."

She raised her lips again and he held her close.

"Still no words of love?" she asked.

"You wouldn't want me to lie," he said.

She sighed. "I suppose not."

She pressed close to him, then after a moment, she asked, "You told her you loved her?"

"No, thank God."

"You *thought* you loved her."

"Which is better? That I thought I loved her or that I *know* I'm very fond of you?"

She tensed and writhed a little in his arms.

"I don't know," she said, with a break in her voice. "I think I'd rather you thought you loved me and told me so. Even if it was only for a little while."

"I do love you, Sally, but it's different."

He felt secure again, having regained his detachment.

She sobbed and pressed against him tightly, her nails digging into his back until they hurt him.

"Different," she said, beginning to cry. "Always *different*. It isn't fair!"

eight.

One day an acquaintance gave him a ticket for a formal holiday dance. In three years of school he'd never gone to a formal. He thought it might be nice and he told himself it was the least he could do for Sally.

She was surprised when he called and asked her.

"A formal!" she said. "A real, honest-to-God formal! With *you*?"

"Don't drop your teeth, kid."

"I'm so surprised."

"I know you're ashamed of me in public," he said, "but it'll be pretty dark in there, and if anybody comes along that you know I can stick my head under my coat."

"I don't know what to say. Gosh darn."

"That's pretty effective. Well?"

"It would be fun, Erick."

"Sure?"

"Of course. I'd like to go."

They made arrangements.

♦ ♦ ♦ ♦ ♦

He was getting assembled in white shirt, bow tie and his dark suit. They called the dances formal but that was for the benefit of the girls. Most men, the bulk of them veterans, didn't own a tuxedo or care much whether they did or not.

"You look pretty good," Lynn said.

"Gad, praise from those pinched lips," Erick said.

Lynn was sitting at his desk, a thick volume of psychiatry in his lap.

"Did you get a corsage?" he asked.

"Yes."

"What kind?"

"Roses."

"The cheapest."

"Gardenias are cheaper."

"How come you missed that?" Lynn asked.

"Drop dead."

Lynn smiled. Sometimes he didn't understand Lynn.

"Why didn't you take Virginia to this thing?" he said.

"I wouldn't care to waste an entire evening with her."

"You'd rather get myopic on that book."

"Quite correct," Lynn said. "I have too little time to read during the school week. Besides, I have to go over some manuscripts for the magazine."

"When are you going to take another of mine?"

"When you stop gadding about with that tit-heavy dancer and write something decent."

"Oh...screw off."

Lynn shrugged. "You asked me," he said.

The night was cold and crisp. The earth and the air seemed tight from the cold, as if they were holding themselves rigidly, waiting for Spring.

Riding out to Sally's house, Erick got into a spell which had been recurring periodically since December started. It was hard to decipher. Generally, though, it was a sense of culmination, the realization that graduation was close at hand and that a rich segment of his life was about to end.

He reviewed the months, the years past. For some reason it seemed that only the moments of happiness stood out. Whether that was from actual predominance or mental design he didn't know. But every once in a while, during these moods, he would get an agonizing desire to turn back the clock. The future seemed cold and threatening, barren of promise. In a few months the trees would burst into renewed life, grass would reach its green fingers through the earth. And he would be gone, severing in a moment all the fabulously intricate webs of relationship the years had woven. With the sharp upward sweep of graduation he would cut himself apart and return to a stale, unwanted life. He would be back home. He couldn't stay with his sister regularly. He'd have to get a room, a job. And he'd never see Sally again. At the moment that was the least of his worries.

What was more important was his desire to move back, to recapture old pleasures, to retain indefinitely those days when he was young and could always turn for help to someone else. When life held only promise of good things, when there were no battles to be fought.

♦ ♦ ♦ ♦ ♦

She was wearing a form-fitting red gown held up by thin straps. A remnant of remaining tan gave her smooth shoulders and upper breasts a healthy color. Her thick brown hair was gathered back with a gold clasp. Under it, the flow of tresses cascaded over the back of her white neck. Her face was bright with color; red lips, pink cheeks, softly tinted brown eyes, the red roses nestling in her dark hair.

She pressed her cheek against his.

"You smell pretty," he told her.

"Thank you. Thank you for the roses."

"They match your dress."

"Yes. Isn't that nice?"

She stepped back and looked at him. She straightened his bow tie.

"Mmmm-hmm," she said. They looked at each other and smiled.

"Shall I call a cab?" he asked.

"If you like."

He knew he couldn't ask her to go to a formal in a bus. He went into the hall and dialed. She passed him and went to her room for her coat. He could smell the trailing essence of her perfume as she passed him in the darkness.

When she came into the living room he was standing by the window. Something cold gripped him as he turned and looked at her. He wondered for a moment if there were ghosts of moments the way there were ghosts of people.

The room seemed to shrink. She stood in front of him and he felt nervous and restless. No words seemed to fit the moment.

"What have you been doing?" she asked.

"Oh, nothing." *Wishing time would stand still.*

"Nothing?"

"School. Studying."

"What's the matter, Erick?"

"I don't know. Just thinking, I guess...about how fast time goes."

"It does, doesn't it?"

"Yes."

"It always does," she said.

"I suppose."

"But this life is artificial, anyway," she said.

"What do you mean?"

"College life," she said. "It's contrived."

"Yes. I suppose it is. I like it, though. It's...free."

She smiled slightly and he saw pain there. "Free," she said. "That's your world."

The honk of the cab's horn split their reverie. He helped her on with her coat and put on his own. Then they went out and got in the cab. He gave the driver the address. On the way he hardly spoke.

"I'll probably fracture your toes," he said once.

"I hope not," she said.

"Leo going?"

"No, she's out of town for the weekend."

"Oh."

He yearned to confide in Sally, tell her exactly what he felt. How lost and afraid he was becoming as all the old things fell away. But the thought of telling her didn't appeal to him. Something had left their relationship. The Spring before, even the early fall before he'd met Melissa, he could have spoken to her. He could have put his head in her warm lap and told her everything without holding back, pouring out the words from his heart because he knew she would understand and comfort him. But the closeness had faded. He tried not to pretend anymore that he wasn't the one who had destroyed it.

It was about nine-thirty as they walked up the sidewalk to the gym.

"Ever been to a dance here?" he asked.

"A few times," she said.

They went in. Erick handed his ticket to one of the men standing at the door. The sound of the band entered their ears, mixed with the swish of dancing feet like far-off breakers.

"Shall we check our coats?" he asked.

"We'd better," she said.

"Okay."

They went down the side hall into the field house. Sally said hello to a young man crouching behind a counter made of a wooden plank balanced on two barrels. The young man was jamming Coke bottles into a dishpan of cracked ice.

"Hi, Sally," he said. "How's my favorite dancer tonight?"

"Fine," she said.

Erick helped her off with her coat at the checking table. The men looked her over and whistled.

"Look who's here," said one of them.

"Danged if it ain't that shapely fizz-ed teacher."

"Oh, you kid."

"Twenty-three skidoo."

"Wow wow!"

"Don't tell me they finally put you boys to work?" Sally said.

"You know us," said one of them.

"That's why I asked," Sally said.

They made noises of mock protest. Erick dropped the coats irritably on the table, and one of the men looked at him briefly, then scraped two checks across the counter. Then he beamed at Sally again.

"Look at that gown! Man, is she showing us a thing or two."

Whistles in unison. Sally laughing. Erick glowering, endless nasty remarks filling his head.

"What are you doing here?" one of the men asked her.

What the hell do you think she came here for, idiot!— Erick's mind snapped—*to play basketball?* He stood there, invisible.

Then he stepped away from the counter, turning his back on her. He felt like walking out of there and going home. He was sorry he'd come, sorry he'd asked her. All the longing and quiet reverie had been washed away. He wanted to be alone, to get away from it all.

Finally her hand on his arm.

"I'm sorry, Erick, one of the boys was telling me about his new baby."

"Legitimate?"

She looked at him and one side of her mouth twitched in the beginning of a smile. They walked down the hall wordlessly. Another member of the football team said hello to her as they passed him. They entered the gym.

It was dimly lit, looking deceptively large. Long curled streamers of red and green were stretched from the beams to the walls and fluttered brightly in the smoky yellow light from the overhead fixtures. Glowing paper discs of every color hung down from the streamers and a giant cotton snowball was suspended from the center of the ceiling. Colored balloons undulated gently around it.

On the left side as they entered the band platform was set up. The members in grey slacks and red corduroy jackets sat slumped in their chairs between sets. Their faces glowed whitely, specter-like, from the standlights. The band leader was leaning over speaking to a girl vocalist who sat, white arms crossed over her breasts.

Around the edge of the sawdust-sprinkled floor almost a hundred couples sat on folding chairs, stood arms-folded or leaned against the yellow firebrick walls. The broken chatter of their conversation filled the air. Smoke ghosts swirled up lazily over their heads.

"Pretty," said Sally.

"Yeah."

She took his hand and they walked over to a large decorated Christmas tree standing between the doors. A sprinkle of colored lights shimmered in the dark branches. The air around it was heavy with the pungent odor of pine.

"Isn't it pretty?" she said.

"Mmmm."

"I love Christmas."

"I used to."

"You mean you don't anymore?"

He sighed. "It's like everything else. You get out of the habit."

"Get *in* the habit."

"I can't very well in my room."

She looked at him in surprise. "You mean you're not going home?"

He shook his head.

"Oh, Erick!" she said, her face filled with sympathy. "How come?"

He said nothing as they walked under the shadow of the track.

"Why, Erick?"

"Oh, mostly finances. But there's nothing to go home to anyway."

"Oh."

"I could dig up the money, I suppose. But I don't want to go."

She squeezed his hand and smiled tenderly. "I'm so sorry," she said.

"Don't be," he said. "I have no one. My parents are dead. My sister and I don't get along."

"Poor Erick."

"Oh, what's the difference?" he said bitterly. "I'll be home for good in June anyway."

She was quiet and he looked at her. The band lights reflected in her eyes and her face was blank.

"For good," she said, and her eyes seemed haunted.

Then she threw off the feeling and looked around the dance floor.

"A lot of people," she said.

He leaned over and kissed her cheek.

"What's that for?" she asked.

"For being nice," he said. "For being sorry about my having no Christmas."

"I *am* sorry," she said. "I think Christmas is beautiful. But not alone."

He put his arm around her and they stood, watching the people. He smelled the quaint combination of odors in the air. Sweat and perfume, roses and old socks. He smiled at it.

Then the saxophones began to moan suddenly as if with an attack of stomach trouble. The beat of the moment died in their groaning. Drums introduced an orderly beat and all complexity departed in a methodical fox trot rhythm.

Erick turned and extended his arms and they moved out onto the floor. Couples slipped out of the shadows and the broad floor was soon filled with them. The music gasped brassily over their heads as their feet glided over the smooth saw-dusted floor.

Erick closes his eyes as they danced. He felt the hypnosis of swaying in darkness. He pulled her closer and their cheeks pressed together. He wondered why he didn't bump into anyone. Usually they crashed periodically into other couples. Usually he made girls gasp as he dug heels across theirs. That night he seemed to weave in and out among the dancers like a radar-driven bat in a black cavern.

"Are you leading me?" he asked once.

"No," she said, but he was half convinced that she was.

When a rumba started he said that was where he got off.

"Can't you rumba?"

"After these years, you ask that?"

"I don't remember ever trying with you."

"Well, I can't."

"Try"

"All right, but God help your tootsies."

They started. He kept glancing at his feet.

"Don't look so grim," she said.

"I can't help it," he said, stumbling. He stopped, started again, losing the rhythm.

"Relax," she said.

"I can't."

"Sure you…oh!"

"Sorry," he said. "Better quit while you can walk."

She shrugged slightly as they left the floor and stood by the wall. A tall boy in a tuxedo gangled over.

"Have this dance, Sally?" he asked.

"No, thank you."

He looked startled. "Huh? Oh. Oh! H-how you been?"

"Fine, thank you," she said.

He goggled, he smiled. He glared at Erick momentarily, then he turned on his heel and strode away rapidly.

"What's this," Erick asked, "refusing?"

"I don't like him," she said.

"I thought you liked everybody."

She looked down at the floor without answering. He looked her over, wondering how many men she knew at the school. It must have been a lot. And *he* was the one. Or had been, at least.

He put his arm around her. "That's some dress," he said.

"Gown. It cost too much to be a dress."

"Gown."

He looked around, back at her.

"Like a Coke?"

"No, thank you."

The next set began and they started to dance. He liked dancing with her, he realized for the first time. She was the best dancer he'd ever known. He couldn't even feel her motion, it seemed to parallel his exactly. No matter what he did, how his motion or timing altered, she followed without a struggle.

"I like the way you dance," he said.

"That's good."

He pulled her closer and their cheeks rested together again. He kissed her cheek, letting his mind go as blank as it could. Their outstretched hands came down and rested on his left shoulder. He closed his eyes again.

He sighed and rubbed his cheek against hers as they danced. Her left hand tightened on his shoulder, her throat contracted and he heard a slight gasp pass her lips. Her breath was warm on his cheek. She made a slight grumbling noise.

"What's the matter?" he asked.

"Oh…"

"Oh, what?"

"I'm…"

"You're what?" He kissed her hair.

"I'm mad at you and…"

"Mad? Why?"

She pressed against him pugnaciously. "Because you're not nice. Because you're…oh, I don't know."

"Oh."

"Every time I want to be cool you do thisssss," she said, the last word extending into a hiss as he kissed her earlobe.

He locked his arm tightly around her. They danced slower and slower, circling in small motions. Finally they stopped completely. He bent over and their warm lips touched. He felt as though he were floating in dark space with rustling winds about them and far-off music playing. *Deep in the dark center of life…*

She looked at him through half-closed eyes.

"*Oh*," she sighed, "here we go again."

♦ ♦ ♦ ♦ ♦

When he took her home, she fried some eggs for him. He liked sitting there at the kitchen table watching her, noting the oddly pleasing contrast made by the homey little apron and the sophisticated gown.

They sat at the kitchen table smiling at each other. He seemed to sense a new warmth coming into their relationship. So much was past. Separations, arguments, everything. They had weathered all of them and were still together, smiling at each other.

But time was passing. He felt that, too, felt a chill in realizing that he would be leaving soon. He had to make up his mind. Yet there was still no consuming fire of love as there had been with Melissa. He wondered why. Sally was just as beautiful, her dark brown hair framing her well-shaped face, her kind shining features, soft with affection. Did love have to burn? Couldn't it just warm?

He reached over and took her hand.

"I like to be with you," he said.

"What, hon?"

"I said I like to be with you."

She smiled and her eyes glistened a little. She shook her head slowly.

"Erick," she whispered, "oh, Erick."

And then sighed with gentle despair as a patient mother might sigh over her impossible son.

♦ ♦ ♦ ♦ ♦

School was out. Like an uptilted saucer, the town drained itself rapidly of the student body. Erick could almost sense the exit of them as he lay on his bed in the room, looking at the ceiling. Lynn was sitting on the other bed in his underwear.

"Why don't you go home?" Erick said. "You've got money."

"Why should I?" Lynn said. "I have less than you have to go home to. At least your parents are dead. Mine is a disgustingly healthy, jowly and repugnant salesman. My mother is a driveling clubwoman. My only hope in life is that my father was the iceman who, as I recall, had some philosophy."

Erick grinned. "Filial affection."

"Yeah," Lynn said, "to quote you."

"Well, you and I will probably be the only ones left in the whole town," Erick said.

"Ho chummy," Lynn said. "Sally gone yet?"

"I'm going over tonight to say goodbye. She leaves in the morning."

Lynn looked over at the package on Erick's desk.

"What did you get her?" he asked.

"A record album."

"Not an engagement ring?"

Erick turned and looked at him, but Lynn's face was unrewarding.

"You nuts?" he asked.

"Thumb me a woman," Lynn said.

♦ ♦ ♦ ♦ ♦

"Hello honey!" she said, throwing her arms around his neck.

He kissed her. "How are you?" he asked.

"Wonderful!"

They sat on the couch and he put his arms around her. She snuggled close.

"This is for you," he said, taking the package off the table and putting it in her lap.

"Oh, thank you, darling," she said. "I didn't want you to get me anything."

He wondered where his present was, then it occurred to him that maybe there wasn't any. So what? But he did feel a little resentful.

She looked at the record album.

"I love that!" she said happily, and kissed him.

"When do you leave," he asked.

She seemed to hesitate a moment, then she said, "In the morning."

"Leo gone yet?"

She nodded. They sat in silence, she leaning against him. He could feel her breath on his neck, fell the warmth of her body through his shirt. It was toasty warm in the house. He felt drowsy as the radiators thumped gently and, a thousand miles away, a bus churned down the icy stretch of Main Street.

They sat there for about an hour, talking a little, mostly making casual love and watching the room get dark. It seemed as if the day was a stage production and the curtain was slowly drawing shut. They were in the audience, sitting in near blackness now that the performance was over, sitting close together in warmth and darkness.

He ran his hand slowly over her arm.

"How are you going home?" he asked.

"I don't know." He heard her throat contract. "I…train, I guess."

"Mmm hmm. How long does it take?"

"Oh. Eight hours, nine hours. I don't know."

"All packed?"

"Erick, I…*packed*?

"Yes," he said. "Are you?"

"Yes. I mean no."

"Which is it?"

She pressed against him and drew in a ragged breath. Her arms slid around him and clamped around his chest.

"Oh," she murmured.

"Oh?" he asked.

She seemed to shake her head a trifle as though she were baffled. The movement of her body against him was a breathless movement in the night.

"Oh," she said again, more plaintively.

"What is it, Sal?"

She sat up and pulled away a little to look at him.

"Erick," she said.

He felt his heart begin to beat rapidly. Suddenly. He felt his hands tremble in his lap. The way she said his name.

"What?" he said.

She drew in another breath.

"I…"

She turned away and he heard her heavy breathing. He seemed to know what she wanted to say but he couldn't help. He was powerless.

It seemed endless, sitting there in the dark room and waiting.

But suddenly, she got on her knees on the couch and moved close to him. She put her hands on each side of his face and kissed him with moist, hot lips. Her teeth were clenched. He could tell by the way she said,

"*Come live with me*," leaning forward and breathing in his ear, "*and be my love*."

He sat there with her body pressing against him. He felt as if he were frozen fast to the couch. Only his heart still moved, moved fiercely.

Terrible silence. He shivered.

"Darling?" she asked.

He tried to speak but failed. He took a deep breath and swallowed.

"What?" he said.

"I'm sorry."

He found himself starting to laugh, then broke it off in sudden shock.

"Why?" he asked, in a thin, wavering voice.

"I…I'm just…sorry, that's all."

The penitence in her voice made him feel strong for a moment. He put his arms around her impulsively.

"Don't be," he said.

Then he twitched as she pushed close. *Now you've done it!*—his mind cried.

Her arms clamped around him, tightly and suddenly, as if trapping him. Her lips were hot and moving in the darkness. Her wet tongue licked over his lips and cheeks and ears. He was struck dumb, he felt his stomach throbbing excitedly and felt heat gushing through his body. He moaned, only half with physical arousing. But she didn't know, she kept on.

His hands moved out automatically and dug into her large breasts, half to push her away. She dragged up her sweater and he felt the smoothness of her brassiere under his fingers. *No!*—his mind shouted. "Oh," he altered it aloud.

Her flesh was burning hot, he felt almost with horror. Automatically he started to unhook her brassiere.

"Let me!" she gasped, and she pulled it open in a quick ruthless movement and jerked it off. Her large, swelling breasts were in his hands. Her lips were torrid under his, her hands kept moving over him. He felt like a driven thing. *No!*—screamed his mind, *baby, baby!*

Futile.

He was shivering, writhing. He wanted to scream out in the blackness. He wanted to leap up and run away into the night. It was much worse than the other time. There had been *some* control in them that time. Now there was nothing but wildness and helpless excitement, trapping him.

God help me!—the words exploded ridiculously in his mind, and then he knew he had to do it because it was a test. It was a trial.

And he was suddenly in the barracks again and listening to men tell about how they'd done it in cars and taxis and rooms and on the ground and against trees and in alleys. And suddenly, completely, without conscious effort, the whole thing seemed to balloon up as something impossibly dirty and vile. He caught his breath and heard her panting and thought she sounded like an animal. He felt her breasts like swollen flesh under his hands and he wanted to push her away with a disgusted snarl, but his body kept dragging him on, the heat welling up like fire, enveloping him despite the mental struggle. *Sex, sex!*—cried his mind—*dirty thing!*

"Erick. Baby. *Baby*."

The tenderness was gone, the love was gone, stripped away. She was only a hot-breathed hungry animal. He pulled back.

"I'll take them off!" she gasped.

No! God, no!—yelled his mind.

"Sally," he muttered, as if trying to appeal. She was against him again like a dead weight that kept returning. He tried to drain every last vestige of desire.

"Oh, *Erick*." Like the groan of a feeble old woman, repelling him.

I have to go to the bathroom, he thought. He almost said it.

"Sal," he started.

She was pulling up her skirt.

"Sal, *wait* a minute, will you?" he said, almost hysterically. He jerked forward and struggled to his feet. He felt the coffee table against his shin and, flailing out for balance, he toppled forward, reaching for support. He crashed across the table and his outstretched hands struck the floor. Pain shot up his arms. He cried out involuntarily and his arms gave way. His face struck the floor then and he felt pain drive a sharp wedge into his brain.

He screamed out and slumped down in a heap, rolling over in agony and pressing shaking hands to his face.

"Honey!" she cried.

He lay there sobbing and groaning and whimpering with pain. The light blinded him for a moment and he winced. Then he saw her leaning over him, her large breasts hanging down from her body, the dark erect nipples pointing at him. He felt blood gushing from his nose, running over his lips and chin and onto his shirt. She gaped at him in horror and he cried out through a square of mouth.

"Get out of here! Leave me alone! Get out of here!"

Cold water. Compresses. Lying down. Sally in her bathrobe, silent and sober-faced, tending him. Blood stopping, bandaging the scrape on his forehead, the abrasions on his hands. The darkness again, the sound of her door being locked, the sound of her feet moving in her room. Silence. Sleeping. And, in the morning, him awakening on the couch in an empty house. On the dining room table a key to the front door, a gift and a note.

Merry Christmas, read the note, *take care of your nose*.

nine.

Lynn looked up at the ceiling, his lips turned in.

"Are you telling me you never laid the girl?" he said.

Erick didn't look at him. "That's right," he said.

"You mean you haven't had the chance?"

Erick swallowed, shook his head.

"What?" Lynn said.

"No," he answered.

Lynn sniffed, then took a long drink from the bottle of wine. He passed it over.

"Here, get drunk," he said. "You can use it. Never got a chance, huh?"

Erick drank a big mouthful of the red wine. He blinked as it ran down his throat like a thin line of flame. It settled in his chest, his stomach, like a pool of heat. He felt the warmth spreading through his body.

"I want to," he said. "I should."

"Get drunk?" Lynn asked.

"Get Sally," said Erick bitterly, almost succeeding in sounding like a virile man driven to the end of patience.

Lynn blew out a heavy breath.

"So do I?" he said.

A cloud of attractive dizziness built itself up around Erick as he kept drinking. They lay like four extremitied growths on the two beds. The bottle was almost empty. It was the third.

"You're gonna get it," Lynn said thickly. "I'll see to it."

"Get what, rabies?"

"Babies. You're gonna fill Sally with a brat."

"By God, I'd like to. By God. Never get the chance. Damn thing. Anyway."

"You'll get it. Seduce her. I'll teach you."

"Yeah. Seduce her." Erick's fingers clutched the pillow vengefully.

Lynn rolled on his side and wrapped one arm under his head to pillow it as he looked at Erick.

"I'll tell you what to do," he said. "I'll give you everything to do. You do it." His eyes were staring and thick, he breathed heavily. He had on a bathrobe.

"Sure," Erick said. "You tell me."

"I'm gonna give you a blow by blow how to do it," Lynn said, "kiss to orgasm." He took off his glasses and put them under the bed.

"Yeah?" Erick lay there staring straight up, twisting a little with the rising heat in him.

Lynn stood up and plopped down on Erick's bed.

"First you gotta kiss her," Lynn said.

He smiled and hiccupped but Erick got the sudden chilling sensation that Lynn wasn't drunk. He turned on his side away from Lynn.

"I have kissed her," he said.

"Well, I'll show you how?"

"What?"

His heart was pounding again, pounding, to his confused alarm, with excitement. He sent out a million hooks for support in his mind but his mind gave back unreflective deadness.

He felt Lynn's hand on his back and he twitched under it.

"Get outta there," he said, drunk enough to be convincingly surly.

"Gotta show you, don't I?" Lynn slurred.

He isn't drunk, Erick thought, *he's acting*. Every thickened syllable is deliberately executed, every hiccup a performance, every body weave a pretense.

"Let's go to the movies," he said.

"All closed on New Year's Eve," Lynn said.

"You're drunk. I'll *kick* 'em open!"

"I gotta teach you."

Erick turned. "You will, eh?" he said, trying to ligh the moment. He grabbed Lynn's arms and shoved, hearii himself giggle foolishly. It turned to laughter as they wei suddenly wrestling.

"The landlady will object," he gasped.

"Fuck her," Lynn gasped back.

"Think we have time?" he gasped back, surprised at how strong Lynn was in his hands and arms. But he was stronger. He clamped his hands on Lynn's forearms. Lynn's hands kept grabbing for Erick's legs and once they seemed to rub accidentally over Erick's stomach and groin. It made Erick lurch spasmodically.

"I said get outta there!"

"Gotta teach you, don't I?"

"Go on back to your…"

Lynn sat on Erick's chest.

"Get off!"

"Gotta teach you, don't I, gotta teach you, don't I?"

It seemed to come from nowhere. He didn't know why. Maybe it was the feeling of being pinned down, of being trapped. But suddenly he shoved Lynn completely off him with a snarl and then he grabbed Lynn by the hair and drove his fist hard into Lynn's face. Lynn collapsed back on the floor without a sound.

Erick sat up, his heart jolting his body, his hands shaking. He looked down at Lynn and felt himself straining to jump on him and pummel him endlessly with his fists.

Then the feeling slid down and away. He sat there breathing heavily and staring dizzily at Lynn's body.

"Lynn?" he said.

No sound.

"Hey, Lynn."

Lynn didn't answer. Lynn was unconscious.

♦ ♦ ♦ ♦ ♦

It was almost his twenty-third birthday. Lynn and he sat in a darkened booth at the Golden Campus.

"I said I'd plan it for you," Lynn said. "I mean it."

He was deadly serious and Erick sensed that he wasn't doing it as an act of friendship but as an act of revenge.

"Since when are you a great lover?" he asked.

"I've been around." Lynn lit a cigarette and blew out the smoke. "I'll blueprint this thing for you."

"What if she's not willing?"

"Listen," Lynn said, "no girl says no indefinitely. A girl's objections to laying are like a wall you come up against. When you reach it, climb over it. If you can't, drill a hole through it. If you can't, burrow under it. If you can't, go around it. If you can't, prove to her that there never was a wall there in the first place."

"How profound," Erick said.

"Listen," Lynn said, almost grimly. "This thing is going to come off. Otherwise you'll go to pot dreaming about it. You need this to show you how stupid you're being."

Lynn had never forgiven him for that night, Erick was sure of it. For weeks after Lynn wouldn't talk to him. Then one day, when Erick apologized for about the tenth time, Lynn smiled and said, "Okay, baby, we'll forget about it." But he hadn't, Erick was sure he hadn't. He could feel it.

"Why don't you major domo?" Erick said. "Lead us around, make us drinks, change records, throw back the sheets, dispose of unwanted garments and lead us into the bedroom?"

"Do you want this or not?"

Lynn's cold eyes surveyed him. No, I don't want it—Erick wanted to say. No, it's none of your damn business, he wanted to say. But he couldn't say it to Lynn. He covered his throat contraction behind the cup of coffee. He put down the cup and said, as casually as he could, "Certainly I want it."

Lynn looked at him carefully. "All right then," he said. "Then listen to me and shut up."

It was strange listening to him. It was a though Lynn were the instructor and Erick the student. Erick couldn't understand where Lynn had found out these things of it he was making them up as he went along. But he listened, feeling again that sense of rising despair, of growing entanglement, with every nod of his head, with every point admittedly assimilated, sinking deeper and deeper into the necessity of going through with it. He felt as though, after a while, he could do nothing but go through with it. It was like a dream.

That night, the next day, the next, he couldn't believe it was all actual. It was a joke, it had to be. But Friday came and suddenly he began to feel the growing tension, the sense of duty, the feeling of *now or never*. He remembered over and over that night on the back lawn. He remembered the night before she'd left for Christmas vacation and he kicked himself mentally. Fool! Those times it would have been simple, it would have been right. Now it would be complex and wrong and cruel.

He began to make hasty plans of his own. He bought a record album for her, telling himself it that it was a belated birthday present for her. But he knew that the album was a symbolic two dollars.

There would have to be liquor. Lynn had said it himself, and Erick knew it was essential. The edges had to cloud up before he could relax and concentrate on love-making. If only he'd been half-drunk those other times there would have been no trouble. He had to fill his mind with dulling opiate and dispel the probing so that he could say and do things that, sober, he could only whisper to himself late at night when he lay awake in his bed.

Throughout those hours he thought out a grand pageant of scenes, long montages, the ends of chapters in romantic novels carried out in full detail. *The rustle of silk in the darkness and, then, heady madness*. He gave them dialogue, he gave them action and thoughts. Every scene ended alike. After a while it all began to assume an air of monotony like the times he'd worked out beforehand everything Melissa would do and say. It made this moment, too, seem stale, as if it were already a part of the past.

Saturday morning after class Lynn and he sat in the Black and Gold Inn, drinking coffee.

"Do you remember what I said?" Lynn asked.

Erick's stomach sank. He felt as if he were boning up for some quiz he couldn't possibly pass because he'd been sleeping in class the whole term.

"I think so," he said weakly.

"You're taking her to the opera?"

"Yeah."

"All right. Take her right home after. You're fortunate she has a house of her own."

The way Lynn spoke made it sound as if Sally were value, a mute, immobile factor in the plan. She was to sit here, recline there, accept there while the plan was affecting itself. That was the fallacy of it, Erick thought, the fallacy of all plans which did not take into consideration the human factor.

"Yeah," he said, "Say, guess who I saw today at..."

"You'll have a fifth," Lynn said. "That should do it. Don't let her keep going into the kitchen to make drinks. Have a bowl of cracked ice on the table in front of you so you don't have to move."

His face was mirthless, he was reciting some unpleasant knowledges.

"How about we roll in the refrigerator?" Erick said, conscious of his desire to ease the air.

Lynn sagged back in the booth, clasping his lean hands on the edge of the table and closing his eyes. Erick noticed the way the right corner of Lynn's mouth kept twitching as he spoke. He paid no attention to what Lynn said.

"Keep drinking until things are a little foggy," Lynn said. "But don't drink so much you get sick or lose control of yourself." His mouth tightened. "Don't pass out," he said.

"Don't pass out," Erick muttered.

"There's a couch in her living room, isn't there?"

"What?" By the silence he knew Lynn had asked a question.

"Is there a couch in her living room?" Lynn enunciated slowly.

"Yeah."

"Start making love to her. Arouse her. Don't hurry it. Get the girl good and hot."

His teeth were clenched as though he were actually saying—Whip the girl until she bleeds.

"Kiss her throat," Lynn said, "her cheeks, her ear lobes, concentrate on her ear lobes."

He opened his eyes. "Understand?" he said.

"Yes, teacher."

Lynn looked at him a moment and then said, "Good."

"Say, you know who I..." Erick started again to change the subject, but Lynn went on talking.

Erick felt rising unrest as Lynn spoke. It was dark and unfriendly there and he was planning to hurt a girl he knew he should only love. Lynn's voice droned on, the words were lost. Erick sat there feeling like a callous monster. The affair tasted of leftovers.

Lynn had her stripped to the waist. Relentlessly, he was putting her through a series of mathematical equations. Erick got the feeling that Lynn was trying hard to disgust him before it even started. He was succeeding.

"You whisper—let's go to your room," Lynn said. "She won't refuse."

"What if she refuses?"

Lynn's mouth curled. "Believe me, she won't refuse," he said. "She'll drag you there."

"Oh," Erick said.

He felt the onslaught of one of those increasing moods of hating Lynn. More and more he found himself looking at Lynn and saying to himself—*God, God, what in hell do I see in him? He's vicious and small.* During those times he looked back with relish at the night he knocked Lynn unconscious with one solid blow.

He remembered the next day, the way Lynn kept shaking his head and saying—*You're psychotic, that's what you are. You dumb bastard, you're a paranoid and you'll kill somebody some day, I swear to God you'll kill somebody.* It made him smile to himself.

"...in on the bed," Lynn was still talking. "You keep making love to her as you take off the rest of her clothes."

Words went on, an endless stream of them. Erick lost the continuity. He was back on the night before Christmas vacation, in the darkness and the heat while Sally's body moved under his hands. Why, *why*? It would have been so right then, so free and joyous.

The memory made him twist his head suddenly and close his eyes as if to shut it all away.

"What's the matter?" Lynn asked.

Erick could hear the expectancy in Lynn's voice. *You'd like me to say I'm disgusted, wouldn't you!*—his mind shouted—*You'd like me to say all right, you win, I can't go through with it, I hate the very idea. Wouldn't you!*

"Nothing," he said. "I have a headache. Is that all?"

"You got what I said about premature discharge, didn't you?" Lynn asked casually. "Think about something unemotional until you're ready."

"I'll think about whales," Erick said.

"Good," Lynn said, the suspicion of a smile on his lips. "Think about black whales floating near icebergs."

A laugh fluttered in Erick's throat. He cut it off.

"Why don't you give a course at the University?" he suggested. "Elementary Seduction; Monday, Wednesday and Friday at 10:30 a.m."

"I can't," Lynn said. "I have a philosophy course then."

Erick drained the coffee cup.

"Well, that's it then," he said, trying to forget everything Lynn had said.

"That's it," Lynn said.

No more, no justification for all the planning. No words of—never mind this part, it will all be right when your body explodes and she's in your arms crying and soft and you both love each other. He guessed Lynn never even thought about that part. He guessed that Lynn didn't know about that part.

They walked through the cold streets toward home.

"It sounds like a steely-eyed strategy for rape," Erick said.

Lynn said, "Rape entails resistance."

♦ ♦ ♦ ♦ ♦

When he called for her she was wearing a dark skirt and a tight red blouse that left most of her shoulders and part of her upper chest bare.

"Hello," she said.

"Hi," he said, holding out the record album. "This is for your birthday, which I, unforgivably, forgot." He held out the bag. "This is for us."

She opened the bag first and looked in.

"Well," she said. Then she opened the package. "Oh, I like that," she said. For a moment the old way of affection spread over the room in her smile, her kiss on his cheek.

Then it ended. She said they'd listen to the records when they got back from the opera. She put down the album and went for her coat. He stood alone in the front room of an unfriendly house. In the front bedroom he heard Leo singing to herself.

They left the house and went to the opera.

Erick couldn't keep his eyes off her that night. For some reason she seemed to be stretching all night, moving her shoulders back and tightening the muscles of her chest. All the men around kept gaping at her breasts. Erick began to feel the tight, sick feeling again, the feeling he had when Lynn was talking to him.

While the opera was unraveling itself, the plan was pulsing through Erick's mind. He couldn't concentrate on the music, the singing, the story, what there was of it. Her presence seemed to surround him. He could smell the perfume of her hair. He wanted to reach out and take her hand but he didn't. He kept looking down at them as they rested gracefully in her lap.

Cracked ice in a bowl. Kiss the hollows of her neck and shoulders.

A soprano was singing a flighty solo. The audience was still except for sporadic coughing. Erick noticed Sally stir at his side. He felt the heat of the auditorium, felt the pressing of the wool suit on his legs. He stared blankly ahead at the back of the woman's head in front of him.

Don't drink too much. Let's go to your room. Black whales floating near icebergs.

His hands clenched, he felt his throat contracting. He was very thirsty. He yearned to have some cold water gushing down his dry throat. He felt dizzy. *Start on the couch. Cracked ice in the…*

During intermission they stood in the lobby.

"Sally," he said, "you know I'd marry you if I had enough money to support you and could still write."

"I know," she said, sounding perfectly unconvinced, hardly looking at him, only the vaguest touch of the old sadness touching her eyes for a moment.

It made him furious to have said it. He hadn't meant it, he was sure of it. In the back of his mind he was positive he had said it in order to arouse her love again so his plan would work.

When the curtain calls were done, Sally turned to him and said, unemotionally, "Well, let's go home and get drunk."

He smiled and helped her on with her coat, his stomach tight and aching. He kept trying to find some combination of words, some action that would let the easiness flow through his limbs again. But there was nothing, everything remained tight and menacing. There was no love in it.

Before they got on the bus, they stopped at the drugstore and bought soda.

"How many times have we ridden this bus?" he asked as they rode out to her house.

She spoke so quietly he hardly heard her. "Many times," she said.

"Sal," he said, and shivered.

"Are you cold?" she asked.

He looked out the window at the dark city rushing by like time.

"Yes," he said, "I'm cold."

She looked at his forehead.

"Still a scar there," she said, and it seemed she was telling him that she knew about his plan and wanted him to know it would never work.

When they got to the house she went into the kitchen to make drinks.

"Why don't we…uh…keep the ice in a bowl to save walking?" he asked.

"Don't be silly," she said, "They'd just melt together."

"Oh. Yeah."

Sitting on the couch, he couldn't help smiling.

"Step number one blown to shit," he murmured.

She handed him a drink and put on the records he'd given her. The swirling strains of Ravel's *La Valse* shivered into his ears. He drank down the contents of the glass in less than half a minute. He felt no effect. She hadn't sat down yet, so she took his glass and brought him another drink. *Good*, his mind said affably, *she's going to get you drunk, you won't have to do a thing*.

"Isn't that nice music?" he asked when she returned with the drink.

"Yes."

She sat down next to him and he took her hand. He blinked. And now, the thought came, in this cold impersonal light, *I am supposed to start making love to her. Bam!*—like that. No forewarning, no talk, no lead-up. Just—*Bam!*—love-making.

Impossible. He knew that.

"How's Felix?" he asked inanely.

"Fine."

Silence.

"How's Lynn?" she asked.

"He's asleep. He has a headache."

"Too bad."

"No. Too good. He deserves worse."

No comment from her. He finished the second drink. *Start kissing down the straps of her slip*. He grimaced. Always the plan. It kept eating at him, stamping impatiently for execution.

"You're drinking too fast," she said.

"I used to resent drinking," he said.

"You don't know what you want," she said.

"I want you."

"Oh, sure."

She got up to make herself another drink. He sat there glumly and felt like crying. He wiped away a tear. You're a maudlin drunk, he told himself, that's what you are, just like your old daddy.

"You know when I got drunk the first time?" he asked her when she came back.

"I have no idea."

"The night I met you."

"Yes, you *were* drunk."

"But clever," he said. "Full of words."

"Full of something," she said.

"I got to you," he said, forcing the smugness.

"Did you?" she said.

"Would you like me to go home?" he said abruptly.

"If you want to."

"I don't want to go home," he said sadly.

He expanded his eyes with a shudder and stared at the floor. The room was beginning to look distorted. But there was no warmth to it, the cold creeping in his stomach kept alive. *Take your time*, croaked his mind, *plenty of time. Get her to put cracked ice in a bowl, that's the whole thing, if you'll only get her to put cracked ice in a bowl.* Ice schmice! he snapped back, get the hell out of here and leave me alone.

"More," he said.

More drinks.

"How's Felix?" he asked.

"He's still fine."

"Did I ask you?"

"Twice."

"I'm very concerned for his future."

"Of course."

"How's Felix?"

She didn't answer. Then she said, "He's going to play pro football."

"Prostitute football?"

"Professional football." She didn't allow him the acceptance of his bad joke.

"Oh." As if the revelation had come.

"He's getting ten thousand a year for it."

"For booting a dead pig around?"

"Jealous?"

"Of *him*? I'm afraid not, no, I'm afraid not." Then, "I'll make more than that someday." He looked up in self surprise at the defensive tone in his voice.

She got up to change the records. "He asked me to marry him," she said.

"Oh? Did you accept?" With a feeling as if he were going to jump out of his skin.

"I haven't decided."

"Why not?" The insides of him crawling. "Ten thousand a year. Blessed security. Cadillacs. Man servants. A mansion underneath the weeping willow trees. Mint Julips."

She sat down again and her hand was limp when he took it.

"I don't know why I shouldn't," she said.

"Surely it isn't me?" he said, wondering if his voice was as thick and stupid-sounding to her as it was to him.

"*You*," she said, bitter for the first time he could remember. "You'll never marry me."

"I want to. I wish I could." He thought he sounded convincing.

She pulled away her hand and turned her face.

"You *could*," she said. "You could if you wanted to."

"I've told you many times why I can't. Many times."

She picked up her glass and took a long drink. "I know," she said, lips drawn back from her white teeth. "Your *art*."

He snickered impulsively.

"You make it sound like masturbation," he said, and she didn't answer.

He pursued it, he kept digging.

"Why do you take it?" he asked. "Why don't you throw me out? Why don't you tell me to go jump in the lake?"

She said it in a flat voice, slowly.

"*You wouldn't believe me*."

She was silent. Then she said,

"If you only realized how much I cared for you last year. I'd have done anything for you, gone anywhere, helped you. I was all yours."

"Mine," he murmured, staring at the swell of her young breasts.

"I was," she said. "Not anymore."

He sank back against the cushions, feeling sick and restless. He couldn't relax, there was something running around in him. On the record player the waltz drew lost and despairing.

"No, of course you're not," he said. "Why should you love me when I treat you so terribly?"

"I don't think I do love you anymore," she said, as if the argument were still going on in her mind. "I can't love in a vacuum."

"No," he said, stroking her hand. "No."

And *this* night I was going to seduce her, he thought.

"I don't love you the same way," she was conceding already. "I guess I always will, though. In some way."

He leaned over and kissed her white throat. He hadn't the slightest desire to seduce her anymore, the tautness had drained away. He looked down at her arched breasts, the inviting valley between them. They were beautiful, he thought, but so was the Mona Lisa, and he didn't want to go to bed with the Mona Lisa. Sally was another person now. This wasn't the girl who was trying to take off her clothes, trying to take his off that night. This was someone else, someone pure and good and incapable of narrow lust.

He put down his glass and slid his arm around her waist. She was passive. The strings throbbed on, the music gained in violence. Now it is the decadent society after the war, dancing to its own death music, he thought. He looked over her body carefully, not caring whether she noticed or not. He tried hard to imagine himself going through with the plan, but it loomed as something outrageous and impossible. He couldn't even visualize it. Cracked ice in a bowl, indeed.

He rested his head on her shoulder and stared dizzily at the floor. She was motionless. *When I think of the tensions in this room*, he thought, *of the currents tearing at the planks, it makes me shudder. And that's how it is everywhere*, he expanded briefly, *talk going on, giddy masquerades held in huge ball-rooms surrounded by abysmal murk. Vast pretenses. Spots of artificial light in the ocean of night. Man.*

He drew back his arm when the front door opened and Leo came in. She seemed to waver in the doorway.

"Well, hello kiddies," she said, "did I interrupt anything?"

Sally got up. "Want a drink?" she asked Leo.

Leo pursed her thin lips.

"Well, I just might," she said. She drew off her jacket so that her slight breasts pointed through the yellow sweater. She saw Erick look at them.

"Pretty?" she said, a smile starting on her face.

"Yup," he said. "Nice music."

In the kitchen Sally ran water from the sink. Leo sat down and crossed her legs.

"Where you been?" he asked.

"Beer drinking," she said, "in dark booths."

"Dark booths."

"Confessionals with beer," she said.

He snickered. "That's good," he said.

Sally came in and gave Leo a drink. Leo sipped. "Whiskey on beer," she recited, "curls your hair."

Sally sat down and started talking to Leo about Felix. Erick sat slumped, pretending to read a book of poetry he'd picked up off the coffee table. Once he thought he noticed Leo nod her head in his direction as if to say—What's with him?

After a while he got up and weaved his way into the bathroom. He stood there dizzily, listening to Leo's voice in the living room, her sharp laughter. When he came back and sat down he noticed that he'd forgotten to zip closed his pants and a bolt of shock ran through him. He zipped it shut, surprised that it didn't embarrass him. *My God*, he thought, bemused, *I'm under the influence, I am no longer accountable. Time for rape*, his mind suggested, but he thrust it aside.

"Well, I have to hit it," Leo said, after a while.

"It's only eleven-thirty," Sally said.

Leo shrugged and went to bed anyway. Sally got up and went into the bathroom.

When she sat down Erick started to read to her. It was the first time in his life he'd read to anyone. He wondered how he sounded but it didn't matter too much to him. Was it a silly voice, an empty voice, a drunken voice? Goodbye, plan, he decided. And felt what amounted to relief.

Suddenly he banged the book shut and pressed his face into her shoulder.

"Why can't it always be like that night?" he begged and, in his mind, he said—*How will this affect her, what will her reaction be to this calculated skein of syllabic effect?*

He felt her body tighten.

"I don't think the furniture can stand it," she said, and he felt another tear in his eye. Then she sighed. "It could have been," she said, "once."

Vacillating thing! his mind insulted her.

"If I could have been human," he said, "if only I'd admit to myself what I know is true. That I love you."

"You don't love me."

"Yes," he said, rolling his face on her shoulder, feeling the warm flesh against his cheeks. "I do. I want to say it. I *do* love you. I love you! See? It's easy to say. It's been eating at me since we met. I have to say it. I won't back down. It isn't a lack of love that keeps me from you. It's what you called... art. Well, it's more than just art. It's life for me. I can't give up my life, can I?"

He moved his face down and pressed it into the warm swelling of her breasts. She began to caress his hair gently, without excitement.

"I love you, Sally," he said.

She didn't answer.

"Please don't think that's the babbling of a drunken author."

She still didn't say anything. He kissed the white tops of her breasts with a feeling of sacred love for them, for her. He rested his cheek against them.

"What are you, really?" he asked. "What do you really think? I don't know you, do I?"

"No," she said. "You don't, Erick."

"No."

"You only know what I've wanted you to know," she said.

"Oh," he said.

He put his legs up on the couch and rested his head back in her lap. He turned his face into her breasts.

"Don't, Erick," she said quietly.

He stared at the ceiling, feeling the heat of her legs through the skirt.

"What's it all about, Sally?" he asked. "Here I am and here you are, two spots in immensity. Why are we together and why should it last or end? There must be a purpose to it. Or else this life is such a terrible waste of time."

She sighed, her fingers brushed back his hair. He looked up at her.

"Sally?"

"Yes."

"Would you kiss me, Sally? Please?"

Their eyes held for a long moment. He felt that every second of their past was flickering in that gaze, that they were searching for some answer. Their eyes never moved.

Then her face seemed to float down, it came closer and closer and more and more of the room and the world disappeared in the shadow of her. Her full, soft lips were almost on his, his mouth trembled. He could feel and smell her breath on his mouth.

She rested her lips on his. Her head was motionless. She just rested there without even breathing as if she meant to stay there. And he thought—*I say my mother kiss my father like that—when he was lying dead in his coffin. It was for goodbye.*

But her lips were warm and he was alive. He reached up suddenly and plunged his fingers into her silky, brown hair, fastening his fingers on her skull. He stretched his body taut to let every bit of the sensation run through him.

She straightened up and he took his hands away. Her breasts pressed against her sheer blouse. He pushed his face against them and kissed the blouse over them. She held his head in tense fingers and pulled him into them.

"Oh, Erick, Erick, Erick," she sobbed.

Then it was over, as suddenly as it had come. She relaxed her grip and he was looking at the ceiling again.

"I planned to seduce you tonight," he said.

She was silent. He looked at her. She was smiling down at him, amused.

"I really had it planned to the last detail," he said, trying to sound amused himself. "I only forgot one thing. Me."

"That you never forget," she said. "You forgot me."

"And you," he admitted. "I forgot you no longer love me enough to forget yourself."

"A woman never forgets herself, Erick," she said.

"You mean there's always something practical in it?" he said, still trying to sound amused.

"That's right," she said.

He was a shifting mass of emotion. He felt cold and resentful. From worship of her he now felt distaste, alien regard. He felt ridiculous in her eyes and knew, in tight anger, that she was a woman and he was a boy. And felt as if a disgusting secret of the ages had been revealed to him.

"I wouldn't do it unless the man married me," she said.

"You mean you'd do it with anyone who said they'd marry you?"

She took a deep breath and didn't answer.

"And what about last summer? And what about before last Christmas?" he said like a hurt juvenile, looking for revenge. Any kind of revenge.

"I thought you'd marry me, of course."

"You never thought that," he said coldly.

Her fingers left his hair, she shifted uneasily. "You're kind of heavy," she said.

He sat up and leaned back against the couch, extending his long legs onto the floor.

"So, it's all a game, eh?" he said lightly.

"All a game."

"And you won't let me seduce you?"

"What do you think?"

He reached out and picked up his glass.

"I think we've wasted a lot of time," he said.

She didn't reply. He felt nervous and tried to tone down his last remark. "Well, at least I don't mind," he said, "as long as I know no one else can seduce you either."

"You don't."

"Oh, come on, Sally, we're not that far apart."

She got up and turned off the record player. She stood there stiffly.

"Couldn't it ever have been?" he asked.

She didn't turn to face him.

"That's a funny question," she said, and he saw her shoulders shake a little. He pushed up, thoughts crowding through his brain, pushing one past the other like people in a rushing mob. He felt sick with loss.

"Sally," he said, moving forward.

"You'd better go," she said.

He went over quickly and put his hands on her shoulders. She twisted away and he stood watching her hurry from the room. He heard her heels on the floor, heard the springs of her bed as she fell across it. He hoped that Leo was asleep.

He went into her room. In the dark he could hear her crying. He sat down on her bed and she kept crying. He reached out for her shoulder, touched her leg. He pulled his hand away and reached for her shoulder. Life seemed to be flooding away from him, he felt as though he were trying to reach down his hands and catch hold of a stream and stop it in its path, keep it from rushing away from him.

"Please don't cry, Sally," he said. "It makes me unhappy."

"I'm sorry...if it does. Y-you can't always be happy, if y-you want to be with o-other people," she said, her shaking voice muffled in the pillow.

He turned her over and without a word took her in his arms. She did nothing. He held her close and stroked her hair gently.

"Sally," he said, "I do love you. I hate to see you unhappy. Why does love always make people unhappy? I want you to be happy. If..."

She was silent.

"Sally?"

"W-what?"

"Nothing. I just thought you were asleep or something."

"No."

"All right."

"You'd better go," she said.

"I don't want to leave you like this."

"Don't worry about it."

He sat there a long moment, indecisive. He almost asked her to marry him. Then he knew he didn't want to marry her. So he kissed her forehead and put her back on the pillow and stood up. He listened to her uneven breathing in the darkness and found himself swaying back and forth in the darkness as if waiting for something to happen.

Then he spoke, trying desperately for some magic phrase that would end all irresolution and make things happy again.

"I'm sorry," he said. "Sorry for whatever I've done to hurt you. Believe me I didn't try to hurt you."

Then he turned and went silently out of the room. He put his coat on and started for the door. He heard a whispering sound and turned. She was standing in the dark dining room, her face white and very serious.

"I'm sorry," she said. "You don't have to go if you don't want to."

"It's late," he said. "I'd better."

She stood before him as he pulled his knit gloves on. Then she opened the door and dutifully held up her cheek as he bent over to kiss it. He wanted to stay. He turned away and walked out, saying, "Good night, Sally."

She said, "Goodbye."

When he was halfway to the corner, the cold air washing over him, he realized what she'd said and wondered if she meant it. Wondered if the cord had been cut after so long a weaving. The simile made him smile for a moment, grimly. Maybe it was that all along.

After a while he got tired of waiting on the corner for the bus and he walked the long way home.

ten.

He hadn't meant to go to her dance recital. It had been almost two months since he'd seen her. But Lynn was taking a course in Aesthetics and was required to attend it. He asked Erick to go with him and Erick thought it would be all right. He knew very well she'd be in it but he pretended not to think about it.

As they went into the oven-hot gym, the striking difference in weather between this night and the last one he'd seen her impressed itself on Erick. He felt heat oozing through the gathering crowd. He kept wiping his face and neck and arms. In a few minutes his handkerchief was soaked.

When the lights went out he put on his glasses. Sweat kept dripping off his eyebrows across the lenses. He kept wiping them off but they kept steaming and blurring. Most of the time he seemed to be watching the dance through a mist.

He saw Melissa. She was in a chorus number. She wore a tight blue leotard and did little arm and leg movements. She looked very graceful. When he turned away from her he felt no sorrow. He felt nothing. Her face was the face of a statue.

Then Sally came on for a solo.

His eyes never left her. He forgot the heat. Sweat ran unheeded over his face. A tom-tom beat filled his ears. Under the glaring lights she leaped around like some pagan indulging in a frenzied rite. The audience was the silent watchers, the judges. They were other members of the tribe, squatting naked on the forest floor and watching her, their dark eyes glittering hungrily in the firelight.

She was wearing the tightest costume he'd ever seen on her. It was more like a dark skin. Every line of her body was revealed and he drank in the sight of her. It was like a hot summer dream weaving itself in the sweltering darkness, the only focal point her leaping on the floor.

LEAVE YESTERDAY ALONE

She was beautiful. She had improved wonderfully since the recital the year before. She was vibrant and quick, she seemed hardly to touch the floor. Her long legs stretched out, twisted as she flew through the air.

Then, suddenly, she was on the floor, writhing in sinuous rhythm. He felt his heart beat faster, his breath caught, his throat moved. One of her legs lifted in a powerful arched motion. He was not conscious of the small, almost frightened sound he made. The muscles in her thighs and calves stood out like white-sheathed serpents. He swallowed again, thirstily. She was an animal, a magnificent animal. He had never seen it before or, if he had seen it, he would not look. That she was an animal, yes, he had admitted that. That she was magnificent, never, and now it was too late. The thought tortured him.

He stared at her. He had her dancing naked. She was bent back with tense grace, her strong uptilting breasts arching with her body, every line moving with the rhythm.

Then, in languor, she swirled slowly around the wooden floor, her bare feet making tiny squeaking noises on the boards. Her long brown hair tossed lightly as she left the floor in a silent leap and landed, catlike and sure. She turned slowly and moved her body snakelike, writing her shoulders sensuously. He felt his stomach muscles tremble. He had a sudden urge to run to her.

It seemed as if the two of them were alone in the dream. He had only to leap up and run to her to touch her warm body, to feel the unutterably sweet taste of her lips, the caress of her arms. To fly in her arms around and around, their hearts beating faster and faster, limbs locking and unlocking, their breaths mingling.

Then to rest while she wove a spell of scented flesh around him, while she imprisoned him with her love, enchanted him with the sinews and muscles of her being.

He held his breath, chained down by a thousand invisible links of tortured desire. She seemed to float before him.

She was circling him, music and throbbing rhythm impelling her on. She was dancing in a cloud that grew thicker with each moment. Her form floated in gentle arcs around him. Head back, hair floating in breeze, breasts in superb mold through her black costume. Around and around, never stopping once from her hypnotizing motion. Closer and closer to him, her eyes on him, her body approaching, in magnetic silence. Her form, her softening form settling on him. Blending of their mouths and...

Sudden darkness. He blinked and shuddered. Nothing. He was bound in dreamless black sleep.

The lights went on and he slipped off his glasses. Lynn sat silently at his side, looking straight ahead, his face blank. Erick's face dripped with sweat, Lynn's didn't. Erick wiped his face and let a shaking breath pass through his throat.

People talked around them. He sat there, a throbbing nerve mass, cleaning his glasses over and over. Finally he put them in his pocket.

When the recital was over they went out into the hall. Sally was there, talking to a woman, still wearing her brief costume. She saw Erick and a quick smile lit her face.

"Well," she said loudly, falsely he thought, "You *came*!"

They shook hands.

"I enjoyed it very much, Sally," he said.

Lynn said, "It was interesting." She smiled through him, then she looked over Erick's shoulder.

"Hi!" she shrieked and ran past them toward an older man who stood near the wall.

Abruptly Erick turned and started down the stairs, not even bothering to see if Lynn were with him.

"She was certainly anxious to see *you*, wasn't she?" Lynn said.

"Oh, shut up, will you?" Erick said.

In his mind the chant went over and over—*Done with, goodbye forever, done with, goodbye forever...*

LEAVE YESTERDAY ALONE

♦ ♦ ♦ ♦ ♦

Suddenly the weeks passed. As if time were an accelerating action, starting out slowly and lethargically at his entrance into the University, gaining velocity and going faster and faster as the years passed until now it was moving so fast in the last few weeks that nothing could be seen clearly. Everything was like landmarks from a speeding train.

The day he came from his last examination it was as though some great weight had fallen from his shoulders. The reaction had not yet begun and all he felt was complete relief at being through with endless studies. Now he could go home and spend all his time at writing.

One day Erick ran into Leo and she told him Sally was sorry about being so rude at the recital. He said it didn't matter. Why don't you give her a buzz, Leo said. If I get a chance, he said.

The final days before graduation Lynn and he spent at the college pool, sleeping in the sun and talking. They both got sunburned. They ate thick steaks at night. They got drunk on gin and lay on the campus grass half the night, evolving a muddled philosophy of the future.

Sometimes Erick woke at night and thought of her. It didn't matter, of course, he was through with her. She had been only a part of college life and with college over now, Sally alone would be only a thin reminder of previous joys. He would leave her, there would be only a few memories.

Yet, deep inside, there was something; an inchoate feeling that disturbed him, that could not be faced. He had to ignore it, otherwise it threatened to well up and submerge him with its unknown waves.

He concentrated on thoughts about graduating. He thought about being young and being free.

♦ ♦ ♦ ♦ ♦

It started out like a mass execution. Somber bell tolls rocked in steady beats through the hot air. The rhythmical waves of solemn sound filled the ears of the black-robed hosts as they gushed methodically from the school corridors. They could hear the rustle of many-tongued hordes who lined the hot sidewalks, armed with cameras and stares.

He walked and ran, stopped and started. Sweat stood out like crystals on his forehead and upper lip. It ran down inside his wilting shirt collar and meandered across his back and chest.

The bell kept hitting the reverberating clang into his moving head. The bell tolls overlapped and soon, under the blaze of the sun, the clanging seemed to merge into one annoying dissonance.

He looked around dizzily. There was no time to see, no time to mark the essence of full moments. It was going too fast. After today, tonight, there would be nothing left. This ground was passing away, this ground which had known all their steps together and apart. He shuddered and tried to forget about it.

Four years had passed, gone. Gone, leaving their indelible marks, but nevertheless—gone. *Memories were worthless*, the thought assailed him. In a mind that desired more, memories could not fill the immensity of the will to remember. Once he had gone he would have cut himself off forever from this spot.

From her.

He kept pushing aside the thought hurriedly, almost desperately. He couldn't think of her. The desire kept coming to call her up, to go and see her that night, propose, marry her. And yet he didn't care for her, he kept telling himself. You don't love the girl, what are you so damned upset about? It wasn't the thought of leaving her that made him sad, he reasoned, it was the thought of leaving everything, the sense of utter completion, of a million happy moments never to be recaptured again.

LEAVE YESTERDAY ALONE

To walk in the hot sun was more than displeasure. The physical annoyance of the heat-absorbing black robe and cap were bad, but they were nothing to compare to the mental agonies. The slipping away of pleasures never recognized as pleasures until their times had passed. The poor inadequate consolation of photographs, notebooks, letters, memories—in the face of complete hopelessness.

There were almost two thousand of them. They walked in double columns. Like a flow of blackness they issued from the administration building, their heels clicking noisily onto the sidewalk. Around the huge square campus they marched. Bugs and cameras clicked their recognition of the scene. Parents and friends looked for a familiar face in the sea of black-capped heads. And smiled to see it, waved self-consciously, or raised ubiquitous cameras to place the moment on silver paper for all time, that moment caught fast as well as man could do it.

Erick wondered how his mother and father would look standing there. He could almost visualize his mother, her stooped body dressed in her best outfit, a white hat on her graying head, the sun glinting off her glasses, the pink-cheeked face glowing with happiness and pride, the little self-conscious wiggle of her fingers as he passed by and the flush of delight to see him for a moment. He was sorry she couldn't be here but then, in the next moment, he knew he would want to be alone. There was too much in these last hours to leave room for sharing feelings with anyone. She would have spoiled it.

Everyone must be feeling the moments falling away, he thought. No, maybe not, maybe the future was all that counted to them. Maybe they were like Lynn, with letters in their pockets from magazines and newspapers and advertising agencies offering them jobs at good salaries starting within the next two weeks. Maybe the world was their toy. It was not his.

The minutes, like intangible racers, gained and kept gaining. Now, in sight of the wire, they were blurs of light.

And worlds had perforce to end because there never was any going back since time began.

His lips trembled as he thought of returning to a world he had forgotten how to use. There was no future for him except the dim hope of writing successfully. There was nothing to look forward to returning to a world he didn't trust or care for. The sense of freedom he felt after his last examination was gone now. He wanted to take it all on again, start from scratch, become a freshman again. College had been the happiest time of his life. Now there was only a couch in a living room or a furnished room and a city he hated.

He had the wild impulse to go to the dean and tell him he'd cheated flagrantly on all his final exams and ask to be put back a term. To ask for a job, any job, just so he could stay at college. He was like a frightened boy afraid to leave his mother. The thought of Sally crossed his mind. For a moment it stood out in sharp clarity. Was the fear of leaving the fear of leaving Sally?

He didn't know. All he knew was that, despite the heat, he felt his bones covered with a chill and he knew that, suddenly he knew that, he would never see her again.

"Sally," he murmured.

The girl in front of him looked over her shoulder. He looked down, then the line stopped moving and he came down heavily on the girl's heel. She turned with a hiss of pain.

"I'm sorry," he said.

He felt the heat like a blast from an oven. Dark waves settled around him and he blinked. Someone pushed his back and he stumbled forward, suddenly remembering the night in Germany when the man behind him had pushed him forward and he had wanted to kill them all. He didn't want to kill anyone now.

He stepped on the girl's heel again.

"Come *on*!" she snapped angrily.

"I'm sorry," he said.

Drops of sweat ran down his wrists. On and on he plodded, thinking that this was the end of rest, that this was his punishment and hell; to walk forever in hot sun in black with the end of happiness etched on his mind.

Passing clouds and visions. Heat, endless heat. Stumbling through the streets lined with people.

They were in the field house. He found himself listening to some bald man telling the graduates how the world was waiting for them. He looked around distractedly, remembering how they used to arrange the field house for concerts, looking at the place where he and Sally had always sat. He turned back, conscious of being watched. He stared at the program-littered floor and wanted to cry. He felt like squirming, like leaping up and screaming—Christ, let me out of here! And running down the long weaving aisles like a maniac into the sunlight. He could hardly sit still, he kept twisting and shifting. *Oh, stop it*, ordered his mind, *what are you bitching about, you don't love her.* And he knew that it *was* her that was upsetting him.

He twisted his head and saw that everyone had their caps held in their laps. He took his off and felt his hair sticky and plastered to his head.

"God, this is awful," he muttered.

"You said it," agreed the young man next to him. Erick glanced at him and wondered when he'd stood up with the rest of them, he couldn't remember doing it.

He heard the dean's droning over the public address system that according to the authority vested in them. Erick felt dizzy, as if he were going to faint. He recalled the time in basic training when he had gotten sunstroke while standing in review on a great open field in Georgia. He had been holding his rifle before him at parade rest and it had an unsheathed bayonet on the end. He had gotten dizzy and almost fallen forward and impaled his throat on the sharp blade. They had caught him and dragged him to a shady spot. He remembered the cool smell of the grass in that shady spot and the feeling of the cool water they gave him.

The ceremony was over. He found himself wandering among the broken masses of happy graduates and friends and parents. It was over. He concentrated on that and tried to understand it.

He stumbled along without seeing, his feet moving automatically for the room. Later he realized he didn't have his diploma and he had to go back to the administration building and stand in a long line to get it. Then he left his robe in the school store and went down into the cool basement into the Dramatics Office. Lynn sat there alone in a sweat-soaked shirt, smoking a cigarette. He looked up.

"That's that," he said mildly.

♦ ♦ ♦ ♦ ♦

They walked through the streets toward the train station. Erick felt like stopping and sitting on the earth. Everything seemed precious to him. There had been nothing so wrenching as this moment in his entire life. To leave such a beautiful portion of existence behind. He couldn't take it with him, it was not to be lifted piece by piece, not to be stored in a trunk and sent Railway Express back to New York.

No, it was ingrained in every spot, in the very ground he had walked on, walked *away* from. And for him, it was on the campus where he had walked in the bars, where he had danced to jukebox music with Sally in his arms. Mostly every spot seemed precious because of Sally. The house she lived in, the streets they walked together. The movies they sat in together, the cafes and restaurants they had eaten in. In all the places they had enjoyed together.

And he could not take those things with him. Like gold, it was too heavy to be carted away in the hand. It had to be left in its place, there to remain a shining memory.

"Glad to get out of this hole," Lynn said, "back to civilization."

Erick felt like stopping, putting down his bags, sitting on them and saying—All right, go on, leave me alone. I'm here to stay.

He kept walking. And every time they passed a public phone booth, he felt a twinge and thought of how easy it would have been all afternoon and evening to call Sally and say—Hello, how are you? But he hadn't. He waited for her to call but she hadn't and the feeling of pain kept growing. Now it was reaching a peak as they walked slowly through the streets toward the train station.

"Damn cab company," Lynn said. "They should have more cabs."

"Shut up," Erick said. "Think about your $120 a week and shut up."

"Oh," Lynn said, "I sense a delicate ire."

"Yeah, yeah, yeah."

Drag me down, earth! Hold me back, don't let me go!

They were in the train station buying tickets. The air was crushing him, his legs felt like running lead. He could hardly walk. *Sally, Sally*, his mind kept speaking her name. His stomach was a rocklike mass, sinking. He struggled along, lugging his suitcase, into which had crept all the elephants of the world.

That clicking. He blinked his eyes, focused.

It was the train wheels!

He lurched as he realized that he was staring through dusty windows, watching the dark city pass into the night, melt away, rush backwards and disappear into forever. As though it were a magic place, an enchanted city which had appeared to his eyes four years ago and now was swept away by a returning curse.

Now there were only stretching plains and black lumps of trees looming up and leaping past the window. The rapid clicking of the wheels on the tracks. He stared dizzily at the passing country.

"Oh, by the way," Lynn said, "Sally called yesterday."

Erick's head snapped around and he gaped at Lynn. Lynn looked back blandly.

"*What*?" Erick said.

"That girl called," Lynn said, "Sally."

Erick couldn't speak, his throat was suddenly congested.

"She called three times," Lynn said. "You were out all day though."

Erick felt himself drawing in, clenching his fists.

"Why didn't you tell me?" he asked hoarsely.

His voice sounded too patient to him. He felt the words screamed in his mind.

Lynn shrugged.

"Why should I?" he asked. "If you didn't want to call her yourself, what difference would it make if you knew she called you?"

Lynn was right. He recognized that a split second before the rage broke up the thought.

"*You stupid son of a bitch*!"

He said it hysterically, not even thinking whether the entire car heard it or not. He felt himself get as hard as rock and knew that he was going to kill Lynn.

"Why?" Lynn asked. "Surely you don't mean..."

Something drove into Erick's vitals and he shoved up spasmodically and lurched past Lynn, his right foot stamping over Lynn's. He felt himself weaving drunkenly down the aisle, his hands shooting out in automatic spurts for support. The whole car seemed to distort and melt and run like wax. His stomach heaved and leaped.

The door banged shut behind him and he stood in the small, reeking cubbyhole. He twisted around, making sounds of disbelief, of incredulous disbelief.

He leaned forward and stared into the spot-flecked mirror. He saw his harrowed eyes and his mouth half open. He felt like a child lost in the night. There were no words for it, all he could do was stand there staring and weaving, running his right hand over his face, sounds of terror and distress moving his throat.

Then the rush of sickness enveloped him.

He spun around with a lurching movement and threw up into the toilet.

Then he was leaning and shivering against the cool metal wall, his brow pressed into it. The wall ran before his eyes and he was carefully reading the instructions about the use of the toilet. He read it again and again.

Then he came back and he closed his eyes suddenly and cried. And he was lost in darkness, rattling, throbbing darkness that moved on and on and carried him away from everything that was in the world for him.

PART TWO

one.

It was one of those New Year's Eve parties where no one knows who invited who and everyone is making love by midnight.

Lynn had invited him.

When Erick came a strange girl let him in and he walked through ranks of strange people, dropped his overcoat in a strange bedroom, and finally found Lynn at the bar, tending.

"Erick, is it thou?" Lynn said.

"It is mou."

"Thrice welcome," Lynn said. "No date?"

"You know women repel me," Erick said, wringing the suggestion of a smile from Lynn. Then he picked up an olive and inserted it in his mouth. He watched Lynn pouring whiskey into shot glasses.

"You have a date?" he asked Lynn.

"No," said Lynn. "I'm with Marie."

"Ah, Marie," Erick said.

"Thumb me a woman," Lynn told him, looking up for a moment and then lowering his eyes immediately to the business at hand.

"Her name was Sally," Erick said.

Lynn didn't look up. "That one isn't any good," he said.

Erick made himself a Vodka Collins. He took a sip and smacked his lips.

"She was a strange, beautiful slob," he said.

Lynn extended his lower lip contemplatively. "Perhaps."

"She wore black lipstick and had crabs," Erick said.

Lynn's narrow lips raised in a smile. "The classic of all time," he said, "but not fair because already used."

Erick stuck a cheese-covered cracker into his mouth.

"Yeah, yeah," he said, looking around the room.

"I thought you weren't coming," Lynn said, finishing up the group of drinks he was preparing. Erick turned back.

"While working on my life story this evening, which story is entitled *From Rags To Rags*, I said to myself—Boy, you must go down to the sea again. It being a prodigious great walk to the Battery, I came here instead."

"Grand," Lynn said. "Simply grand."

He examined the drinks, dropped in appropriate cherries.

"On the way over, I saw the three following sights," Erick went on, taking another sip. "First, a lady disguised as a bridge lamp boarding a bus. Second, a dog with no teeth. Last, but oodles from least, three victims of good cheer lying sprawled in the gutter surrounded by mountains of vomit."

"Tasty," Lynn said. "Vaporous."

"And, on the basis of these three signs, I have decided that my mission in life is to be floorwalker in a morgue."

"Possible," Lynn said.

"Look at them," Erick said.

"At whom?"

"The women of the city."

"Must I?" said Lynn. "It requires quite enough abdominal fortitude to maintain a steady gaze on Marie."

"Marie," Erick said, "who cuts her hair and her morals short."

Lynn bowed. "You have captured her," he said.

"What the hell do you see in her?"

"A vice-presidency," Lynn said. "Her father owning the agency."

Erick's face lost lightness and he stared at the women, his mouth curled down.

"She's like all of them," he said. "Look at them. Corrupted. Drinking, smoking pseudo-sophisticates trying to be gay." He raised his voice to a falsetto. "We must be gay! We must have gay parties and get gay drunk and throw up gay vomit and have gay hangovers."

"Quite," Lynn said.

"What's the point?" Erick said. "They're dead, working in their mills of hypocrisy, losing their personalities. Sad, *sad*. God, think of how they were at school, with their pink cheeks and their sweaters and skirts, healthy and full of bounce and young."

"Young," echoed Lynn, putting the drinks on a tray.

"Now they're old. They wear sophisticated clothes and effect sophisticated manners and laugh about lesbians and gigantic immoralities. Old but not mature. Still with their rah rah minds, with their little town college minds—and with these poor little undernourished pulps in their heads, they try to cope with the monstrous forces that live in the city, that thrive in grottoes of stone and steel. And they can't figure it out, they can't fight it. They lose their personalities, they all start to look the same and talk the same."

"Think the same," Lynn contributed.

"Yeah," Erick said. "Think the same. Give us freedom!—they cry. Run off to the city, crying—I must have freedom! And, here in this sprawling dung heap of a city, do they find freedom?"

Lynn didn't say anything. He watched Erick.

"In a pig's eye they find freedom! They're more slaves than they even were. Free of parental interdict, yes, and as long as they have that freedom, they consider themselves willful creatures. But they aren't. They're slaves to this great sucking vampire of a city, its mores and its demands. Not free to abstain because everybody smokes and it gives at least one arm something to do instead of hang helplessly. Not free to abstain because everyone drinks and it is smart and clever to throw up your guts periodically and joke about it at the office the next day. Not free to abstain because moral laxity is the very cant and cachet of our times. One must not be thought a prude. It's easier to lose the soul."

Erick took a deep breath and finished his drink with a gulp.

"What the hell did I come here for?" he asked.

Lynn patted him on the shoulder.

"Sit down, baby," he said. "Get drunk and drift away. Daddy will bring you back."

"Oh, shut up," Erick said irritably, and moved out across the room.

He saw a full drink on a table and, quickly, exchanged it for his empty glass. Then he moved on, searching for something. The room was crowded with young men and women arranged in asymmetrical groups, some slouched, some seated on couches, some draped with affected ease on armchairs. They all chattered brittle-like. *They are all gay*, Erick thought, *they are all lousy with gaiety.*

"People," he said, and stopped for a long swallow of the drink. He screwed up his face. "Who in the hell made this drink?" he asked the air, "Lucretia Borgia?"

A short, plumpish girl with high, pointy breasts moved past him.

"Hi, Erick honey," she said, digging her pudgy fingers into his arm.

"Good evening, Madame," he said, and walked on past Marie.

"Thumb me a woman!" she giggled over her shoulder, and he paid no attention. She asked him a lot now since she'd started going with Lynn.

"She had a breath that smelled like the spaces between toes," he murmured to himself as he leaned against the wall, listening to a recording of "Sing, Sing, Sing," while some bushy-haired aficionado cracked knuckles in time.

Nearby a small group was listening to a young advertising executive discoursing on the insidious and vicious aspects of the Communist plague, which threatened to upset the United States government. While listening to the young man without hearing, Erick stared at the flaring bodice of a tall, red-haired young woman who seemed to have given little definite thought as to the question of whether her bust should be covered or not.

When she noticed his stare she looked over at him with a look, Erick thought, that lady novelists called "dark." What happened was that her brow knitted and her mouth turned down slightly and, involuntarily, her hand sought the folds of highly unconcealing silk at her swelling breasts, attempting to veil them more adequately.

"I know the so-called liberals will keep calling your attention to the small percentage of these Communists in the country. Well, I say," said the young man, "if one termite eats hard enough, the whole house will come down."

"If his belly is big enough."

They stopped talking and the red-haired girl looked at Erick with a what-the-hell-have-we-here? look. The man gave Erick a blasé glance and then went on speaking with the talent that opinionated people have of ignoring anything that smacks of disagreement.

Erick stood there stiffly, damned if he would move away. His brain struggled vainly to assure him that these were just poor people struggling to be important. But it didn't help. He suddenly felt ridiculous, out of place. He felt a rising heat of awkwardness and wanted to run.

His face remained the same. Without a ruffle of lost composure. He had learned to do that through the years. He gave the girl's rising chest one more candid look and then pushed away from the wall and walked off.

Immediately he was sure they were speaking of him. He straightened his shoulders as if a parting sight of him that was more or less impressive would ease the acidity of their comments. Then his brain grew furious with him for being so obvious. He hated himself as he was growing to hate himself more and more when the gaps and rents began to appear in his cool façade.

"People," he said quietly, bitterly, indicating at once his distaste and his fear.

He sat drinking and his body seemed to float even if his mind kept sagging. It seemed that he moved around the room like an apparition, and that last drink, a particularly large one, just about did away with self-criticism, leaving only the small core of acid reflectiveness that never slept.

After passing Lynn a few times and peregrinating about the room a few more times, he sank down on a vacant chair and watched people. He looked at the redhead more and more, feeling a vicious heat course his body. The thought kept occurring—*a penny for your tits*—as he stared directly at her bust. Which more and more appeared undecided between remaining in her dress or plopping out into the smoky air for the plaudits of the assemblage.

He looked around the room that swelled with chatter and young straining laughter. He watched the slack-postured girls standing as one, right arm crotched against their hips, cigarette held loosely between two Churchhillian fingers. He watched clean-shaven young men in wide-spread collars and immaculate suits draining their small minds in attempts to be amusing. And he thought of all the fraternity men at the house where Lynn had lived the first two years of college. And thought that all those young men had added to themselves was years, and no glory, but only increasing dandruff had been heaped on their futile shoulders.

"New Year's Eve!" Marie lisped to him once, pogoing past with a cigarette and a drink. "Be gay!"

He watched her pound off into the crowd and thought of getting her cornered in the bedroom and tearing off her clothes, raping her, and beating her skull in with a hammer.

"Charming party," he said. "Perfectly charming."

♦ ♦ ♦ ♦ ♦

It was close to midnight.

"I will retire to the white house," Lynn said.

"I gotta fix my face," Marie said.

"Really an insuperable task," said Lynn.

"Ha ha," said Marie.

Erick said, "Goodbye."

He watched them move away and, for a second, as Lynn's back receded, he thought of the past moving away. He remembered the months prior to graduation, when the sense of time was so strong on him.

Then he saw the girl by the window. She was standing alone before the picture window that overlooked a glittering celebrant called New York.

He felt a sudden tugging at his stomach and got up abruptly, impulsively. His first inclination was to get his coat and leave fast. But he couldn't. He didn't know why he couldn't.

There was a great deal of noise and she didn't hear him. He stood behind her a moment and looked at her hair. She stood very still, an unheeded cigarette hanging down at her right side, a half-filled glass sticking out of her hand like a sweat-covered growth.

"Are you the light in the window?" he asked.

She started a little and he saw the liquor splash up the sides of the glass. She turned quickly to look at him, her breath caught, then a smile started.

"Well," she said, shaking her head, "I didn't see *you*."

"Gazing out on the gaudy bug heap?" he asked, feeling himself grow tighter and tighter. She was like a ghost, he thought, a scrap of past suddenly jolted into the present, thoroughly out of place, making him ill.

"Bug heap, Erick?" she asked.

He made a noise. She was looking into his face as if trying to find something. She looked into his eyes, then up at his blonde hair, and her lips twitched a moment, as if they were undecided between frowning and smiling.

"How are you?" she asked.

"I'm alive," he said.

He saw her temples move, saw the lips draw back a little from her teeth. "It's quite a surprise, really," she said.

He tried to relax, to smile. "Yes, isn't it?"

My God, where is she, how is she?—cried his mind.

"Got your wife with you?" she asked, her smile a trifle labored.

"What?"

Something crossed her eyes, he didn't know what exactly. Maybe pain, something that etched a thought on her face, a thought that seemed to say—Everyone is married. And he knew she wasn't.

"You're married, aren't you?" she asked.

"No, of course I'm not married," he said. "What the hell gave you *that* idea?"

She blinked. "I don't know," she said, smiling awkwardly. "For some reason...I thought you were. Someone must have told me you were."

"Why did you ask, though?"

"Oh, I don't know," she said. "Maybe I don't want any raging wives clawing out my eyes." She said it lightly but Erick got the fleeting sensation that there had been many raging wives in the past who had wanted to claw out this young lady's eyes. Amorousness had always seemed her major talent at college.

Thinking of that made him want to touch her. She'd never attracted him at school except in spurts. They he realized that he wanted to touch her because she was suddenly the past to him and he wanted to grab hold of the past and pull himself back. To...?

"Heard from Sally?" he blurted out, unable to bear the conversation any longer when the question was eating his brain out.

"Mmm-hmm," she said lightly. "She got married last October."

He stood there smiling dumbly, his body suddenly devoid of all feeling.

"Oh," he said, "that's nice."

"She said if I ever ran across you to give you her regards."

Leo smiled.

"Regards," she said.

♦ ♦ ♦ ♦ ♦

He was drunk and he felt a driving need to get drunker and drunker. He wanted to numb his brain with liquor, drown it, destroy it. He was sitting next to Leo, his arm around her. The room spun around him and he kept getting the impulse to stand up and leap out the window.

"Who *are* you?" she asked, half drunk too.

"I'm Erick Linstrom," he said.

"What do you represent?"

"The poor huddled masses."

"Me too," she said.

"Me too," he said.

"What else do you do?" she asked. "Beside represent the poor huddled masses?"

"I write prose and pose in the nude for the girls from Battle Creek, Michigan."

"Lucky girls from Battle Creek, Michigan."

"Lucky."

"Save next weekend for me," she said, and he wanted to punch her right in the nose.

"Sure," he said, without knowing why. "I'll save 'em all for you."

"Good," she breathed, and her hand was on his leg. *Get your filthy hand off me*!

"And you are…?" he asked.

"Leo Peck."

"I never knew a Leo," he said, "who was a girl."

"Short," she said, "for Leonora, which is a girl."

"Is a girl. Is a girl."

"And I pose nude for the boys from Battle Creek, Michigan."

"Oh."

He took a long drink. *I'm going to die now*, he thought, *I'm just going to die*.

"I'm really a poor but honest working gal," she said, and the phrase smacked tritely in his ears. *You have no sense of the cliché*, he thought, but let it pass. *May I tear off your underwear?*

"You're still writing, huh?" she asked.

"Still writing, huh."

"Sally said you probably would be."

"Gracious of her." Her name made him shudder.

"You write stories?"

"Stories."

"What kind?"

"Unsalable."

"Are they salacious?"

"Salacious and unsalable."

"I'll have to read one some time." She pressed her leg against his.

"You're a modest boy and I love you," she said, and she suddenly leaned over and kissed him. Her lips were narrow and hot.

"Remember the Alamo to keep it holy," he said.

She looked at him with a drunken smile. "I'm Leo," she said. "I'm with you and I can be had." He wondered how many college boys had heard that line, how many had taken complete advantage of it. He felt his stomach muscles tighten. *I'd better leave her alone*, he thought, *I don't want to spoil even my memories*.

"You sold stories?" she asked, as if she'd seen his thoughts.

"One story. One magazine. One nation indivisible with…horse manure."

"Whish magazine?"

"*The Undertaker's Trowel.*"

"Tha's nice. Tha's awful nice," she said. She was close again. He could smell the liquor on her breath. He noticed Marie getting necked on another couch. It wasn't Lynn. As Leo leaned against him, Erick watched Marie's body writhing and saw how wide open she had her little red mouth.

"Like a bird waiting for a worm," he said.

"Who's that?" Leo asked.

He dropped his mouth on hers suddenly and dug his fingers into her back. Her breath caught and it seemed as if she had turned to shaking stone. Her nails raked over his arms and one hand clamped behind his head. Her tongue slipped like an attacking snake into his mouth. *Oh Sally! Sally!* his mind cried out, and he opened his eyes for a moment, getting the brief sensation that he was back in Sally's house, kissing Leo, and Sally was just about to come in the room and find them like that.

He drew back so fast she didn't have a chance to close her mouth. She looked as if she were gasping for air. Her eyes were thickened, animal-like, her mouth twitched.

Then she tightened too, her face grew hard as she reached for her drink. And he saw that she, too, held some fashion of jealous guard over herself, afraid, like him, to reveal the true self. He'd seen hints of it at school but never really looked. Now he felt as if he must know all about her so that his memory of Sally would be consolidated and placed in a firm mold. Maybe she could even tell him things about Sally, how…

No. He didn't want Leo to even mention that name to him. It was too close. How casually she'd said—Oh, she got married last October. He'd almost been unable to go on breathing.

He glanced at Leo and saw that her eyes were brown like Sally's, but not soft like Sally's. His throat contracted and he pretended that he was distracted by a sound on the other side of the room. He turned in that direction just in time to see Lynn lower his head. It made him angry that Lynn had been watching him.

"What have you been doing since you left school?" he said.

"Working," she said, and drank some more. He accidently brushed his hand over her shoulder and she stiffened.

"Working where?"

"In an agency," she said.

He noticed her thin face, her sharply-cut features, so different from Sally's full face. He noticed her narrow but firmly resolute shoulders. He glanced at the black dress cut deeply at the bodice as if she had reasoned that a young business woman at a New Year's Eve party must be sexy and she had made the concession without considering that sexiness meant more than dress. The firm arching of her breasts helped a little and so did her white wrists and slender hands, half hinting that she was some frail creature who could be expected to be a raging temptress in the sanctity of one's bedroom.

"Excuse me," she said, and she went across the room quickly and down the hall. He sat there staring at the rug. *She hates me*, he thought. *Who cares, I hate her, too.*

♦ ♦ ♦ ♦ ♦

"Happee new year!" howled a young, very drunk man, and an equally drunk Leo pushed against him with a silly smile, sliding her arms around his neck.

"I *like* you," she said, gritting her teeth.

Her mouth settled like wet wings over his and he held her tightly; the ghost of something long forgotten or, at least, attemptedly forgotten. A horn blew. Everyone screamed and clapped their hands and slid forward to lock lips with the nearest convenient member of the opposite sex and the year exited in a sudden, slurping silence.

"Happy new year, baby," she muttered in his ear.

"Happy new year," he said tensely, and buried his face in her hair, trying to pretend she was Sally. Without hesitation he cupped one hand over her right breast and drew in his fingers. She trembled violently and pushed it harder into him. *First sign*, he thought calmly, back again in the present. Thoroughly vindicated by the way her breath spurted out hotly and her fingers opened and closed like the jaws of a trap on him. *Trap me*, he thought, *destroy me, I want to be destroyed.*

Her hotel was two blocks from his room and close to the party. He was sober enough to be glad of that, to feel grateful they could walk from the party and he wouldn't have to pay a cab.

He was conscious enough too to be aware of how shabby his overcoat was. He wondered if she remembered it was still the same one he'd worn at college.

"I had a crush on you," she said as they went down the stairs. "You know that?"

"No."

"Ooh, I used to wanna jump ya when big Sal went out of the room."

Don't call her that, you drunken slut! his mind exploded. He didn't change expressions, he smiled thinly. Only his muscles contracted suddenly under his clothes and the murderous rage churned in his stomach. They went out of the building and he didn't care if he ever saw her again.

"Are *your* parents alive?" Leo asked.

"No."

She held onto his arm. "We're both orphans," she said.

It was past four. Erick felt almost a cleansing to come out into the sharp biting air of the street. It cleared up the fuzziness in his head, leaving only the slight dizziness, the tilted gyroscope that made walking seem easy. It was good, too, to get out of that party that was still dwindling on in dark corners, where moans and rustles of opening dresses could be heard. Lynn had gone home long before, leaving a half-stripped Marie on the couch with a married executive whose wife was presenting impromptu bounties in the bedroom.

They walked along, listening to their shoes clicking on the cold sidewalk, walking under the grayish morning sky and, crossing the main arteries, looking down toward the Battery to see the light coming from the East.

Her arm was hooked in his. The front of her fur coat was open and she breathed deeply as she walked. He said once that she'd catch cold.

"I don't give a damn," she said, almost exultantly.

As they walked along he felt the icy air creep through his suit and chill his body.

"I love it like this," she said. "This is the time to live. When everybody else is asleep, when the city itself is all yours."

"The city is no one's" he said.

"You know what I mean."

"I suppose," he said. "It does have a certain dignity in the morning. The carping and the haggling are done with. It washes out its scaly hair and composes its filthy limbs to wait, in supine drabness, for the coming day."

"Someone is bitter," she said.

"Yes," he said.

She slid her hand into his pocket and her strong fingers knitted with his. They kept walking in silence. He hardly felt the cold now. He kept wondering if she did look like Sally as she sometimes appeared to; the eyes, the cut of her hair, the walk. Leo looked very pretty with her cheeks so red from the cold, ringlets of her darkish blonde hair hanging around her face, framing it. When she smiled, it revealed her small even teeth, very white.

In the lobby of her hotel they stood face to face. He was almost sober by then. The cold in his body was beginning to make him shiver fitfully. He wasn't going to kiss her there, with the desk man observing them in sleepy detachment, the door porter leaning against the wall. Besides he didn't want to kiss her anyway.

She took his hand.

"Good night, Erick," she said. "It was swell running into you again. Thanks a lot for taking me home."

"You're welcome," he said. She was something remote now.

They stood in awkward silence a moment, then he blurted out, almost automatically, "May I call you?"

She smiled pleasantly.

"Sure," she said. "I'd like you to."

"Okay," he said.

There was a brief verbal scuffle while they straightened out the fact that if he forgot the number she gave him, he could easily find it in the directory. Then she squeezed his hand and her eyes were warm for a moment. She walked into the elevator, which yawned conveniently.

He walked back to his room, shivering, coat buttoned up to the neck, feet getting numb.

What did he ask her if he could call her for? Who wanted to call her? Just because she reminded him of Sally—that was a dumb reason for seeing anyone. *Leave yesterday alone*, he told himself, *that's a fool's game*.

Sally married.

As he shut the door of his room, the words struck his mind and he realized he'd been obsessed by that one thought all night. He felt his chest tightening as he leaned against the door. He coughed hollowly and looked around the drab room.

Then it all seemed to pile up in him and he sat down quickly at the table and took the cover off his typewriter.

Sally is married.

I met Leo tonight and she told me.

It is two things. It is possibility and impossibility. I can believe it and I cannot believe it. It is all so irrevocably bound up with memories, with half-recognized hopes, with long disappointments.

I love Sally.

I have no right to say it now, not when it's too late. No use trying to recapture that magic. It was a particular brand that is not repeated.

Too late. That's my trouble, I say things too late. I hope for something to happen. I lie awake at night and dream of possibilities but never a concrete move do I make. I wait and dream and then the bubble is burst and I am thrown down on rocks.

That is me.

I love her. I have loved her for some time now. Why didn't I tell her? Why didn't I ask her to wait, to come to New York and be with me? Why didn't I tell her I wanted to share my life with her? Why?

God only knows. Hidden childish hopes for better things when, rationally, I knew all along there was nothing better than her. There is nothing.

I know I shall never find another woman in my life that will mean as much to me as Sally. Not only because it is her, not just because of that. But because all the ties that bind us were of non-weakening nature. She is always associated with the period of fruitage in my life, with that period when I first found my fulfillment. Because when I think of happiness, I think of Sally.

I never knew one like her. Never. I don't expect to. She could make me feel delight. She could make me happy. I enjoyed being with her. Love came long but when it came it was no suspicious burst of juvenile fire. It was a growing realization that, for a long time, I had become increasingly fond of her and I didn't want to face life without her.

Then, why? Why? Why didn't I tell her? Why didn't I write, telegraph, phone and say—Sally, I love you. I know I have no right to say it now, but I love you. Will you come to me and will you hope and work with me and will you let me share my poor life with you? Will you be my wife?

I never said it.

And I never can now. It is too late, much too late. I am desolate to think that I shall never hold in my arms that warm, pervading comfort of her presence. To sleep with her, to have those warm arms around me, to feel that comforting body against mine. To talk with her in the darkness, to make love to her. To feel her love in the very nerves of my body. Oh God, how powerful a love she had.

Well, what's that to the matter? I'm lost, done for. I've no chance of having her now. I surrendered, I gave up. I was a fool that didn't know a miracle when it was in my own hands. And, if I'm unhappy because I've lost the only girl I ever loved—then I deserve it! I deserve each moment of misery richly. I have been owed these moments of sorrow, they are long overdue. They came before but not without rays of hope. Hope for possibilities, for something to happen without me lifting a finger. Providence, fate, good fortune. Sally coming to me without me even asking. How stupid I am and have always been!

Well, it's over. I can't have her anymore. I'll never marry. I want too much. To expect another girl like Sally is ridiculous, impossible.

I hope she will be happy. I hope she will be brilliantly happy. I hope she has a fine home and beautiful children and I hope she is always at peace. I want that for her. At least I can send my love to her in that respect. I will not envy. I will not be jealous or hate because some other man has been intelligent enough to see her worth and embrace it.

No. I wish her every happiness. I hope she will always receive every goodness she deserves. I love her. Blood of my blood, heart mine. I send my love to you. You will never know it but my heart is with you and always will be.

My Sally.

Later in bed he thought once of Leo. Of the fact that he'd never call her up. That was certain.

two.

And he wouldn't have. It was just of those rare circumstances which seem to fall under the category of fate. Lynn had known a girl named Virginia Greene at the University. This girl got a job with a woman travelogue producer after she graduated and, since graduation, had been buzzing around the world making pictures with this woman, Adelaide Cross.

Now they were ready for a New Year's season of touring the country and their first engagement was in New York City. So Virginia, remembering Lynn with affection, got in touch with him and sent him four complimentary tickets to the performance—*Mexican Magic*. Erick was amused when he found out that Lynn wasn't even going to ask Virginia to go with him. Lynn suggested that only the two of them go. Then Marie found out about it and insisted on going. Lynn, vice-presidency bound, dared not refuse. Erick needed a date, Leo was the only girl Erick knew. Reluctantly, Erick called her and the date was made.

♦ ♦ ♦ ♦ ♦

"Hi," she said over the phone. "Why don't you go in the bar and order us a couple of Sidecars?"

"What?" he frowned. "Oh, All right."

"I'll be right down."

He moved into the dim bar that smelled of leather and liquor and smoke. He slid into a booth and took out his wallet. He had three dollars. He hissed in displeasure. She must have known he had just about no money.

"Two Sidecars," he ordered irritably, almost asking, "How much are they?"

As the drinks were brought in to the table, he thought he might have told her his stomach was upset and ordered only the drink for her. He sat there fingering the stem of the glass in front of him, staring moodily at the table.

Money, he thought. *Damn its endless power*. He took a sip of the sharp-tasting drink. Then he looked up to see if the girl who came into the bar was Leo, but it wasn't.

Leo came down twenty minutes later. By that time Erick was just about ready to get up and leave her. His body was tight with anger, as she slid in across from him.

"Mmmm," she said, picking up the glass. "Sidecar."

"We have to meet them soon," he said coldly.

"Sorry I'm late," she tossed off.

♦ ♦ ♦ ♦ ♦

It was a big place. Erick hadn't thought it would be crowded but it was. Mostly with old people. They were filing in fast like a sluggish stream. The four of them moved in with the aging assemblage. Men in tuxedos and wearing painful expressions on their faces were telling everyone to go upstairs. They went downstairs and found four seats together. They squeezed in, begging pardons, and slumped down.

"I think we got into the old folk's home by mistake," whispered Leo. He smiled thinly. *If you don't like it, get the hell out*, his mind said to her. He looked over at Lynn, looked around with a half-disguised amusement.

"Pretty sharp, haah Lynn?" he said.

Lynn smiled weakly.

"Haah, Lynn?"

"Quiet," said Lynn.

Erick looked around. In front of him were two women who could have been nothing but school teachers. As a matter of fact the place was a veritable hotbed of maiden school teachers. He could almost smell them, a faint odor of starchy clothes and chalk and drying away. Two of them sat in front of Erick. That they were old maids shone from their unwrinkled and sexless features, in the botanical hats they wore over graying hair. One of them, a skinny one, didn't laugh. She trembled with amusement as though shaking a bug off her shoulder or coughing. She was laughing at what the other was saying.

Erick looked around the theatre, feeling a sense of crowding and of noise. Hearing a hundred voices billowing like ocean spume, rising waves of sound. Seeing the walls rise sheer and parabolic into the high arched ceiling, spaced with glittering circles of light. Seeing a chandelier encrusted with geometric china shining like a crystalline moon. Deep-cut scrollwork on the walls. A stout harp, chipped with brittle age, leaned upon by round-bellied urchins leering down in narcissistic detachment at the squash of assembly. Curves, elliptic plaster turns, sweeping falls of paint-thick walls with periodic announcements in sober-glassed red: EXIT. Tiers of side boxes dipping from the second balcony and ending at last, a hovering pinnacle of plush and tarnished brass above the orchestra. And down again to the floor, the long segments of living ellipses that formed the rows of seats.

"Sure is old," Leo said.

"What?" he asked.

"I said it sure is old." Louder. The old women in front stopped talking a moment as if she'd insulted their collective chastities. Erick couldn't help smiling and that relaxed him. As they spoke of various things, what he'd done, what she'd been doing, he heard the creaky voices of old folks all around. He felt out of place. Where were the young people, he thought, the vital people, the people who could change old things? Why did the old always crowd into one place and never have the young with them? Why were they so far apart?

He shook his head once. They were not here, the young, nor ever would be. They were out, by Christ, downing a fifth and jazzing their old flames in a beat-up hot rod on some lonesome country road or socking it in hard to the strains of some hirsute combination that plied its ungodly wares in some near-dungeon on the outskirts of obscurity. Or in movies munching popcorn and fumbling for brassieres. Or in darkened living rooms, making springs squeak. Was that the only way?

He looked at Leo. She was looking at him.

"Welcome back," she said.

He smiled a little. "I drift away," he said.

She put her hand on his. It was more like a claw, he thought, maybe not in actual appearance so much but in the way she drew the fingers in and sort of scratched his flesh without bruising it. But it wasn't like Sally's touch, no girl could ever touch him like that. He looked at Leo and noticed her breasts rise once sharply and her lips moved a little.

"Club people," Lynn said, "an unnatural tribe of underdeveloped people who thrive on forced enthusiasms."

"Have you been working all this time on that?" Erick asked.

Lynn snickered. He looked up.

"Time to start," he said.

As if responding to his command, the lights flickered and went down. In the darkness Leo's hand gripped at Erick's and she leaned toward him. Her hand was hot. It wasn't like Sally used to do. It wasn't warm and loving, it was hungry and possessive and he didn't like it. He felt her fingers drawing in on his hand.

An aging man, white-crowned and portly, stalked out of the wings. He strode casually to the podium, there was a murmur of interest from wrinkled lips. Aha, Erick thought, this is nothing new, I see, these are the old troupers, smug in their knowledge. This is their club, their lodge, their sewing circle, their political ward.

"Oh God," he muttered.

"What's the matter?" Leo whispered.

He leaned over. "I think that..."

Then he stopped as he realized that she was moving her head a little as his breath touched her ear. He felt a lump rise into his throat and he turned back front quickly, exhaling quickly.

All the old people murmured now, there was an expectant rustle. *What in the hell is the man going to do*, Erick thought, *take to the wing?*

"And how are *you*?" said the man.

Giggles. Old women half-swooning and clutching for their lace collars. Old men cackling deep in the hollow recesses of their bony chests. Raw, bloody amusement, Erick thought.

The old man went on. The four of them were like usurpers, Erick thought. He started to imagine. The others would smell them out, they would rise up in vengeance and eject them, sever their bodies from their heads and poke their heads on the ends of their black umbrellas. They would burn them up in a fire of old snuff and asephetida bags.

The man spoke proudly. All was pride there that evening. One hundred twenty years of continuous seasons, said the old man with a husky, patriotic ring in his voice. Mad applause, loud and raucous. People applauding themselves. *Who knows*, Erick thought, *maybe some of these people were there when the first session of this culture organization began those one hundred and twenty years ago*.

The man kept talking incessantly. Erick glanced at Lynn and saw him sitting there as if anesthetized. A bored Marie was trying to read a magazine she had with her with not much success, since it was practically dark.

"We must support the Institute," said the man. He spoke about all the functions of it, the museum and the concert series and the operas and the lectures. Then, after twenty minutes, the man said he wasn't going to make a speech. He left but not until everyone had applauded various people in the Institute, various customs of the Institute, and just plain the Institute. Erick kept applauding vigorously, once crying,

"Hurrah!" in a fit of levity. The old school teachers, suspecting cynicism, looked back at him from beneath irate eyebrows.

The applause rang on. Erick could just picture all the old men and women there. He could see each one of them sitting there, glorying in each moment, wishing to make each passing second of such import that, even on their death beds, it would be memorable.

I'm young, he thought, *and will not understand. But life to the aged is a fast one, a cruelly rapid one. It flies past, the days are moments, the months are winks of the eye. It gains velocity the older you get until it goes so fast by your eyes that you cannot even see it clearly and it makes you want to cry aloud*. It was the way he felt near graduation, when days seemed to go and come with blinding speed.

And this affair was glorious business for the old people. They were all together and they were going to see a show and they had a whole glorious season of shows and lectures and concerts and marionette shows and operas before them. Ahead were palmy days, bounties for the decrepit, a boon to the palsied. So they applauded. They felt good. They felt as if every moment should be heralded, feted and given the honor so due it. To them each moment was a precious jewel to be held tightly and not let go of without a sign and a backward look that brought tears to the rheumy eye. And if these moments could be made auspicious by singing them out, by applauding them away, by shouting their departure as a crowd shouts departing passengers away on an ocean vessel—then all to the good. Farewell sweet moments! Never can you come again, but I have treated you kindly. Treat me equally so in our next meeting. The next time around.

Erick tried to shut his eyes and sleep. Finally the man left the stage and, except for slight mumbles and chattering, silence fell down like a tent.

"Now do we see the pitcha, Lynn?" Erick asked. "Now, haah? Lynn?"

"Shut up or I'll buy you a season ticket to this place," Lynn threatened.

"No, not that!" Erick begged.

The old ladies grew more irate. The curtain went up. Erick murmured, "Uh-oh."

It was a ballroom scene. There were pillars of canvas that trembled as if with the ague. There were doors of canvas painted on the backdrop. There was, for reality, a great lumpy grand piano standing boldly and forcefully on the stage.

"Is that the movie projector, Lynn?" Erick asked.

Lynn looked uncomfortable. "I thought this was a picture," Marie said. "Lynnie?"

"Oh, quiet," said Lynnie.

"Next week is the picture," Erick said. "This week is the Mills Brothers."

Four men filed out on the stage, five. The four were middle-aged youngsters held in by trusses and character. The fifth was old. They strode in manly strides. Over the wings and into the stage. They walked with a good walk and with a true walk. They had tuxedos on. They smiled. They were a quartet.

The fifth man was desiccated. He was an old grey potato in a tuxedo. He had no hair. He plopped down at the piano and struck at the keys savagely, as if they pit vipers all in a line. He bounced his fingers on the whiteness and the blackness. The keys screamed, there was noise. It was music. The men sang.

They sang old songs and new songs. Cowboy songs and songs from the Deep South. The second baritone introduced the rest of the quartet. This is Gene Cole from Alabama. Applause, sighs, laughter, muffled sobs, as though Gene Cole from Alabama was the greatest thing since the crucifixion. This is John Foster from Kentucky…

They weren't a bad quartet, they sang in tune. But it seemed funny to Erick. It had an air about it; old people and the old opera house and a quartet singing humorous songs in Negro dialect while an old raggedy man stabbed at a keyboard.

"This is glorious, haah, Lynn?" Erick said.

Lynn put his hands over his face and moaned softly. Erick laughed.

The quartet finished and strode off stage. They strode on again. Lynn sank deeper into his seat. The quartet sang an encore—*Moonlight on the Campus*. A sad memory song. What a mockery of sentiment, Erick thought, a stupid song about college days. He ignored the contraction in his throat. He went on thinking about the old people. What were they dreaming now? Of youth? *When I was young*. The words probably hovered in a thousand heads. When I was a boy. When I was a girl. You don't appreciate. If I only had the things that. Why if someone had offered me a. You young folks have no idea what.

"Yup," he murmured to himself.

The red curtain went down. He looked at Leo.

"Glorious?" he asked.

"Absolutely," she said.

"*Is* there a picture, Lynnie?" Marie asked.

"I've lost contact with reality," said Lynn. "You'll forgive me. I thought I was coming to see a film partially made by a young lady I knew at college. Instead I have been subjected to a hideous round of shocking sights and sounds. I apologize to you all. Shall we depart?"

"Maybe next, Lynn," Erick said. "Maybe is the pitcha next."

The curtain went up. A white screen hung down.

"Thank God," Lynn said.

The lights went out and a stocky woman bustled out. That would be Adelaide, Erick thought.

"Good evening, fellow travelers," she simpered.

Erick thought the film was asinine. Adelaide Cross kept rattling off platitudes about the lovely Mexican women who never wore mascara while behind her on the screen were pictures of writhing, pop-eyed fish gasping for life in a fisherman's net. She spoke about beautiful cape work and the camera reported the dragging of a dead bull from the arena.

A lot of the film was about bull fighting. First the film showed Mexico in recent times, the horses padded thickly around the body. You see how they are protected from the bull's horns, Adelaide Cross said. Then the picture showed Spain in the 1920's, with the horses getting gored and lying in a heap with their blue guts hanging out and throbbing on the hot bloody sands.

"So you see," Adelaide Cross said, "Things are much better. Oh, what excellent cape work. How indomitable the man is."

In went the razor-point banderillo into the muscle of the bull's neck. A banderillero misses. "He'll get boos," said Adelaide Cross, "then, like a flash, the sword is plunged into the heart of the bull. It drops dead instantly."

It wasn't a travelogue, Erick thought, it was a satire on a travelogue. Sunsets every few moments bringing inevitable applause. Shots of idiotic women giggling as they picked flowers. Rooftop shots of various capitols. And Adelaide Cross giving full measure of clichés.

"The women never have to wear mascara," she said for the fifteenth time.

♦ ♦ ♦ ♦ ♦

"Good God," Lynn said despairingly, "my poor friend Virginia Greene teamed up with that female cretin."

They were in a small Village restaurant, stone-walled, travel posters slapped on the walls. The white-covered table glowed in the candlelight and shadows flickered on the walls. A recorder played Shostakovich's Fifth.

"It sure was interesting," Erick said, mockingly earnest.

"That woman was incredible," Lynn said.

"Can I have some more wine, Lynnie?" Marie asked. Lynn poured from the bottle. Erick offered Leo some but she still had a little in her glass. He looked at her as he asked her. Her eyes sparkled in the candlelight. The jacket of her grey plaid suit was open and her firm breasts showed through the sheer white silk of her blouse. She held the wine glass with both hands and smiled at Erick. He turned away.

"How'd you like that stuff about bullfighting?" he asked.

"Sickening," said Lynn.

Erick mimicked, "The bull drops dead instantly." Then his face sobered. "As if that condones it," he said. "As if it isn't a grisly sport."

"One of man's most monstrous entertainments," Lynn said, "on par with lions eating Christians."

"It is," Erick said, noticing how Leo looked intently at him as he spoke. For a moment he got the sense that life was one great endless conversation with one girl or another looking at you while you talked. At least his life was. Rather monotonous. But he went on.

"Man at his lowest ebb," he said. "Not that death is unnatural. When it's done for food, for self-preservation, then it's natural, a part of evolution, each seeking to survive. It isn't cruel or uncruel, it simply *is*."

Marie looked around the restaurant, bored. Leo still looked at him.

"Killing for sport," Erick said, "to destroy a life to amuse a bunch of jerks on a hot Sunday afternoon. To give the psychotic bull fighter a chance to realize his death wish."

Leo took a breath and, for a moment, her eyes were Sally's eyes and she was Sally sitting across from him in the picked up his book and affected the look of pure hat he managed so well.

dnight," he said. "Go home and write yourself a ”

little cellar place they used to frequent at college. He liked the feeling.

"Well, at least it's honest hypocrisy," he said. "They're killing outright. They don't try to hide it. Like our prize fighting."

He drank some wine and felt the heat roll down into his stomach.

"In prize fighting," he went on, "death comes slow, treading on the footsteps of a ruptured vessel, a severed connection, a swollen lobe. That's the prime cruelty. The same crowds, the same betting, the same roar of the beast. Only the crowd is the beast now and the thing that dies is man. The making of dollars on the loss of vitality, the presentation as entertainment of the destruction of man."

"Why not?" Lynn said. "Let man punch himself to extinction, one by one."

Erick noticed how Marie stared at the tablecloth, running her fingers over it. Does it remind you of the sheets in someone's bed you've been in—he almost said.

"Really they ought to drag a boxer out by his heels, too," he went on. "The dead and bloody victim of sport. No. He walks out. Maybe he smiles and raises his arms in victory. But he's closer to death. There are differences. His muscles are different. His brain is less efficient. His eyes see more poorly. And with every fight he dies a little more, more of his greatest gift is dissipated. He trods quickly and yet more quickly toward the grave. And even if he dies in bed, he's dead sooner because he gave himself up to the lights and the punches and the flailing of commercial demand. He gets slaughtered, piece meal. He makes money and pays his bills and digs his grave with clotted blood vessels."

"I don't like boxing, anyway," Marie said. "It's boring."

"Yes, dear," Lynn said, patting her on her foolish head.

"And so much for Hemingway," Erick said.

Lynn grinned. "I thought there was something behind that tirade," he said. Erick ignored him, but he felt embarrassed, as if Lynn had suddenly stripped him before their eyes.

"I like it here," Leo said, as if changing the subject. "Who discovered it?"

"Columbus," Erick said.

"No, who?"

"Lynn."

"No, I did," Marie said. "I used to come here long ago when they first opened, and nobody used to come here during those days."

"That was during the Harding Administration, wasn't it?" Erick said.

Lynn and Leo smiled. "Who's *Harding*?" Marie asked.

Lynn told her and she looked at Erick and said, "Ha ha ha," but she wasn't laughing.

"You know," Erick said, "if it wasn't for sex, I don't think men and women would stand for each other."

Marie asked casually, "Have you two had sex yet?"

"Not yet," Leo said.

Erick felt himself start unexpectedly and he almost spilled his wine glass. Leo had spoken so simply. *Not yet*. The words haunted him the rest of the evening. Maybe she'd said it just not to be fazed by Marie's impertinent question. Then again, maybe she hadn't. It was as if she'd said—*Well, we just met, but as soon as things get a little settled, we'll pop into bed together and have at it*.

Sally, he thought without knowing why, *what would Sally say*? Why did he always feel responsibility toward Sally for anything he did to Leo? It was crazy, unrealistic. But he did.

He kept on talking all night and no one noticed at all that he was upset, because he had spent twenty-seven years keeping revelation from his face.

"Thumb me a woman," Lynn would say, and Marie would groan, "Oh, not again!"

"Her arms reached the floor," Erick would say, and the rest of the night he forced himself to be light. Before the evening ended Marie impulsively insisted that they all have

three.

When he called for Leo on Saturday night, she told him to wait for her in the bar and order two daiquiris. He hung up the phone angrily and moved into the bar. There he sat in the booth, waiting for her, thinking about their first date, about how when they got back to the hotel she insisted on looking in her mail box when it was obvious there was no mail. But it gave her a chance to stand with him out of sight of the night clerk. He'd held her in his arms and kissed her coolly. Then she pressed her cheek against his and he felt like a fool, bent over like that.

"Thanks a lot," she said, "I had a swell time."

"Quartet and all?"

"Quartet and all," she said, as if it were some obscure declaration of love.

"Shall I call you before next Saturday?"

"I wish you would."

"All right," he told her, and then kissed her again, and she caught at his elbows and held tight.

"Good night, baby," she said.

He thought of it as he sat there staring down into the untouched daiquiris, watching the delicate frothy surface break down. He felt a desire to have Leo alone somewhere, to seduce her. It was almost a sense of duty, the duty of the red-blooded American male. But the way she kissed him, the way she spoke so glibly of sex, her shadowy past at college—they all seemed to indicate that the idea was quite mutual. He remembered her at Sally's house, always stretching out. That night she'd come in when he was drunk. The way she took off her sweater and swelled out her breasts. *Nice?* He could hear her words again.

After a while she came down, wearing a tweed skirt and a light brown silk blouse. She carried a waist length tan jacket in her arms. She came up and slid in beside him with a smile and pressed his hand as he kissed her cheek.

"Hi, baby," she said, then picked up the drink and took a sip. "Mmm, that's good," she said. "I go for daiquiris."

♦ ♦ ♦ ♦ ♦

Lynn let them in.

"Hi!" Leo said to him.

"Hello." They all went into the living room.

"Where's Marie?" Erick asked, glancing around.

"She's ill," Lynn said.

"Oh, that's too bad," Leo said, and Lynn looked stage-sad.

"What's wrong with her?" Erick asked suspiciously.

Lynn sort of half shrugged then headed for the kitchen. Leo looked after him.

"That spoils it for him," she said softly.

"Oh, yes indeed," Erick said. "Give me your jacket."

They went into the bedroom and Leo looked around.

"Oh, I like this," she said. "I wish I had an apartment like this."

"Do you?" he asked.

"What's the matter, baby? You look upset."

"Nothing," he said.

Dinner was a somber affair. Erick sat morosely while Lynn acted out the role of perfect host, bringing in the well-done roast lamb and potatoes, lighting candles, moving from kitchen to dining room with his quick, sure motions, a smile always half-written on his face.

"More salad?" he would ask, "Broccoli?" Sitting and eating only a little himself, his gaze on Leo always that of scientist on microbe. Or procurer on client, Erick thought. He wondered how Lynn had managed to keep away Marie. Probably by getting her an introduction to some handsome young radio or television star. Marie was fickle.

"Thumb me a woman, Mr. Linstrom," Lynn said once, so irritatingly that Erick wanted to hurl his dish at him.

"She was a man," Erick said as pointedly as possible.

Lynn pursed his lips. "What do you think?" he asked Leo. Then he moved back into the kitchen looking interested and pleased.

After dinner there was a bottle of wine, two glasses on the shiny-topped coffee table before the couch. The bottle rested in, oddly enough, a bowl of cracked ice.

Erick twitched uncomfortably when he saw it. He almost expected Lynn to start lecturing casually on the importance of concentrating on black whales floating by icebergs. One thing was certain, though. He wasn't going to touch Leo. It was too obvious with Lynn hovering, waiting like a pale-faced pimp for the commencement of business. He sat beside Leo on the couch, sipping red wine. Lynn sat in an arm chair, chatting politely. From the Magnavox steamed Wagner's *Love Death Music*. Lynn let his words stop and watched Leo as she lay, her head back, listening. She moved against Erick and Lynn's face registered slightly. Erick glanced at him. Lynn's features committed nothing. Erick waited but he couldn't catch Lynn's eye. He turned back with a heavy breath and felt his arm tingle as Leo touched it idly with her white fingers. *This is Leo Peck*, he thought, *she lived with Sally. Years and years in the same house with Sally, with…*

He closed his eyes. It was terrible to remember.

♦ ♦ ♦ ♦ ♦

Promptly at ten, Lynn got up and said, "I believe I'll do some reading."

He grabbed a book and went into the bedroom with another bottle of wine and an, "Excuse me, both." The door shut behind him and Erick wondered what sort of look was on Lynn's face, now that he was hidden away. Elation? Or shaking rage?

"He feels bad," Leo said.

"What do you mean?"

"About Marie not coming. I think probably she stood him up. I feel so sorry for him."

Erick snickered.

"That's not nice," she said. "Isn't he your friend?"

"Yup. My pal."

"It doesn't sound like it."

"You should only know," he said.

They were silent a while.

"What does he do?" Leo asked then.

"He needles."

"No, I mean his job."

"Public relations."

"He does all right for himself," she said.

Erick blew out a weary breath. Then he said, impulsively, "You want to go out with him?"

She turned quickly and looked at him.

"What are you talking about?" she asked.

"You like his job, you like his apartment. You want to go out with him?"

In another moment, he thought, he'd strike her silly empty face.

"You want to?" he asked again, louder.

"Stop it." Her voice was cold, as cold as his look. She smiled a little then. "Stop it," she said again.

With complete perverseness of desire, he pulled her against his body and kissed her. He hated her, he suddenly thought, and that's why he kissed her. He wanted to hurt himself. She was a part of Sally and he wanted to punish himself. No, that was silly, what it really was was…

All the time this went on, she was moving her hips to rub her stomach against his. Her breath came quickly and he didn't even know when he put his hand on her left breast. She shuddered violently. Excitement began fluttering down through him and he realized that the idea of Lynn being in the next room excited him even more. He knew Lynn had planned it, had managed to talk Marie into doing something else. But he was amused because he was going to enjoy it.

Leo pulled her lips away suddenly.

"Oh no," she muttered.

He almost laughed in her face. He got a vision of the great game it was, replete with ohs and ahs and refusals and eventual grantings. Strange how oblivious he seemed to it now. It wasn't frightening or wild or anything. It was amusing and he craved it. To him there was no question about it and he was sure she felt the same way; they were going to have each other. It was as casual as Marie's stupid question. They might laugh and joke and talk of something else. She might look desperate and say "Oh no," but every path of activity led to the same highway and that highway led straight and true to the bedroom. To love? That was doubtful. He didn't think he needed the delusion anymore that he loved what he desired.

They lay there a long time making love. Every once in a while she'd get too excited and pull away and turn a little to the side, breathing torturously and staring at the ceiling with an expression of self-disgust on her face. Then she'd come back, she kept coming back and, like a machine, he pulled her on, all the elements in his fingers, pulled and woven together. *Wouldn't Sally be surprised now*, he thought. *Wouldn't she be surprised to see how easy it was now for him, how well he did it.*

He didn't even jump when Lynn came staggering out. He only thought, as soon as he heard the door open—*Lynn can't stand it anymore, he has to know.*

"By God, I'm drunk," Lynn said, blinking at them. "I sat in there reading and I couldn't focus my eyes. I kept reading and drinking, drinking and reading. The book started to fade, I couldn't see what I was reading anymore. I thought the lamp was burning down or my eyes were going bad. Then I knew—I was drunk."

Leo was laughing quietly as Lynn stood there weaving, then leaned against the wall. Suddenly Lynn slipped down slowly and sat on the rug.

"My good God," he muttered in a hollow voice.

"Good book, Lynn?" Erick asked.

"I don't remember," Lynn said. "All I remember is the room getting fuzzier and fuzzier. And I thought maybe my eyes..."

"Were going bad," Erick finished.

Lynn stared dizzily at the rug. Then he looked up at them.

"It's a secret," he said, "but Marie isn't ill. That was just a deception. She's really out with another man. Probably in the reclining position by now."

"Who broke the date, Lynn?" Erick asked. "You or Marie?"

Lynn shook his head as if to clear it. He looked at Leo.

"Don't you listen to me and don't you believe anything I say," he said. "I'm drunk. I'm a monkey. Where is my cap and my cup? Where is my simian appurtenance thereunto?"

"Unquote," Erick said. "Erick Linstrom."

Lynn's mouth twitched. Then he looked at Leo brightly.

"Why don't you spend the night here?" he asked her.

"Why Lynn," Leo said.

Oh, you can do better than that, Erick's mind commented.

"I mean with the big Swede here," Lynn amended. He threw out his arms in a gesture of artificial gratuitousness. "Be my guest."

"Couch isn't big enough," Leo joked, and Erick found his mind racing through all impending conversations. His heart started to beat rapidly at the thought of how close it was. He didn't know whether to sit there quietly or join the ruse or get up and kick in Lynn's face. The last was definitely a possibility. The thought of committing violence on people he disliked seemed to come up against no conscientious opposition anymore.

"I mean in the bedroom," Lynn went on. "I'll sleep on the couch."

You're getting a little obvious now, Erick told him without words.

"I don't think so, Lynn," she said.

Lynn lurched up and started for the bathroom.

"Think I'll bladder out," he said with calculated coarseness. The door slammed shut behind him.

"Why don't you stay?" Erick asked, feeling the words come out by themselves, something to say.

She looked at him with an expression he took for pain.

"If I do," she said, "you know what will happen."

"I know," he said. He didn't.

She clenched her teeth and rubbed a hand over his chest.

"Oh God, I *want* to, Erick, but..."

"Then do," he said casually, suddenly imagining that Lynn was on his knees at the bathroom door keyhole, listening. The vision was hilarious.

"I can't," he heard her say. "I can't get involved again."

"Involved?"

"It's a long, sad story," she said. "You wouldn't be interested."

"Maybe I would."

He didn't care about anything. He wanted to go back to his room and go to sleep.

"No, you wouldn't," she said.

Lynn came back in and fell down into the armchair.

"Why don't you spend the night here?" he asked.

She shook her head.

"I'm discreet," Lynn said.

"You're drunk," Erick said.

"I'm drunk, I'm engaged, I use..." he broke off and flung out a melodramatic arm, "God!" he cried, "Stop the world, I'm getting off!"

Leo laughed nervously.

"Oh, God, where am I?" she said.

"In the House of Love," Lynn said, looking pleased.

"You don't give up easy, do you?" she asked him.

"Not I," said Lynn, then he turned to Erick quickly. "I have it!" he said. "Give us your lecture on Man as Animal!"

"I don't remember it," Erick said.

"Sure. Come on, Man as Animal."

"What's that?" Leo asked.

"Work of art," said Lynn. "If our boy would write stuff like that he'd sell and get out of his introspective rat hole."

"Why don't you go blow your brains out?" Erick asked.

"Man as Animal," Lynn said. He applauded. *I'd like to squash you*, Erick thought, *like a bug, a big fat bug*. He leaned back and closed his eyes and saw himself as he was when he'd read it to Lynn at the Golden Campus that night while, out on the floor, Sally danced with another man. He had just run into Sally accidentally that night, while she was on a date with Felix Karis.

"The title of my speech is Man as Animal," he has said. "This is not such an outrageous title as I will, at minor length, prove to your skeptical minds. So list."

He was back there. He didn't care about the present, the only thing he knew about the present was that he was reliving the past in it.

"He remembers every word," he heard Lynn say. "I shudder before such memory, I give obeisance."

Erick closed his eyes tightly, getting the foolish hope that when he opened his eyes he would be back in the Golden Campus again.

"Man," he said, "the animal who hides like a thief behind the whitish veil of human flesh. Man's actions are his basic qualification for the animal world."

Leo snuggled against him and he suddenly realized that she had been part of his college life, too, and it drove him back further.

"Yet, not withstanding this, there are notable physical aspects which also may give him admittance into the world of the jungle. So list.

"Now. Scornful of the decent fashion, this animal Man no longer stands on all fours. Instead he has strained all muscular function so that he now stands in a painfully unnatural erect position, somewhat like the anthropoid, though hardly as attractive."

Lynn snickered. "Man as Animal," he muttered.

"His skull is tightly covered with a loathsome white skin, which peels off when sunlight makes it red. The skull and this skin are in turn covered with a vulgar growth that the beast has clipped at intermittent periods so the two bulbous growths through which sound permeates its dull mind may not be covered. The features of this animal..."

"Man as Animal," Lynn mused still. "How true. Stop the world, I'm getting off." He looked up. "I apologize," he said. "I wish you to continue with the masterful delectation."

"No," said Erick.

"Go on, baby," Leo said. He did. He liked it because it was the past. Lynn was right, he thought, as he started in again, he should have married the past. It was the only happy time.

"The features of this animal," he said, "are ugly in the extreme. Sticking out horribly from the absorbent flesh is a structure which looks like a bastardized snout."

"Ugh," said Leo, "maybe I made a mistake to tell you to go on."

"A proper comment," Lynn said. "Man does arouse disgust."

Leo looked at Lynn, newly curious, and Erick went on, curious only about how much of the past he could recapture in his mind.

"This structure mingles with the face in that same loathsome skin covering. Underneath are two nostrils, through which air is taken and through which..." He hesitated. He wasn't at college and it was all rather poor. He wondered, with a twinge, why he had been so impressed with his cleverness once. Maybe in college, in a campus beer cellar, many things sounded good that were only juvenile. Because it was another world, with its own conditions, its own standards.

"Through which..." Lynn prompted.

"Through which the disgusting phlegm in blown when this animal falls prey to the north wind," he said.

"Erick, that's not nice," Leo said.

"Man is not nice," Lynn said. "Man is a motley growth."

"He's a public relations man," Erick said.

"Uh-huh," Leo said.

"Go on!" summoned Lynn. "Sail on and on!"

"No."

"I insist," Lynn said. "Tell about the eyes."

Erick sighed. What did it matter anyway? If he didn't go on the conversation would somehow work itself back to he and Leo spending the night there. He wanted to forget that.

"On a higher level than the nose and on each side of this growth we find..."

"This *nasty* growth," Lynn amended.

"Adjectives, he remembers," Erick said. "All right—nasty growth. On each side of it we find the eyes. They have...uh."

"They have what?" Lynn asked.

"Rhythm."

"No," Lynn said.

"They...have...tiny hairs sticking from their top lids, which whisk up and down frequently, thus keeping bits of flying matter from the blank eyes."

He went on quickly, the words flaring up on his mental screen.

"These said eyes are often hidden by glass and steel or shell or plastic devices which distort the muscles even more than they are already distorted by the beast's own overindulgence in sights."

"That's me," said Lynn animatedly, "distorting the muscles."

"Oh, the hell with it," Erick said. He was ready to leave and never see either one of them again.

"One shall not leave this abode alive unless one completes his talk."

Silence, another drink, change of mood.

"Directly under the nose a slash is found. This opening leads to the mouth. Into this ugly cavity goes the food which sustains this creature. This self-same food, I might add..."

"Yes," said Lynn, "self-same food?"

Erick signed. "Emits from this entrance when..."

"Erick," Leo said.

He laughed out loud. "Oh, shoot," he said, and went on, enjoying the thought of shocking her.

"...when the beast is inclined to his usual greed in eating. This is known in the culture as puking. Furthermore from this mouth comes the aforementioned phlegm..."

"My God, I'm going," Leo said.

Good!—yelled his mind. *Go fast!*

"Bits of alien matter unwanted by the system," said his voice.

"God," Leo said, still on the couch.

"...as well as a perfectly hideous variety of sounds which constitute the communicable capacities of this vile beast."

"Communicable capacities," Lynn said, scratching his stomach. "Toothsome."

"The shape of this beast's head is generally nauseating. It may be square. It may be egglike. It, further, may be round."

"I know, I know," Lynn broke in. "It may even be flat if a trolley car runs over it."

"Correct!" Erick said, feeling a minor spurt of enthusiasm.

Leo laughed. "You two really are a pair."

"You have a pair, too," Lynn said.

Leo looked undecided between smiling and frowning.

"Didn't think you noticed," she finally said.

"Why don't you spend the night here," Lynn said.

"We'll see," Leo said casually, and Erick was conscious of her warm body against him. He ran one hand over her stomach and felt her shudder and look at him with that heavy look again, as though desire had been poured over her like a hot thick syrup.

"Man as Animal," Lynn said, looking at Leo's legs.

"No more," Erick said.

"More," Lynn said, "or the Madame will throw out the customers."

Erick smiled thinly. *He's trying to disgust me*, he thought, *he's sorry again that he's started it. Really, in a way, he's as bad off as I am.*

He rolled unto his back again and looked at the ceiling. He felt his heart throb slowly and heavily as Leo ran one hand endlessly over his chest, her fingers searching. He hoped Lynn was looking as Leo ran her hand lower and lower until she was pushing her fingers under his belt and pressing them into his stomach. He let a look of enjoyment cover his features and turned slightly toward Lynn so Lynn could see. Then he went on talking, as she started to pull out the ends of his shirt and, finally, was stroking his bare chest and stomach with warm-feeling fingers. It was different from Sally but he liked it. *Who cares?* he told himself, *what's the difference what I do?* As he talked he tried to make believe it was Sally beside him, touching him with such intimate fingers.

"The indefinite outlines of this skull," he said, "are an indication of vacillation in the animal's very structure, not to mention its brain functions. A connecting structure joins this head to the trunk of the animal. Prouder than the giraffe, it has more than seven bones in its neck. And, around said neck, hangs many a chain with a tiny replica of a murder rite."

"True," Lynn said, eyes closed, his head leaned back against the wall. "Fitting and true." *He wants attention*, Erick thought.

"The neck blends with the..."

He shuddered as a ripple of excitement ran down his stomach and muscles to his groin. Leo immediately dug her fingers into that point as if she'd been searching for it. Erick didn't have to look at her to know she was too excited and too drunk to care about Lynn being there. *I know your kind*, he thought scornfully, *you'd probably make love to me in front of Lynn and not be bothered at all.*

"The neck blends into the horizontal bony structure, which tends to bend inward after a period of inactivity. The trunk varies from a column-like structure to various degrees of curvature, which indicates the physical well-being of the creature."

Leo kept caressing. *I wish she'd go down further*, he thought, almost asking her. He didn't care what she did to him. Somehow it made the physical sensation more intense to keep talking as if nothing were happening to him, working both body and mind against each other.

"On each shoulder end hang long, outlandish flesh-and-bone structures called the arms. These end in two extremities, both of which have five claws of various thickness and length, which flex and bend in their fashion. These have nails on them under which dirt is stored."

He forgot where he was for a moment. He was drifting into a hot jelly night with her hand stroking him, his voice going on and on without effort, Lynn against the wall half-unconscious, his slender body slumped down, hands inert at his sides like whitish lumps of flesh and bone. Music coming from the record player: Ravel's *Waltzes, Noble and Sentimental*. And the entire scene moving toward its climax, none of them making the slightest effort to stop it.

"These self-same nails are often used by the female of the species to scratch their opponents. Or to caress their..."

He stopped and looked at Leo, then leaned over and kissed her ear and blew into it. She shuddered and pushed her hand far down under his belt, making him twitch on the couch.

"Man as Animal," Lynn mumbled, "go ahead." *He knows!* Erick thought triumphantly.

"On the chest of male and female are discovered the mammaries," he said. "In the case of the male, these have atrophied through lack of use. In the female, however, these structures have flowered."

"Like Marie," Lynn said. "Always budding."

"Generally they sag down so that mechanical devices are necessary to keep them from sending the rest of the pack into convulsions of..."

"Mine?" Leo whispered heavily, and she put his hand on one and closed the fingers.

"No," he muttered.

"Go ahead!" Lynn said. "Who's sleeping?"

"These fleshy baubles are used to feed the young of the species," Erick said. "However, oddly enough they have established what amounts to a cult in the minds of the male animals. The very simplicity of their prognathous structure has been known, and I do not exaggerate, actually known, to drive the males insane. At this juncture of madness and lust he often attacks the female and attempts to cohabit with her forcibly. For this, the unhappy male is usually put away by the remainder of the herd."

He felt Leo shaking a little and looking over he saw that she was laughing quietly.

"So vital, indeed, is this flesh that the female members lacking this possession have been known to acquire artificial devices which serve to imitate the very thing they lack. These devices worn on the spot often deceive the male of the species, but not permanently. And, when he finds out, he usually dies a little."

Leo took his hand again and put it over her breast. Again she drew in his fingers.

"Mine?" she asked again, and he swallowed. He began to perspire and feel breathless.

"Below this," he went on, without even knowing why he did, "below this we find the stomach and...and the reproductive organs, which..."

"Here?" Leo asked, tensely, excitedly. His eyes closed and breath tore at his throat. He didn't care if Lynn saw her or not. He was gone now, he knew. It was only a matter of time now.

He skipped a part of the speech, wanting to end it.

"I will wind up the speech by saying this," he said, "the abounding idiocy of this animal tribe is the custom known as dressing."

"I agree," she whispered heatedly in his ear. "Let's strip." Lynn started to snore.

"The fallacious minds of these beasts have inculcated insane mores which require the clothing of their frames for reasons moral. Where they evolved this moral stricture is something lost in the fogs of history."

His mind kept working. He wanted to drag out the pleasure.

"That it is so at all is manifestly humorous. The most hilarious aspect of this mad system is that the sole aim of the male concerning the female is to remove these outer wrappings so that he may view and utilize the unclad limbs. This absurd contradiction forms one of the most serious drawbacks to the well-being of the animal."

Lynn had opened his eyes and was looking at them. Leo's hand was still down there. He felt himself drawing in tightly.

"For, torn between clothing and h-his desire for nakedness," he said, "the animal often loses all sense of reason and goes berserk."

Lynn pushed up and stumbled into the bedroom. Leo turned on her side and pressed against Erick. Lynn came in again with a white robe and tossed it on top of them. Erick saw that it was Marie's.

"Here," Lynn said, "get comfortable."

"Oh good," Leo said, sitting up. "Excuse me," she said, and went directly to the bathroom.

Erick got up and stood looking at Lynn. He noticed how dizzy Lynn was. Lynn nodded once and smirked. Then, abruptly, he walked by Erick and tumbled down on the couch, his head snapping back heavily on the arm. He lay there immobile and slumped. Erick stood on the rug staring down at him. *Well, it's worked*, he thought, *it's about to happen*. Wild excitement was pouring through his blood. He kept shivering, couldn't believe it was true, that it was really going to happen.

When he heard her unlocking the bathroom door, he almost turned and fled. But he stopped and looked anxiously at Lynn. Lynn was asleep or pretending to be asleep.

She came in wearing the robe, carrying her clothes. He saw her skirt and blouse, her dark brassiere and pants. She tossed them all down on the armchair and looked over at Lynn with unconvincing curiosity.

"What happened to him?" she asked lightly.

He wanted to shout in her face—*You know what happened to him! He's on the couch and now we go into the bedroom*.

"He conked out," Erick said.

"Guess we can't sleep on the couch," she said. She seemed very calm about it. His heart hammered against his chest as she pushed against him and slid her arms around him. He could feel her soft nude body through the robe.

"You gonna stay here, too?" she asked.

Oh, why don't you stop pretending, you…!

"Come to bed, baby," she muttered, and grabbed his hand. She led him into the bedroom and closed the door authoritatively behind them. Almost in a daze, Erick took off his shirt and pants. Then he was standing naked in the darkness. He heard her drawing back the covers briskly and saw her standing in a patch of light from a street lamp. She stood there so he could see her. Then, slowly, she let the robe slide from her shoulders and fall with a whispering of cloth to the parquet floor. He saw her standing there naked with dark shadows covering her body. His heart hammered insanely, his legs shook. She put one knee on the bed.

"Come to me, baby," she said in a low-pitched voice, and put her arms out.

four.

He rolled onto his back in the darkness, breathing heavily. She was very silent. The wildness of her, the crazy, biting, clutching thing she had been a moment before disappeared. She lay like a dead woman there, staring up, large-eyed, at the ceiling. She turned her head away from him and he heard her hair rustling on the pillow case.

He sensed what she felt. She wasn't going to sleep, he knew. Somehow he knew she'd just lie there staring at the ceiling and feeling betrayed. He didn't know what to say. He lay there, almost holding his breath, hoping she would speak, hoping she'd relax and slide her arms around him once more. He felt cold and alone and he said, almost timidly,

"Thank you." It sounded ridiculous.

"Don't talk to me," she said, her voice cold and distant.

He took a deep breath and lay there in the silence, staring at the dark ceiling with her. Done, done, he thought, hic jacet. He'd known it would be like this, he always knew it would be like this. Why had he been such a fool? He'd always had this terribly unrelieving premonition and yet, when the time came, he had ignored it. There was no love, no bliss, no sense of relaxing affection.

"I didn't come," he said morosely, half to open up a conversation.

She turned to him.

"Really?" she said. She sounded concerned; as if this was something she knew of and could grasp and understand. The sound of concern in her voice made him feel happy, although he resented the happiness.

"That's right," he said.

"Well, it happens like that a lot," she said, "the first time."

He didn't know what she meant and he spoke quickly, without thinking.

"How did you know it was the first time?" he said.

"I meant for us," she said.

But then she was suddenly quiet, as though someone has struck her hard. He felt the silence vibrate with something new and his heart beat loudly and savagely. Surely she'd hear it.

"Erick," she said quietly.

"Yes."

"Are you trying to tell me that…this is your *first* time?

He licked his lips and shivered.

"That's right," he said and, though he tried to make it sound unconcerned, his voice was husky and it shook a little. He had the horrible feeling that he might start to cry. It made him want to jump up and run away. Now she was looking at him in the darkness, he could feel her eyes on him. He twitched a trifle as she touched his arm.

"Oh my God, Erick," she said, "I never even dreamed."

"Well," he said, fighting to keep his voice even, "you see how important you are. This isn't just another affair."

You're lying, the thought came, *she doesn't mean a thing to you*. He wondered over it as she pushed close to him and kissed him.

"Come here," she said in a motherly tone and pressed the warm length of her body against him. She kissed him again, gently, and he thought—*the first time, and instead of Sally, it's this*.

"You big dope," she said.

He swallowed before he could speak. "Is that affection?"

"Yes," she said, "it is."

She held onto him.

"I can't believe it," she said.

"It's true."

"But…"

"I don't know whether to feel proud or ashamed," he said. "Whether to blush or take credit."

"Take credit," she said. "It makes…makes me feel almost unclean."

He kissed her damp neck.

"I thought when you were in the army," she said.

"No, I was a dear little boy in the army," he said. "I didn't dream of it."

He thought of the nights he and a buddy would go to the movie in the town and how he used to walk quickly by the girls who gave him bedroom smiles in those sleepy Southern streets.

She sighed in bewilderment.

"I'm your first woman," she said. "You're incredible."

Does she really mean that? he thought, or did she really think he was a dope? But he couldn't get to think anymore because she put her hands on him and it started all over again, the violent breathing, the sweating, the half-articulated words. And when it was over she asked him.

"No," he said miserably, frightened and in pain.

"Oh, darling," she said, "I'm sorry."

They lay there quietly a while. She smoked a cigarette. In the glow of its tip he saw the contours and dark places of her body.

"Do you think it's love?" he asked.

"Of course not," she said, "it's sex."

But later, when they had done it twice more, she kissed him and said, "I think you love me a little." And it made his heart jump, for there was a wistfulness in her voice he had never heard. As though suddenly he mattered to her. For a brief moment he saw her, self-isolated, self-castigated, reaching out one frightened and trembling hand and asking him, despite all, to love her.

They kept on talking, exchanging thoughts in the darkness. It was a new thing in itself, almost the most enjoyable part if it for Erick, this lying there, naked body to naked body, and talking quietly of many things. There was no pain in it.

Mostly she told him about a man she'd lived with for two years after college because she thought he was going to marry her and he never got around to it. It gave Erick a strange, restless sensation to hear her talk about the man while she was lying beside him.

"I'm impotent," he said in the middle of the conversation.

"Don't be ridiculous," she said. Then she shuddered and touched his stomach with one hand. "You're not impotent," she said, and then went back to her story.

Later she said, "I don't know why you should attract me. Your type never does."

"What's my type?" he asked.

"Oh, the tall, clean-cut boy type."

"That's me," he said. "Clean out."

"Oh, stop it."

"You're after my money."

"Huh."

He lay there thinking of how impossible it was for anything to happen between them. Because he was poor and she was outspoken in her desires for material things; a house and a car and furniture and clothes and all the things that he couldn't give her. He didn't know why he even thought about marrying her just because he'd slept with her. It was probably because of the way he was, the way he'd been raised. This was his first sex experience and he thought it should mean something, it should culminate in a fresh, radiant feeling, not a degraded one.

But he could see nothing for them and, even though he wasn't sure he really cared for her, it made him unhappy. He was a prophet looking into a future he had only repugnance for, a seer repelled by his own hideous talent.

Later in the morning they did it again. He was almost relieved, he felt a wild thrill coursing his body. But nothing happened. The darkness lost its sparkle and the stars and it was just a plodding blanket of night again. And he became him and she became her and together they found nothing.

She smoked again. She had smoked about six cigarettes since they had got into bed. She smoked them nervously, with deep inhalations and a quick blowing out of smoke, as though she wanted to get quickly rid of the thing she had just drawn in with all her power and might.

Later they went to sleep and, in the early morning, his stomach began to ache. He woke up five times and had to go to the bathroom. He looked at himself in the mirror and it surprised him to see that he looked the same. The great romance had done nothing to his appearance. He resented that. He had, childishly perhaps, expected that something would be different. It wasn't. It was just the same and he comforted himself in the way of his boyhood and went back to the bed bitterly.

As it began to grow light, she threw off the heavy comforter and flung her arms over her head on the bed. He looked at her shaved armpits, her slight breasts and her stomach and her face. She was sound asleep. Her legs against his were burning hot. She kept putting them over him as she lay diagonally on the bed. The legs kept wrapping over his body and the weight hurt his stomach. He tried to take them off but they kept coming back and that made him angry. He wanted to be alone in the bed so he could lie in between cool sheets and stretch out and be privately sick. She kept putting her legs over him. He visualized himself as married to her, suffering this every night. If he *were* married, he thought, there would be single beds, this damn business of legs all over him…

She began to snore a little. He looked at her hair. It looked dingy. He felt his stomach ache and burn and he kept thinking that daylight and soberness could be a terrible thing to romance. Leo wasn't pretty. The sharp angles of her features seemed exaggerated now, she looked almost shrewish.

She would be ugly when she got older, he thought. The hard look was on her face as she slept.

He shut his eyes quickly as the door opened and he heard Lynn's bare feet on the floor, heard him taking clothes from his dresser closet. He knew that Lynn was looking at Leo and the thought made him shiver. The door shut again and he looked up. There was a note tacked to the door. He got up to look at it.

I have gone to commune with the bees, it read. *Back shortly*.

Erick went back to bed. But, after a short while, it hurt too much to lie down. He got up and took a shower and dressed slowly, then he went and made himself a glass of orange juice and a cup of coffee. He made the same for Leo. He went in and put them down on the bedside table, feeling like a dutiful husband and not sure whether he liked the feeling or not. He sat down on the bed and nudged her.

She opened her eyes sleepily, without comprehension in them. He had the momentary feeling that she wasn't looking at him. *Who was she looking at?*—he wondered—*in that first moment of wakefulness was his the shadowy, amorphous face of every lover she had ever looked at in the early mornings?*

"Coffee?" he said timidly.

She smiled drowsily and he almost resented how pleased and relaxed she seemed. And he thought—*I'm sorry I told her I was never a lover before*. He wished desperately to convince her that she was only one in a long line. He wanted to hurt her.

"Hi," she said, and pulled down his head and kissed him as he bent over. He felt the cramps in his stomach, making him wince, but she didn't notice. She glanced over at the orange juice and coffee.

"I have to wash my teeth first," she said cheerfully.

He handed her the terrycloth robe and went into the living room without watching her get up. He turned on the radio and started to listen to The Masterwork Hour on station WNYC. People were singing *A Lament For Beowulf.*

Later she came out of the bathroom and they sat on the couch. He watched her drink the coffee he'd had to heat up again. She drank it and smoked cigarettes chain fashion. He kept his arm around her and felt repelled by her flat-colored hair, her small wide-hipped body, the sharpness of her face.

♦ ♦ ♦ ♦ ♦

He was in his room thinking about it.

He could see its power now. Gradually it had come on him. What had happened had brought him out of the pit and enmeshed him in the world where, as a writer, he rightfully belonged. It was a little thing while it occurred, because it did occur. He felt it with his senses and it was easy to accept because he was living it. That night with Leonora had worked itself effortlessly into the pattern of his life.

But now he was back. He had returned to his small crouching room and had to make a bridge from past to present. It was a tie that had to be made and that in a matter of hours. He couldn't go on as he did before, there and then he had to adjust. He didn't want to return. Having Leo had changed everything, it seemed. Whether she was worthy of this feeling, he didn't know, whether it was sickness and not strength he didn't know. All he knew was that sex had been added to his life, the rich and baffling mystery of it, and it had to hold its own relative position in his life. It was no longer the stuff of dreams, wet and not wet.

But perhaps that was too much to expect. Maybe he was just in a cloud. God knew he ached, and at times, when he thought about Leo and the pain was severe, he resented sex and wanted no part of it. Surely a reaction would seep in, the conglomerate of physical pain and dazed wonder would pass, and his own higher selfishness would take over again. He would sweat over the possibilities of her becoming pregnant and hate himself and consider himself a fool for doing what he did.

And Lynn would triumph.

But, for some reason, lying there with music in his ears, he gloried in the sense of new wonder in his life. It was all magnificent. Almost certain that he held it beyond proportion, he could not stop it. It was there and, oddly enough, it didn't frighten him. He wanted to be with Leo, wanted to hold her fast in his arms, that sweet wild flesh that so incredibly linked what he was to what he had been such a little while ago.

♦ ♦ ♦ ♦ ♦

Monday afternoon he called her at her office.

"Hello," she said.

"Hello," he said. And felt disappointed. He didn't know what he'd expected. It was just that he'd slept with her, the first woman he'd ever slept with in his entire life, and he thought that something more should be said than just hello.

"How are you?" he asked.

"Fine."

Pause.

"I'm still sick," he said.

"That's too bad, Erick."

Another pause. He swallowed. "Say, I'm going to be over Lynn's tonight. We're going to try out a television script together. Like to come and kibitz?"

"Well," she said, "all right."

"You don't have to if you don't want to," he said awkwardly.

"Won't I be in the way?"

His mouth turned down. "No," he said.

Pause.

"Well, all right."

"She'll be in the way," Lynn said, just before she got there.

"For Christ's sake," Erick said, "just because your pretty plan backfired, don't take it out on Leo."

Lynn looked bland. "My plan?" he said. Then his face hardened. "Listen boy," he said, "we were supposed to do some work on a T-V script tonight. We're not going to get any work done with…*that* sitting around."

"Why not?" Erick said stubbornly. "For Christ's sake, is writing a T-V script such a big thing?"

"You don't have sluts around when you're working."

"Trying to get a rise?"

"Not at all. She's a slut. I'm simply stating a fact."

"Why don't you give up, you big frustrated jerk!" Erick flared up.

Lynn smiled, holding tight.

"I was here. Remember?"

"Oh, you're a great little bastard," Erick snarled. "A *great* little bastard."

"Let's face it," Lynn said, "she likes to give it."

They didn't get any script done. They sat around and talked distractedly and everybody was bored. Then Lynn went into his bedroom with wine and a book and Leo and Erick sat on the couch.

"What's the matter with *him*?" Leo asked, a little edgy.

"He's still mad because he set us up and it worked."

"What!"

She looked at him with shocked rage.

"I'm just kidding," he said quickly, afraid of the look on her face.

They sat there a long time without talking. He felt sick. His stomach muscles were still tight and aching. He put his head in her lap and didn't know what to say. She kept her hands to herself.

"You have a girdle on," he said.

She didn't answer. Her mouth was a thin line. He lay there on her lap in the silence and couldn't relax. It seemed something must be said. They had given their bodies to each other. There had to be some explanation, some resume, some recapitulation. It was too much to just end, there were too many strands that had to be drawn tight and woven into a credible pattern.

"I have to get up early," she said after a few moments.

As they walked silently through the streets, he turned and looked at her profile. Finally, he said, awkwardly,

"Well…what do think of our relationship?"

She looked at him curiously. "What do I *think* of it?"

"Yes," he said. "Where does it end?"

"*I* don't know," she said, and it sounded utterly callous to him, as if the entire subject were a matter she didn't care to discuss. It made him feel sick to his stomach.

"I don't know, either," he said weakly. "I've been thinking about it and…and I'm still confused. I…"

He stopped, angry for letting her know everything all the time, giving her all the advantage. All the things he meant to hide were coming out; his need to love her because he couldn't just sleep with her and let it go at that.

"I'm sick and exhausted," he found himself complaining, "and I don't know what to make of it."

She didn't talk, she kept walking. And he went on, unable to stop himself.

"It's that we don't know each other," he said. "It's that it's a pity we didn't know each other mentally before we knew each other physically."

He didn't see her wince as though someone had slapped her across the face violently. When he looked at her, she had the same expression, the same blank, staring eyes.

"I see," she said.

"I mean," he said, thinking it was an explanation, "like the way Sally and I knew each other mentally. Going around a lot together, talking about everything, and…well, just getting to know the way…we thought."

She walked a little faster.

"I just don't like it," he said. "You seem to be drifting through this thing without the slightest concern. It hasn't affected you at all."

Still she said nothing. They turned up the street her hotel was on. Her eyes stayed straight ahead, her arms hung at her sides with the fingers of her right hand curled limply around her handbag. Her eyes were lusterless.

"I don't want this to end," he insisted, "but it's up to you. I…I just say it's too hard to have physical love without mental love to go with it. Maybe you can do it but I can't. Oh," he gestured futilely with his hands, "I don't know!"

From there on he said nothing either. She went directly into the lobby with him behind her. She turned at the elevator and looked at him a moment, her face utterly dead.

"Goodbye," she muttered, and turned and walked into the elevator.

He walked out of the lobby and down the street. The city spun around him like a Coney Island ride.

five.

He waited a week. He lay on his bed and thought of her. He walked the streets and thought of her. The memory of that night with her grew and grew in his mind until it displaced everything else.

Then one day, after he'd signed for his unemployment insurance check, he came back to his room and wrote her a letter, thinking as he wrote it of the letter he'd written to Sally. And, once, he stopped writing and felt a shrinking sensation as he realized fully all the years that were gone. And, for a moment, he looked at the world with clear eyes and the room and himself and he didn't like any of it. He thought it was frightening to live in an empty present.

Then his particular grief came to the fore and he finished the letter. The very second he dropped it in the mailbox he regretted it. The letter hadn't said a thing really but he was afraid it would start everything all over again. He didn't want that, even though he was becoming convinced that he loved her. He didn't want to start spending useless days again though, sleeping late, going to the movies with his dwindling money, pounding the streets, throwing rejected stories in a pile rather than send them out again.

Three days later he was at Lynn's place. Lynn was home from work nursing an ingrown toenail. He was stretched out on the couch, his leg hanging over the edge, the foot stuck in a pan of hot water.

"What the hell are you moaning about?" he said. "She isn't worth it. No girl is and you know it."

"Ask the man who owns one," Erick said peevishly.

"What the hell do you want from me?" Lynn said. "Sympathy? I told you I didn't like her. I told you it would make you sick and it did. What can *I* do? Any girl that spends two years laying with a man and then starts acting fussy… well, to coin a phrase, fug her."

Erick was in the bathroom when the phone rang. Lynn had limped into the kitchen to make coffee. He came out into the living room with a disgusted look on his face.

"Well, there she is!" he called, then, when Erick came out, added, "I hope you're satisfied. I should have followed my impulse to tell her you were dead."

Erick felt a sudden burning sensation in him and his hands were shaking as he picked up the phone.

"Hello," he said, suddenly struck with the futility of the word.

"Hello, Erick," she said.

There was silence a moment. "Did you…get my letter?" he asked.

"Yes," she said. "I got it this morning. I've been away for the weekend."

"Oh," he said. "I wondered why you…didn't get it before."

"I've been away."

"I…yes," he said.

Silence.

"Erick, could you come over to the hotel tonight?" she asked. "I'd like to talk to you about something."

"Tonight?"

"Yes."

"What time?"

"About nine-thirty."

"Oh. All right. Shall I call your room?"

"I'll meet you down in the bar," she said.

"All right," he said.

She hung up and he want back into the living room, breathing nervously. Lynn looked up from his book.

"Well?" he asked, something threatening to break in his voice.

"We're off again," Erick said.

It took an apparent effort but Lynn managed to shrug and look disdainful. "Well, it's your life," he said casually.

"I'm glad you admit it," Erick said.

"She's probably knocked up," Lynn said with a smile as he started to read again.

Erick's body jolted.

"In two weeks?" he said, his voice thin.

Lynn looked up blandly. "Sure," he said, with cruel confidence, "Why not?"

Pregnancy. The idea appalled Erick. A child of his own growing in her body. He knew it was impossible, he'd read enough. But still, it might be true. It was too close, too much of an emotional thing for him to think clearly. What if it were true? What had she said? I'd like to talk to you—*about something*.

It horrified him. He never wanted to see her again, he wanted to push away the whole world with a shudder of revulsion and run. Fast.

Lynn looked up again, timing his words perfectly.

"Trouble?" he asked. Then he put down his book. "Male and female create them," he said cheerfully. "Gad, what a mistake."

He looked amusedly at Erick staring at his hands.

"One minute you're hot for her and the next minute you're scared to death of her," Lynn said. "Don't you ever..."

"Is it possible, Lynn?"

Lynn spoke clearly and slowly, turning the knife.

"Anything's possible," he said, wringing out his point.

"Oh *God*."

Erick looked as his watch. It wasn't even eleven in the morning. He got up and paced around, stood restively before the window, looking out, feeling Lynn's eyes on him.

"How the hell can I go all day without knowing?" he said.

Lynn shrugged.

Erick was in agony by lunch. Lynn looked up from his plate and shook his head, eyes half closed.

"Oh, for Christ's sake," he said wearily, "I was only kidding you."

"Yes, but…"

"Listen," Lynn said, "bitches don't get pregnant. They haven't got the time to spare nine months for anything natural."

Erick twisted away. "Oh, how do you…"

"Call her up, then," Lynn interrupted irritably. "Tell her you have an appointment. Tell her to meet you earlier. Tell her anything, just stop whining!"

Erick leaped at the suggestion, even knowing that it was wrong. But he couldn't stand the waiting. He couldn't even eat, he was so wracked by fear and worry.

He called her after lunch, when Lynn was back in the living room, soaking his toe.

His stomach pulsed as the phone buzzed in his ear. When the secretary answered the phone he forgot at first and said, "Hello, Leo?" and she said in a cool, impersonal voice, "With whom do you wish to speak?"

He shuddered and swallowed fast. "Miss Peck," he said.

"Thank you," said the secretary.

A long pause.

"Hello," she said.

"Hello, L-Leo?"

"Yes." Coldly.

"Look, Leo, when you called before I forgot that I have an appointment tonight."

He knew immediately that she'd realize he was lying. He didn't know anyone to have appointments with and she knew it.

"So I thought," he went on, "I…could, maybe, meet you after work and we could…"

"I'm sorry, I have an appointment then."

"Oh," he said.

"Never mind," she said. "It isn't important."

His first sensation was one of relief flooding mercifully over him, relaxing every knotted torturing fear in him. Then, almost immediately, he was torn by a similarly disturbing pang of ambivalence. It wasn't what he had feared and that relieved him but, with that fear gone, he heard her voice objectively again and heard the sorrow in it. And knew she just wanted to see him and talk to him.

"Don't say that, Leo," he said. "I want to see you. You know that. I just can't, that's all."

The sound of sincerity in his own voice almost made him shudder. For the first time in his life he realized how wonderfully sincere a liar he was and felt deeply the shame for it.

"It doesn't matter," she said.

"I wish you wouldn't say that," he said, feeling twisted by regret and yet feeling a certain sense of elation that he was in complete mastery of the situation now, and could afford to be generous.

"Look," he said, "if you change your mind, let me know."

He hung up after she did and suddenly, the feeling of elation departed. He felt like an ass. It was incredible, he thought, how one feeling succeeded another in our minds. From fear we slide to elation, then sorrow mixed with elation and then a sudden shame can bathe us. All these in the space of moments. What a fantastic quick change artist was the brain, with its wardrobe of sensations.

He went back into the living room. Lynn didn't look up.

"It wasn't a baby," Erick said. "She just wanted to see me but now we're not getting together."

"That's awful," Lynn said.

♦ ♦ ♦ ♦ ♦

They were watching television when the phone rang. Erick went into the kitchen.

"Hello?" he said.

"Lynn," asked the voice, "is Erick there?"

"This is Erick."

There was a pause. "This is Leo." She sounded dreadfully ill.

"What is it, Leo?"

"Can you...come over to the hotel? I'd like to talk to you."

There was no hesitation.

"All right," he said. "I'll be right over."

"All right."

"Will you be in your room?"

"I'll be in the bar."

He hung up and passed through the living room to get his coat from the bedroom. Lynn looked up.

"*No*," he said flatly.

"Yes."

Lynn shrugged and Erick thought that in the old days at school if something like this happened, there might be earnest discussions, heated demands, cries of "For Christ's sake, stop butchering your talent!"

Now Lynn shrugged and Erick left him behind.

He walked to her hotel quickly, his mind always running ahead of him like an anxious child, looking behind to see what his slowpoke of a body was doing. He wanted to run but he didn't. He felt every urge to break into a dash and run until his side was cut with stitches but he just walked. He reached the hotel twenty times in his imagination before he reached it with his feet.

She was in the bar. He went in and took off his coat and sat down beside her on the cool-feeling, cool-smelling leather.

"Hello," he said.

She smiled a trifle. She looked terrible, half-drugged. Her eyes were dark rimmed. A tray full of half-smoked cigarettes lay in crushed heaps before her on the table. There were two sidecars standing there, hers half empty.

It was silent for a moment and he felt that moment in every nerve, the surroundings, the darkness, not intimate somehow but cool and crouching about them like an animal waiting. The dull wall lights, the music flowing from the speaker over the bar. Her sitting there in a low-cut black blouse.

She drew deeply on her cigarette as if he had come uninvited and she had not the slightest intention of speaking to him.

"Well?" he said, feeling his heart beat sharply and erratically.

She looked at him, then turned away with a convulsive swallow.

"I...don't know," she said. "I can't tell you now. I thought I could. I had it all made up but now that you're here I can't get started."

She sighed again and stamped out the cigarette with shaking fingers. She bit her lower lip. He never felt stronger that she was a helpless girl, afraid and timid.

"I...probably wouldn't have called you if I wasn't full of sleeping pills," she said. "I'm groggy."

She snickered to herself. "But I can't sleep. Can you beat that? Full to the brim of sleeping pills and I can't sleep. That's the first time that ever happened."

He swallowed. He didn't like it, her smoking so desperately and gulping down her drink and being full of sleeping pills. It struck him as terribly unnatural. Yet he didn't want to leave her.

"You look tired," he said.

"I am," she said. "The office work is killing me. And that weekend..."

Her voice trailed off and, instantly, he saw the weekend as some hideously carnal debauch she had thrown herself into to forget about him.

"I shouldn't have gone," she said.

"Where did you go?" he said, trying not to sound nervous.

"To a friend's house in Connecticut," she said.

He took the drink in front of him and sipped. Then he felt a sudden shaming alarm which he tried to ignore but which could not be eradicated.

He swallowed, then said, "I…hope you have some… some money. I'm broke."

"I'll sign for them," she said.

Silence. It hung over them. He held onto the narrow stem of the glass and stared at the circles of wetness on the slick table top.

"I…guess the letter didn't help much," he said.

She lit another cigarette.

"It didn't say much," he admitted.

"It didn't say *anything*," she said.

He almost flared up and said—*Oh, is that so, well, I thought it was rather expressive myself, and furthermore…*

"Well," he said, suddenly hating the word for a poor man's way of getting talk started, "I…think it said something. I still think it's impossible for…impossible to go on without…well, love. I don't know whether you're capable of it but I'm not."

"At least it might have told me more," she said.

"Like what?"

"Well," she said, "how you felt. After that night I thought you were the cruelest person I'd ever met. I thought it was all a lark to you. Just another one-night stand."

He turned to her, incredulous. "What!" He stared at her. "You thought that?" he said. "My God, you should only know how I've…suffered." He finished weakly. It sounded melodramatic but it was the only word.

She sighed heavily.

"I'm glad I'm not the only one," she said.

"You mean it actually meant something to you?"

She turned to face him and her face was the blank one he'd seen the night they'd parted. He saw now that it was a face that bespoke complete unhappiness.

"Look at me," she said. "Do I look as if it didn't mean a thing to me?"

"I...never knew," he said. "I thought it was...well, unimportant."

She shook her head, breathing with difficulty.

"Well," he said, as if winding up a pedantic conversation, "it's obvious that we've both been laboring under a misapprehension."

Hic jacet, he thought, *that's that, good night all*.

They sat in silence unrelieved by the mutual realization that they'd both been disturbed by the incident. After a while he finished his drink and put it down.

"Where does that leave us?" he asked directly, as if it were her place to answer.

She didn't answer. She skirted the edges of it.

"I've never been so happy since I was a kid," she started. "With you I mean. It made me feel like a college girl again instead of like an older woman. I felt young and excited. It was wonderful to act my age again."

"I'm glad," he said. "I was happy with you, too."

Why did he keep lying? He knew he was saying it because it was called for.

"I've known a number of girls," he said, "but outside of...Sally, you're the only one who..."

He noticed how her mouth tightened when he spoke of Sally and it made him nervous to speak of her with the girl who had lived with Sally. Sally was a secret in his heart, too precious to take out into the light and hold it up to prying eyes.

"I'm glad," she said, as if he had finished what he was saying. "I thought I...I could love you. But now I...don't know."

She turned to him, softness in her face for the first time that night.

"I'm glad you're not cruel," she said.

"Believe me," he said, feeling an overwhelming desire to tell her everything, "I suffered. And not only physically."

They sat in silence again. The red neon lights around them shone on the green leather and on them sitting there in the dimness. It was a make-believe world, divorced of reality. He felt her hand touch his and then their fingers locked. He felt two things. A sudden rush of pitying love for her and a sudden rush of fear that it had started again and his freedom was gone. Responsibility tottered over him again like a menacing giant.

"Was Sally so much to you?" she asked.

He swallowed. "Not really," he said, shivering at his own words.

After a moment, she said, "I'm glad you called."

"And if I hadn't?" he said. "It would have ended?"

"Probably."

She smiled weakly. "Thank God for sleeping pills," she said, and her fingers tightened on his. He put his arm around her and they rested their cheeks together.

"You're shaggy," she said. "How long since you've shaved?"

"Two days," he said.

"My God," she said, "it scratches."

"Would you rather I had peach fuzz?"

"No."

After a while he kissed her. Her lips were warm and yielding. He could smell the cigarettes and the pills on her breath and it excited him. He slid his hand down and felt the soft flesh of her stomach through the skirt.

"You don't have on your girdle," he said.

She smiled tiredly. "No."

Then she pressed close.

"I didn't mean for this to happen," she said, her hand closing over his leg under the table. She kissed his neck and he felt heat rising in him. The words tore themselves loose without effort. He wanted to say them.

"Shall we talk of love?" he whispered, kissing her cheek. "Is it too soon, is it wrong?" He wondered if it was himself talking.

She was breathing harshly now, her throat kept moving.

"*Do* you?" she whispered in his ear.

"I *do*, I *do*," he muttered heatedly, kissing her earlobe.

"Oh God, Erick, I love you so!" she muttered suddenly and passionately, her fingers clutching his leg.

Their mouths locked in the darkness and her tongue slid quickly into his mouth, warm and wet. She pulled away with a gasp.

"Leo," he said, breathlessly.

"Oh Erick, *darling*."

Issued the voice from his hidden brain, from the man sitting in his dripping cold catacomb and yawning—*What is all this estimable horse shit?* Voice like a cold trickle of water on the wall of a crypt. *You're gibbering, boy, you're gibbering, don't blow a nut now.*

"Is your mind working again?" she said, making him start.

"No," he said.

She kissed him on the mouth and her hot breath clouded down his throat. She muttered into his ear, "*Good!*"

He wondered why she didn't say anything about marriage. He waited, afraid to bring it up himself. Then he realized he was hardly the prototype of the successful man. One story sold for $25 and that receiving no comment at all. All his efforts futile. It made him angry. He wanted to throw away his typewriter and try something else. But he knew there was nothing. If he worked in one of his favorite banes—a den of nine to five—he would likely commit suicide in a month. He was sure of it. It all gave him an empty hollow feeling, as if this talk were just stale wind, hopeless and worthless. He sat there limply while she caressed him and got more and more excited. He kept saying, "You should get some sleep," and she kept answering, "I know but I don't want to leave you."

So they sat and she ran her hands over him and he touched her body and she shuddered and kept saying angrily, "*Damn* this hotel for making it so hard to get a man in my room!"

Not "To get *you* in my room," he noted. It made him feel empty, as though he had given his love to her for nothing.

Finally, about three, they went to the lobby and she pressed against him and looked up.

"Erick, I love you," she said. "I always loved you. Even at school. I used to hate Sally." Then she added, as his face reflected unpleasant surprise, "Sometimes..."

"Thank you for calling," he said. "It was..."

Her face clouded. "*Don't* you love me?" she asked plaintively.

"Yes," he said, without looking into her eyes. *Tell her anything*, his mind said, *anything, just get out of here*.

Leo smiled.

"Oh God, if I hadn't called." She looked up at him and her eyes were Sally's.

"Oh please," she said, and it was Sally's voice, and he embraced Sally and kissed Sally and told Sally he loved her.

He walked back to his room. There in the silence he listened to the el and the trucks and the cars. Later he heard someone walking down below, coming up the stairs as if they were climbing a mountain of prodigious height. It was the man in the next room. Erick heard his drunken, phlegm tenor in the hallway.

"*Onward Chrishin So-oh-jers!*" Belch. "*Marshing as to warrrrr!*"

Erick dreamed about Sally.

six.

What was she? That was the question he asked himself repeatedly. Was she Sally over again, the past in different form? Was that what he was trying to do—live the past in the present using her as his link between both? That was why the question always came - What was she?

Still in his mind when two weeks later Lynn told him he was going to be out for a Saturday night and would let Erick use the apartment.

"I'll let you have the key," he said, "but I'll be back early Sunday morning and I expect you to have that bitch in heat out of here."

He felt like punching Lynn in the nose, but it was the only place they had.

"All right," he said sullenly.

Saturday night Leo and he made love on the couch. And, about midnight, she put the chain on the front door and, coming back into the living room, she languidly pulled her tee shirt over her head, unhooked her brassiere, slid off her slacks and pants and stood there naked in the bright lamplight. She held her arms over her head and writhed a little.

"Oh, I feel wonderful," she muttered, and knelt down by the couch where he lay, watching her. Her teeth were gritted, she started to unbutton his shirt.

"You love me, baby?" she asked, as she reached in and began to rub his chest.

He swallowed and she looked up quickly into his face, her hands abruptly motionless on his chest.

"Yes." He framed the words on his lips.

She opened her mouth almost in a frenzy then and drove it over his, pushing his head deep down into the pillow, her hands running over him like wild spiders, her saliva running down his throat.

In the bed she was wild again. She bit his shoulder until the skin broke and asked him to bite her. "Harder," she muttered, "harder! *Hurt* me!"

And, after every time, she asked him, "Erick, do you love me?"

And he kept answering—yes, yes, - and kept getting sicker and sicker because he found no relief with her.

About three they fell into an exhausted sleep. And when he went into the living room next morning, he found Lynn sitting there grimly, looking through a bulky *Sunday Times*. He glanced up at Erick coldly and then looked back to his paper without a word.

Erick had to go back to the bedroom and wake her up. She was lying naked on the bed, stretched out, her legs spread wide apart. At first she smiled sleepily and kissed him and asked him why he'd dressed. Then he told her Lynn was back and they had to go and her face grew hard. While she dressed in jerky, angry motions in front of him, her face was the face that turned him away.

Erick suggested they have some coffee and toast before they go but she said no. Then she insisted on washing the dishes they'd used the night before. She stood tensely at the sink, washing the dishes meticulously, as if she didn't want to give Lynn the slightest excuse for complaining. She was quiet.

"What's the matter?" Erick asked.

"Nothing," she said.

They left without Lynn saying a word. As they walked silently and quickly toward the subway he kept looking at her hard, bitter face. Only after they'd gotten out of the subway near her hotel did she speak with venom. "I *hate* him," she said, "God, how I hate him!"

When they got to the hotel she took him up to her room by the stairway, right past the desk clerk.

It was a small room, hardly more than a closet with an adjoining bath. Once inside she sat on the bed a long time.

He sat helplessly beside her. Finally she got up and jerked off all her clothes and lay there staring at the ceiling, her chest heaving with angry breaths.

"No one can come here," she said bitterly. "*Strip*."

He was sick almost a week after. His muscles ached and he lost all his appetite and was sick to his stomach for days at a time. He kept feeling a rising fear of her, especially since he'd kept asking her if he should have worn something. She kept saying it didn't matter, but when he pursued the subject a little she always said, "Let's see," and started to calculate what the chances were of her becoming pregnant. Then she'd shrug at last and say, "*I* don't know," and usually follow that with a, "Don't wish *that* on me," as though a baby were something she knew could happen but not to her. Almost the way he had felt about death in the army, knowing it was all around, a highly tangible possibility, yet being completely removed from it, positive that it would overlook him indefinitely.

And afraid of her, thinking of the time he'd asked, "How...*many* men have you had intercourse with?"

It took her five minutes to recount them. He lay on his back next to her as she told of them, especially the ones at college, some of whom he'd known. And, with every name she spoke, his body and mind drew back into itself and asked—*What was she, what was she*? And he found no relief with her, although her hands and lips kept exciting and arousing him over and over and over.

In pain, in dreamless sleep, he kept whimpering in his mind—*Sally, Sally, Sally*...

♦ ♦ ♦ ♦ ♦

He was in his room the night she knocked on the door. He was half asleep and the lights were out. He turned them on and stumbled over the dusty rug to the door.

Leo stood there in her tan jacket, a skirt apparently thrown quickly around her body.

"What's *this*?" he asked sleepily.

She came in, hurriedly, as if she didn't want anyone to see her.

"I...just wanted to see your room," she said. "I just wanted to see what it was like."

Her voice was nervous and shaky. She looked around the room and he watched her. She had no makeup on but lipstick. She wore socks, crookedly pulled on, a pair of white sandals. And, when she opened her jacket he saw her dark nipples through the sheer silk of a white blouse. He knew why she'd come and the thought repelled him. It had been the only factor in their relationship in the last month. The thought of it repelled him.

She sat on the bed gingerly and patted it.

"Hmmm, soft," she said. "Do you like it here?"

Sure, he said in his mind, *you can see what a lovely room it is, with its French windows and patio and built-in swimming pool.*

"It's all right," he said, sitting down beside her because he was tired.

She leaned against him, then suddenly took off her jacket and pulled open the buttons of her blouse. She put his hands inside her blouse on her milky, soft breasts. He felt the endless tugging in his body again.

"Erick," she said.

He put his arms around her, feeling the sense of completion in the move, knowing she would never go now without getting what she came for. And he wanted her to go, the thought of having her didn't excite him at all. It repelled him. As Lynn said it would. Lynn was always right.

But she started to press hands on him and he had on only pajamas. Before he knew it she had jumped up and pulled the light string with a jerk and plunged the room into darkness.

She almost tore off her clothes, tossing them all over the floor, her breathing tortured in the night. He watched her tear off her shoes and toss them down. She pushed him on his back on the bed.

"I want you," she muttered. "I want you and I'll have you."

Her mouth on his was hot and demanding. She did everything and it was over before he realized it, leaving him tight and sick while she lay panting and exhausted beside him. He closed his eyes and wondered if he should ask her to leave.

"I wish..." she started after a moment.

"What?"

"Nothing." He could see her face, hard, like a mask of sullen anger.

She climbed over him and sat on the edge of the bed. He saw her eyes glow from the street light. She was motionless.

"Do you have a cigarette?" she asked.

"No."

"Oh, that's right," she said, "*you* don't smoke."

He was silent.

She reached down to the floor and, after a moment, said irritably, "Where the hell's my other sock?"

He didn't answer. She breathed disgustedly. "I had the damn thing right here when I stripped."

She had to kneel on the dusty rug and feel around with a slapping palm on the floor. The dust rose and she sneezed.

"Damn!" she muttered, then, "You *might* help me."

"I might," he said, and lay there stolidly. "Why don't you turn on the light?" he finally said.

"I don't want to look at this damn room."

She found the other sock and sat on the edge of the bed putting it on.

"What's wrong with this room?" he asked.

"It's the ugliest, dirtiest room I ever saw in my life."

"It's home sweet home to me," he said acidly.

"I'll bet," she said. "I could just see us living here."

"I don't believe I asked you," he said.

"Don't worry, I wouldn't do it, little boy," she said. "I have no desire to marry a one-shot author."

His muscles contracted. He lay there breathing heavily while she looked for her sandals. Finally she had to turn on the light. She grimaced at the room.

"Don't you have any self respect?" she asked nastily.

"Look who talks about self respect," he replied, feeling as if his body were contracting into a tight, hard ball of hatred.

She looked up at him quickly, her eyes burning. He sneered at her.

"What a difference between you and Sally," he said.

She straightened up suddenly.

"Oh, *really*!" she snapped at him. "Maybe I should tell you a little something about your precious Sally."

"Don't you say *anything* about Sally," he warned, feeling cold and deadly.

"Poor sweet Sally," she said in a tight, vicious voice. "Angelic virginal Sally. Oh, why don't you grow up, you big dumb kid!"

That trembling in him, starting deep down in his stomach.

"I'm telling you," he said, sitting up.

"You're telling me *nothing*, little boy! I'm telling *you*! Sally was a bitch from the word go. She'd sleep with…"

"Shut up!" he cried. "Don't throw your filthy little lies at me!"

"Lies!" she answered. "Ha, that's funny! If you only knew how funny it is, little boy!"

"Get out of here!" He lurched to his feet.

"Not until I prick your stupid dreams, little boy. Not until I kick out the props from under you and watch you fall."

She seemed to lean forward and he thought she was the ugliest thing he'd ever seen in his life.

"Sally was a bitch," she said.

"I'm warning you, Leo." His muscles were drawing in again, he could feel them shaking with tautness.

"Would you like me to tell you about the time Sally went to Lincoln City with..."

"I said get out of here!"

"With who, you want to know with who?" she cried. "I'll tell you—with *Felix Karis*, that's who!"

She might have kicked him in the stomach, the way he jolted and gasped, the breath sucked out of him in an instant. He couldn't speak, he couldn't smother her words with shouts and curses, and they kept on banging off the walls of his brain again and again. He stood there numbly and felt the fires start to creep up from his stomach into his chest, his throat.

"*Yes*. Felix Karis." She seemed to relish the words. "That big, dumb Polak! And you thought she was such a *good* girl. You fool, you stupid little boy! She went to bed with him, she slept in his *big, fat* arms and let him..."

He moved faster than will, than reaction. His hand shot out and slapped hard across her cheek. Her words were cut off as she reeled back, her eyes wide with shock. For a moment she looked at him in stunned muteness. Then her lips drew back and lunged at him, swinging.

"You filthy...!"

He caught her hands in iron grips, feeling as if he could break them off at the wrist without even trying. Then she jerked one loose and it slapped across his mouth. With a hiss of anger he drove a violent blow against her chest and she cried out and backed away clutching at herself.

The room spun around him as he lurched forward and grabbed her by the hair. He jerked up her head with savage fingers.

"You lied," he said.

"Let go," she whimpered.

He drove the back of his hand across her face.

"You lied, you lied!" he screamed. "Say you lied!"

She tried to pull free but he wouldn't let go. He grabbed her by the blouse. Her white, pain-taut face hung in front of him.

"Let go of me!" she cried in anguished fury. "You dirty son of a..."

"You *lied*, didn't you?"

Her body went rigid and her eyes spread out wildly. Her words tumbled out hysterically.

"Sally was a *bitch*, a *bitch*, a *bitch*!"

All the hate and frustrated fury of years was behind the blow he smashed into her face.

She toppled back with a gagged cry, her arms flailing out for support, then fell to the floor and the back of her head struck the radiator with a loud thud.

Erick stood there, his chest shuddering with breaths, his eyes blurred.

"You lied," he gasped. "You lied about her. She was good."

A sob broke in his throat. "Sally was a *good* girl."

Then his eyes seemed to focus and he saw her lying very still on the floor, her right leg twisted under her and her chest motionless.

And, just before the horror and the fright swept over him, he suddenly realized exactly what she was.

She was yesterday. And she was dead.

— The End —